Hippocrene U.S.A. Guide to
WEST POINT
and the
HUDSON VALLEY

Hippocrene U.S.A. Guide to

West Point and the Hudson Valley

Ellen Boraz Heinbach
and
Gale Gibson Kohlhagen

**Introduction by Lt. General Dave R. Palmer,
Superintendent of West Point**

HIPPOCRENE BOOKS
New York

For information, address:
Hippocrene Books, Inc.
171 Madison Avenue
New York, NY 10016

ISBN 0-87052-889-0

Grateful acknowledgment is made for permission to reprint the
following: illustrations on pages 255, 259, 261, and 267 by Mark Miller;
Adair Wine label, courtesy Adair Vineyards; excerpt from *Cradle
of Valor*, copyright © 1988 by Dale O. Smith; Hudson Valley
Wineries map, courtesy Hudson River Region Wine Council; Hudson
Valley map, courtesy Hudson River Valley Association; West Point
map, courtesy United States Military Academy, West Point; Army
Athletic Association symbol, courtesy Army Athletic Association,
West Point.

Printed in the United States of America.

To our families—
Harvey, Michael and Sarah—
Steven, Tron and Kristoff—
who traveled with us,
endured hours of discourse on the Hudson Valley and the Cadets,
and courageously accepted empty larders and infrequent meals.

To our constant writing companions Bud and Spenser.

And to Steven, our editor,
for his endless hours reading the manuscript,
his insightful and discriminating suggestions,
and for setting the standard with his Saturday lists.

CONTENTS

Part II: THE HUDSON VALLEY

ACKNOWLEDGMENTS

We would like to thank several people at West Point who have helped us in our research. Colonel James N. Hawthorne, Director of Academy Relations, enthusiastically supported our project and offered us books and materials relating to the United States Military Academy. Andrea Hamburger received our endless questions with grace and good humor and arranged numerous meetings, tours of behind-the-scenes sites on post and interviews with cadets. West Point's Historian, Dr. Steven Grove, read our history section and made many valuable suggestions. Suzanne Christoff opened the USMA Archives to us, and she and Dorothy Rapp helped us learn the system and find the information we needed. Particular thanks go to Judy Sibley, USMA Library, Special Collections, who was able to track down the most obscure detail and was always willing to help us at a moment's notice. Whether it meant working late to identify photographs or answering a desperate call just before our deadline, she eagerly fulfilled our requests. And, of course, thanks go to the cadets who gave us their insights and shared with us their first-hand experience of life at West Point.

From Lieutenant General Dave R. Palmer, Superintendent of West Point, we gained an understanding of the Academy's pivotal role in the nation's history and the spell it casts on visitors from every state in the Union. Our thanks also go to Major General Chester V. "Ted" Clifton, a member of the Board of Trustees of the Association of Graduates, who saw a need for this book and encouraged us to tell the West Point story.

We also appreciate the many site managers, tour guides, historical societies and vintners throughout the Hudson Valley who helped us during our two and one-half years of research. Jim Adair of Adair Vineyards, Vice President of the Hudson River Region Wine Council, provided us with up-to-date information on the region's wineries. Special thanks go to Mark Miller of Benmarl Winery who shared with us his personal stories and helped us to understand the fascination of winemaking. He graciously allowed us to reproduce some of his illustrations and revealed to us the potential of the Hudson Valley.

INTRODUCTION

Lt. General Dave R. Palmer
Superintendent, United States Military Academy

Two matchless American treasures are described in this book: the United States Military Academy at West Point; and the Academy's dramatic setting—the neighboring reaches of the Hudson River Valley. Visitors to both unfailingly come away with a feeling of having been touched with a magic wand, a sense of wonderment at so much history and tradition and natural beauty packed into so small an area. This book captures that magic.

Americans reserve a special corner in their hearts for West Point and the United States Military Academy. For reasons flowing out of the deep cultural and historical wellsprings of our nation, this piece of ground is revered, this institution admired. It is a magnet for visitors. Graduates feel the attraction, of course, but generally shrug it off as merely the tug of memories associated with their youth and their *alma mater*. There is more to it than that, however. One glimpses in the eyes of visitors—whether first time tourist or long time resident, old or young, man or woman, military or civilian—a gleam of mingled awe and pride and admiration. Not infrequently, those eyes are moist.

That surprising effect on people has some partial explanations. West Point fairly resonates with reminders of our nation's history, and, to a degree not normally seen by Americans, the Academy's reputation is world-renowned, with its traditions widely copied both in our country and abroad. But those reasons still don't adequately explain the immutable magic in the way this place captures the imagination. There is in addition an indefinable element, a rare presence casting a spell over people, a spell that has sparked a two-century long love affair between the citizens of America and their Academy. An Englishman, Charles Dickens, visiting West Point in 1841, sensed that presence. In describing "the Military School of America," he wrote: "It could not stand on more appropriate ground, and any ground more beautiful can hardly be."

11

West Point is indeed a remarkable spot—it provides a unique environment to foster the development of leaders. Besides being hallowed in history, it is also a place of spectacular scenery— framed by rock-ribbed mountains, embraced in a fold of the Hudson, marked in Gothic magnificence. Standing sentinel around the sweeping parade ground, monuments to heroes of America's wars invoke ghostly images of the "Long Gray Line"—two centuries of Academy graduates whose tradition of valor and service provide the standard by which future leaders will be measured.

The growth of West Point parallels that of America. George Washington camped the Continental Army either right here or nearby, rarely marching far away and always returning as soon as he could. West Point was the "key to the Continent," he said. Today, links to our Revolutionary War heritage lie in honored presence all about the grounds—artifacts and monuments recording our nation's birth and growth. After the Revolution, our newly independent country retained an army "to provide for the common defense." The nature of the young American republic demanded that its officers possess democratic values and unquestioned character. To meet that need, Thomas Jefferson founded the Military Academy in 1802. As the nation has matured, the need has grown. More than ever, our military leaders must be exemplars of the values that frame the nation; and West Point is an enduring source of those values. As America moves into the twenty-first century, and its Academy starts its third century of service, the bonding between the two is more powerful than ever. That linkage makes West Point an extraordinary place to visit.

The book's second part looks beyond the walls of West Point to other sites just a scenic drive away. All are on the Hudson's shores, or very near—the grand river is the common connection.

The river rises some three hundred miles from the sea in an Adirondack Lake with a storybook name, Lake Tear of the Clouds. Gathering size and strength as it rushes down from the mountains, it joins the Mohawk near Albany and there takes on its singularly stately manner. Only six feet above sea level at that juncture, the waters continue their journey to New York Harbor in silvery elegance, shaped by both tide and current.

From that September day nearly four centuries ago when Henry Hudson first opened the waterway to European settlement, the river has been a major element in the development of America. At first a highway for settlers, then an artery for commerce, for a century a strategic constant in the equation of war, and throughout a matchless example of nature at her best, the river and its shores stand as primary witnesses to a significant part of the story of America. Just a short trip from West Point the visitor will discover a variety of sites recalling the excitement of our past and reflecting the vitality of our present.

That excitement and vitality are captured in the authors' descriptions of the neighboring area—towns and business ventures, stately homes, romantic routes, scenic spots, historic sites, all sharing and defining the unusual ambience of the Hudson River Valley.

We at West Point feel fortunate to be situated here; every American can feel pride in the unique aspects of this corner of our great country. This book will help all of us appreciate it— and enjoy it. Come, see for yourself. Feel the touch of that magic wand.

PART I

The United States Military Academy at West Point

From The Plain high above the Hudson rise the fortress-like buildings of the United States Military Academy. With traditions as deep-rooted and solid as its stone foundations, West Point instills in its cadets the time-honored values of steadfast loyalty and devotion to duty. Guardian of our fledgling nation during the Revolutionary War, West Point was chosen by George Washington as the site for an academy to train military officers. Since its founding in 1802 by Thomas Jefferson, the United States Military Academy has sent forth leaders to defend the nation and to preserve the principles of liberty upon which our country was founded.

The roll call of its graduates is filled with names of illustrious leaders who have served the nation in times of peace as well as war. In the nineteenth century, West Point was the premiere scientific institution of its day. Academy graduates explored and charted the vast Western territories and built America's railroads, canals and highways. On the battlefield, Academy leadership proved crucial as well. During the Civil War, West Point men led both sides in fifty-five of the sixty major encounters. And in the twentieth century, MacArthur, Patton, Eisenhower and Bradley carried on the tradition of leadership and service.

West Point's mission is to mold leaders of character, and its rigorous four-year program prepares cadets to take their places as officers in the United States Army. From reveille at 0600 to taps at 2330, cadets march from classroom to athletic field to parade ground. Realizing that under battle conditions the smallest detail may mean the difference between life and death, the Academy holds cadets accountable for their every action. Since leadership is built on trust and trust is built on honor, cadets are expected to live up to the high ethical standards of the Honor Code.

The young men and women of the Long Gray Line represent the best of America's youth. The Academy challenges them to meet every obstacle head on. Surrounded by statues and monuments of those who have gone before them, by patriotic words carved in marble and by emblems of the nation's past, cadets are inspired to perform at levels far above even their own high expectations.

The first of our nation's service academies, West Point has always captivated visitors with its natural beauty and the Gothic splendor of its barracks and halls. Standing on the heights fortified by Washington, walking the paths trod by Eisenhower and MacArthur, and reviewing the Corps in precision drills on The Plain, visitors have an overwhelming sense of America's past and the promise of its future.

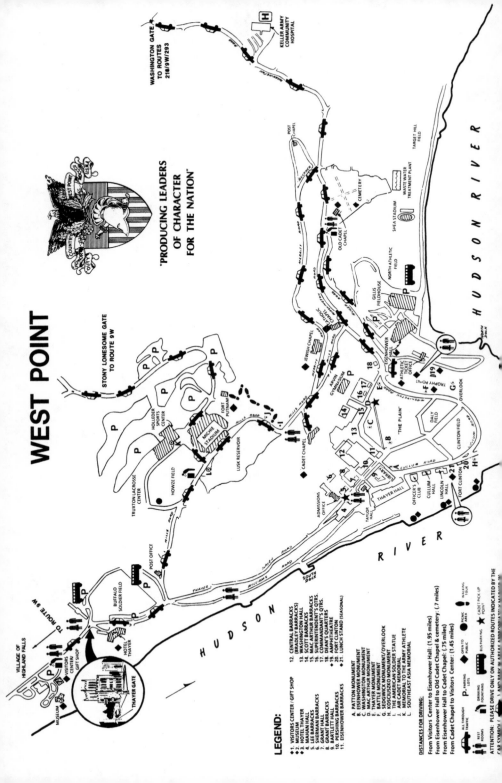

WEST POINT

"PRODUCING LEADERS OF CHARACTER FOR THE NATION"

LEGEND:

1. VISITORS CENTER / GIFT SHOP
2. MUSEUM
3. HOTEL THAYER
4. MAHAN HALL
5. LEE BARRACKS
6. SHERMAN BARRACKS
7. GRANT HALL
8. GRANT BARRACKS
9. BARTLETT HALL
10. PERSHING BARRACKS
11. EISENHOWER BARRACKS
12. CENTRAL BARRACKS (BRADLEY BARRACKS)
13. WASHINGTON HALL
14. SCOTT BARRACKS
15. MAC ARTHUR BARRACKS
16. SUPERINTENDENT'S QTRS.
17. COMMANDANT'S QTRS.
18. DEAN'S QUARTERS
19. AMPHITHEATRE
20. FORT CLINTON
21. LUNCH STAND (SEASONAL)

A. PATTON MONUMENT
B. EISENHOWER MONUMENT
C. WASHINGTON MONUMENT
D. MAC ARTHUR MONUMENT
E. THAYER MONUMENT
F. BATTLE MONUMENT
G. SEDGWICK MONUMENT/OVERLOOK
H. KOSCIUSZKO MONUMENT
I. THE AMERICAN SOLDIER STATUE
J. AIR CADET MEMORIAL
K. MEMORIAL TO THE ARMY ATHLETE
L. SOUTHEAST ASIA MEMORIAL

DISTANCES FOR DRIVING:

From Visitors Center to Eisenhower Hall: (1.95 miles)
From Eisenhower Hall to Old Cadet Chapel & cemetery: (.7 miles)
From Eisenhower Hall to Cadet Chapel: (.75 miles)
From Cadet Chapel to Visitors Center: (1.45 miles)

ATTENTION: PLEASE DRIVE ONLY ON AUTHORIZED ROUTES INDICATED BY THE

To Begin With . . .

First Stop
Visitors' Information Center (VIC)
  Main Street
  Highland Falls, N.Y.
  (600 yards from Thayer Gate, main entrance to the
  United States Military Academy)   (914) 938-2638

Visitor parking, maps of West Point, 15-minute introductory film, gift shop, general information, guided bus tours

Highlights of the Academy
Cadet Chapel
Trophy Point
Michie Stadium
West Point Museum
Hotel Thayer
Old Cadet Chapel
West Point Cemetery

Special Events
Army Football Tickets
  Army Athletic Ticket Office
  United States Military Academy
  West Point, N.Y. 10996   (914) 446-4996
  Free shuttle bus from parking areas to Michie Stadium and Parade Grounds on game days

Cadet Parades
  Late August to early November
  April and May
  Football Saturdays
  Call Visitors' Information Center for schedule   (914) 938-2638

United States Military Academy Band Concerts
  West Point Amphitheatre   (914) 938-2638

Performing Arts (plays, concerts, opera, dance)
  Eisenhower Hall   (914) 938-4159

DIRECTIONS:
From New York City: Palisades Interstate Parkway north to Route 9W north; at Bear Mountain Circle, follow signs to West Point.

West Point open year round. Closed Thanksgiving, Christmas and New Year's Day.

CHAPTER 1

Landmarks of the Academy: An Insider's Tour

The desire to come to West Point grows on me. There are very few good Americans who do not wish to see the place. There's something to be said about that cradle of so many of our great men that makes men feel better when they see it and have watched the boys drill. It's the "long grey line" of the past they see. Pickett, Grant, Lee—an endless parade and the feeling of security and pride about what is best in us and our country.

—Alfred Merritt Smith
father of Major General Dale O. Smith
(USMA Class of 1934)

West Point opens its gates to almost 3,000,000 visitors a year, many of whom return time and time again. No visit is complete without a stop at the major landmarks of the Academy. Trophy

21

Point, the Chapel, cadets on parade—all are universal symbols of West Point. Other sites less well known offer visitors glimpses of the workings of the Academy and day-to-day life of cadets. Some are open to the public; others may be viewed only from the outside. But discovering the stories and traditions behind the fortress-like buildings gives an added dimension to the standard tour. The magnificent setting of the Academy high above the Hudson and the memorials to its historic past inspire visitors with the glory that is West Point.

VISITORS' INFORMATION CENTER

The first stop on a tour of West Point is the Visitors' Information Center (VIC). Located on Main Street, Highland Falls, it is 600 yards from Thayer Gate, the main entrance to the United States

The United States Military Academy at West Point. *U.S.M.A. Archives*

Military Academy. The center provides visitors with maps, general information and schedules of special events of the day. A fifteen-minute introductory film, "Leaders for a Lifetime," shows cadets in the classroom, on maneuvers and on the athletic fields. At the information desk, tickets are available for a fifty-minute guided bus tour (highly recommended), led by West Point officers' wives. Receptionists are on hand to answer specific questions and to explain procedures for visitors on post. An extensive gift shop run by the Army Athletic Association is filled with sweatshirts, footballs, calendars, books, cards and other USMA souvenirs.

The spacious brick and glass Visitors' Information Center, carpeted in cadet gray, opened in September 1989. Lifesize photographs and videos presenting cadets' daily routine illustrate the Academy's purpose: "To provide the Nation with leaders of character who serve the common defense." The West Point experience emphasizes intellectual, physical and military training, and the rigorous program continually challenges cadets to perform at levels far exceeding their own highest expectations.

A time line on the back wall graphically presents the cadets' day. Beginning at 0600 with formation and mess, it continues through a tightly regimented schedule of classes, military duties and athletic competition and ends with taps at 2330. A model room illustrates the regimentation which extends even to the cadets' living quarters. The arrangement of shoes, uniforms, firearms—even the specific number of items allowed on the desk—are prescribed by regulation. Nearby photos of rooms dating from the 1870s to the 1940s show little change over the years. As visitors tour West Point, it is clear that much remains from the past, and the cadets of today hold fast to the traditions of the Corps.

CADET CHAPEL

Since 1910, the Cadet Chapel has stood high on a hill, commanding a magnificent view of the Academy and of the majestic Hudson River below. Built of native granite, the Chapel's battlements and towers befit West Point's military purpose and are in

Cadet Chapel. *U.S.M.A. Special Collections*

keeping with the architecture of the Academy. The polished stone floors and the arches and vaulting give this Gothic structure a medieval feeling. Over the entrance is a representation of King Arthur's sword Excalibur, calling to mind the warrior's code of chivalry. The chimes in the bell tower honor General Robert Anderson (Class of 1826), defender of Ft. Sumter.

Inside, battle flags carried in the Civil War, the Spanish-American War and the Philippine Insurrection hang from the triforium. Stained glass windows by William and Annie Lee Willet on each side of the nave are dedicated to individual West Point classes. Traditionally, each graduating class donated two panels, one in honor of the class which had graduated one hundred years before and one for itself. By 1976, all the original clear glass had been replaced with the vibrant reds, blues and greens of the stained glass. (Throughout the years, the Willets never increased the price they charged cadets for these windows.)

Niches containing the coat of arms of the United States and that of the Military Academy flank the altar, which is carved from a single piece of marble. To the left is the east chancel organ screen, dedicated to the mothers, wives and daughters of the Army. The organ itself, with over 18,000 pipes, is the largest church organ in the world. It can simulate the sounds of bugles, drums and chimes, so appropriate to military music. The sanctuary window above the altar depicts Biblical heroes and symbolizes the "Genius and Spirit of West Point." The Academy's motto, "Duty, Honor, Country," appears in the stained glass, is repeated in stone below and is stitched on the red kneelers at the altar rail. Also on the cushions are needlepointed links symbolic of the Great Chain (see below) which stretched across the Hudson River from West Point during the Revolution.

The right front pew, reserved for the Academy's Superintendent, bears name plates of all those who have served in that capacity since the Chapel was built. A lighted candle in the nave reserves a place for "comrades missing in action and those held as prisoners of war."

The Chapel can seat 1500 people, and the Sunday morning service held at 10:30 during the academic year is open to the public. The beauty of the setting and the solemnity of the service are enhanced by the cadet choir. Marching four abreast, the choir proceeds down the center aisle, and each row of worshipers begins to sing as the choir passes. The music builds until the entire congregation is joined together in song.

The Chapel is used for weddings as well. Since cadets may not marry during their four years at the Academy, many are anxious to do so as soon as the prohibition is lifted. On Graduation Day and for many days thereafter, wedding follows wedding, and each hour a new bride and groom pass under the crossed swords of classmates to begin their life in the Army. Whether in a wedding ceremony, a candlelight service at Christmas or weekly Sunday worship, the Chapel provides an austere and dignified setting where the Long Gray Line reaffirms its link to the past and its dedication to the nation's future.

Battle Monument, Trophy Point. *U.S.M.A. Archives*

TROPHY POINT

Ulysses S. Grant (Class of 1843) called West Point, "This prettiest of places . . . the most beautiful I have ever seen." Of all the sites at the Academy, Trophy Point, with its "million-dollar view of the Hudson," is extraordinary in its beauty. The river winds its way past Storm King Mountain on the west and

Breakneck Ridge on the east, a view immortalized in scores of Hudson River School landscapes. Above the river, the grassy plateau known as Trophy Point has become an outdoor museum for artillery and trophies of America's wars. Here are cannon captured in battles from the Revolutionary War through World War II. Here, too, is the imposing monument that for many symbolizes West Point. Forty-six feet tall, the Battle Monument, designed by Stanford White, bears the names of 2,230 Regular Union Army soldiers who died during the Civil War. It is the only memorial in the United States to these men who fell defending the Union. A winged statue of Fame, presumedly modeled after White's mistress Evelyn Nesbit, tops the granite column, and engraved on the muzzles of the guns surrounding it are names of Civil War battles. For years, soldiers of the Regular Army set aside six percent of their monthly salaries to pay for this tribute to their fallen comrades.

Of all the artillery collected at Trophy Point, the only gun still in use is the post reveille gun. Daily it is fired at 0600 to signal the beginning of the cadets' day, and it is fired once again at sunset. It is said that when Douglas MacArthur attended the Academy, he and a few other cadets dismantled the gun and reassembled it on top of the clock tower. The gun was out of commission for two weeks. Fortunately for MacArthur and his friends, they were not found out until long after graduation, as the seriousness of this prank would most probably have led to their expulsion.

During the Revolutionary War, a 600-yard iron chain was floated on log rafts across the Hudson from the rocks below Trophy Point to Constitution Island. Here the river doubles back on itself in an S-curve, forcing ships to slow as they navigate the strategic bend below Fort Clinton. The Great Chain's dual purpose was to cut British supply lines and to prevent Britain from dividing New England from the other colonies. For five years, the Chain proved a successful deterrent. No British ship ever tested it, and after 1778 most of the fighting took place in the Southern colonies. Today, a circle of sixteen of the Chain's massive links stands at the west side of Trophy Point.

During the Revolutionary War, the Chain Battery below Trophy Point was fortified. From this position, the colonists planned to fire upon any enemy ship which attempted to break the Chain. In the middle of the nineteenth century, Superintendent Richard Delafield (Class of 1818) designed a footpath winding down to the Hudson past the old battery. Originally named Chain Battery Walk, it is now known to all as Flirtation Walk.

Delafield was a great student of the Revolution. During his second term as Superintendent, he ordered the names of three famous battles chiseled into rock ledges along the walk. The inscriptions, "Saratoga, 17th October 1777" near Kosciuszko's Garden and "Yorktown" facing Constitution Island, still remain; "Bunker Hill" was removed in the 1920 railroad depot expansion. "Old Flirty," Flirtation Walk, is reserved exclusively for cadets and their guests. This steep, wooded trail is closed not only to the public, but it is off-limits to officers as well. Everywhere else on post, cadets are forbidden public displays of affection. Only on Flirtation Walk are they permitted to walk freely with their dates, and many make certain they pass the large, mossy outcropping known as Kissing Rock. According to tradition, if cadets and their dates do not kiss beneath this rock, it will fall. It still stands.

THE PLAIN

The flat ground between Trophy Point and the cadet quadrangles is known as The Plain. Its largest field is the parade ground where cadets pass in review and practice military formations and maneuvers. Baron von Steuben first used The Plain to prepare troops for the Revolutionary War Battle of Stony Point. Parades are held two to three times a week from August through November and in April and May. The Visitors' Information Center (914/938-2638) has dates and times of parades, and signs are posted on The Plain as well. Part of the excitement of home football games in the fall is watching the disciplined Corps marching in review to the music of the 100-piece United States Military Academy Band. Nothing can beat the sight of the immaculately-turned-out regiments and the precision of the drills combined with the stirring, patriotic music. It is on The Plain that new cadets gather at the end of their first grueling day at West Point. Here, before their families, they take the Acade-

Cadets on parade. *U.S.M.A. Archives*

my's Oath of Allegiance, and on this historic field, surrounded by the fortress-like buildings that will be home to them for the next four years, they officially begin their training as future officers in the United States Army.

STATUES AND MONUMENTS

Over the years men important to the Academy have been memorialized in statues and monuments on West Point's grounds. Graduates of the Academy who have gone on to serve their nation with distinction and men who won and have preserved the nation's independence are honored with statues on The Plain. Other memorials pay tribute to America's fighting men and women. From The Plain to the reservoir, cadets pass these statues, daily reminders of the heights to which they may aspire.

Statue of General George S. Patton, Jr.
(Class of 1909). U.S.M.A. Archives

Patton Monument

"Erected by his friends, officers and men of the units he commanded," the statue of George S. Patton, Jr. (Class of 1909) stands directly in front of the library. Turned back his first year, Patton took five years to graduate from the Academy, and many feel that the library is the last building he would have wished to face. In actuality, he was extremely intelligent, and today it is thought that he suffered from dyslexia. Patton's brilliant tactics in World War II won him the esteem of his men and made him the Allied commander most feared by the enemy. One of the statue's bronze hands contains the general's gold cavalry insignia which was worn by Mrs. Patton during their marriage. His four silver stars are melted into the other hand. With binoculars raised and his famous pistols at his side, Patton stands as he did all his life—ready to press forward.

Eisenhower Monument

Dwight D. Eisenhower, the 34th President of the United States, graduated from the Academy in 1915. He was a member of the "Class the Stars Fell On." Over a third of its 164 members attained the rank of brigadier general or higher. Its distinguished graduates also include General Omar N. Bradley and General James A. Van Fleet. General Eisenhower was Supreme Commander Allied Forces Europe during World War II and engineered Operation Overlord, the successful invasion of Normandy on D-Day, June 6, 1944. The statue of Ike in his World War II uniform, located on the southeast corner of The Plain, was dedicated in May 1983.

Washington Monument

George Washington believed that West Point was the most important defensive position in the colonies and had this "key to the Continent" fortified during the Revolutionary War. Throughout his presidency, Washington urged Congress to build an academy on the Hudson to train the new nation's future military leaders. Although not established in his lifetime, it was his unrelenting advocacy that laid the groundwork for the Academy's founding in 1802. The statue of Washington on horseback, a replica of the one in Union Square in New York City, stands in front of Washington Hall, the 4500-seat cadet mess.

MacArthur Memorial

A graduate of the Class of 1903, Douglas MacArthur returned to West Point as Academy Superintendent in 1919. Under his leadership the curriculum was expanded to include humanities and social sciences. MacArthur recognized that military leaders need an understanding of men and political interaction as well as of the arts of war. During World War II, General MacArthur served as Supreme Commander of Allied Armies in the Southwestern Pacific. The bronze statue of MacArthur, standing across from the Superintendent's Quarters near Washington Hall, is a popular meeting place for cadets. Inscribed in its base are lines from MacArthur's stirring farewell address to the Corps and to his beloved Academy. ". . . But in the evening of my memory I always come back to West Point. Always there echoes and re-echoes—Duty, Honor, Country."

Thayer Monument

Sylvanus Thayer, Academy Superintendent from 1817-1833, is known as the "Father of the Military Academy." West Point was floundering until Thayer completely redesigned the curriculum and training. Under his guidance, West Point became

Sylvanus Thayer, "Father of the Military Academy."
U.S.M.A. Archives

the premiere scientific institution of its day, and its place in American military tradition was assured. Thayer's statue overlooks The Plain, across the road from the Superintendent's and Commandant's Quarters. On Alumni Day each year, graduates and their guests gather at Thayer's statue to honor their comrades who have died.

Sedgwick Monument

Toward the river east of The Plain is a statue in memory of Major General John Sedgwick (Class of 1837). Dedicated by his men of the 6th Army Corps in 1868, only four years after Sedgwick was killed in the Civil War Battle of Spottsylvania, the monument was forged from captured Confederate cannon. Tradition has it that a cadet in academic trouble will pass his final exam if he spins Sedgwick's Lucky Spurs at midnight. The catch is that he must not be caught breaking curfew.

Kosciuszko Monument

Thaddeus Kosciuszko, the Polish patriot who fought for the Americans during the Revolutionary War, worked for more than two years designing and constructing all the fortifications at West Point. Appointed head of the Engineering Corps, he attained the rank of Brigadier General and was instrumental in the Continental Army's defense of the Hudson. In honor of Kosciuszko's contribution to the Revolutionary cause, the Corps of Cadets in 1828 dedicated what today forms the base of the monument. The inscription "Saratoga" recalls the important role he played in this decisive battle. In 1913, Polish-Americans commissioned a statue of Kosciuszko to be placed atop the pedestal. Nearby is a rock garden Kosciuszko designed for his brief moments of rest. Kosciuszko's sword is part of the West Point Museum's collection. Engraved on its hilt is: "Draw me not without reason, Sheathe me not without honor."

The American Soldier Statue

At the north end of Lusk Reservoir stand three bronze, life-sized infantrymen, a tribute to the American soldier. Sculpted by Felix W. DeWeldon, creator of the famous Iwo Jima Memorial, it was presented to the Corps of Cadets by the Classes of 1935 and 1936 with the admonition that, "The lives and destinies of Valiant Americans are entrusted to your care and leadership."

Air Cadet Memorial

In memory of cadets who were killed in flight training while at the Academy, the Air Cadet Memorial northeast of Michie Stadium was dedicated by the Corps of Cadets in 1945. Until the United States Air Force was established by Congress in 1947, many air operations were performed by the Army Air Corps. During World War II, nearby Stewart Field served as a training ground to prepare officers to fly missions over Germany and Japan. The names and dates of death of those who lost their lives while in training are recorded on this monument.

Southeast Asia Memorial

Shaded by trees at the edge of Lusk Reservoir, the Southeast Asia Memorial honors those who died in Vietnam. A granite boulder bears a bronze plaque, and the monument, with its five granite benches, dedicates this peaceful site to the memory of the fallen. The memorial was commissioned by the Classes of 1960 through 1969, the classes which suffered the greatest losses in this conflict.

MICHIE STADIUM

Named for First Lieutenant Dennis Mahan Michie (Class of 1892), Michie Stadium has been the home of Army football since 1924. Having played football at prep school, Cadet Michie arranged for friends at Annapolis to challenge West Point to a football game. Never able to resist a challenge, the Academy accepted. Although only two cadets had ever played before, Michie organized a team and was its first captain. On November 29, 1890, the first Army-Navy football game was played, and it has become one of the great rivalries of all time.

Michie Stadium, which seats 40,000, has always brought good luck to the Black Knights. Army went undefeated in its first thirty-nine games at the stadium. Not until October 17, 1931, did Army lose, and then only by one point to Harvard. Today, cadets dress in battle fatigues the Friday before each home

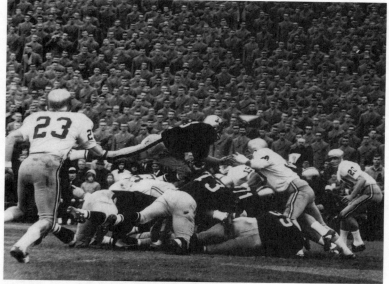

The Sea of Gray, the "twelfth man on the field." *U.S.M.A. Archives*

game. On Saturday, in full uniform, they stand throughout the entire game. A sea of gray, they consider themselves the twelfth man on the field.

Across from Lusk Reservoir, the stadium sits high above the Academy grounds. *Sports Illustrated* has called it one of the ten most beautiful college stadiums in the country. From the second deck of the west stands, fans look down upon the Cadet Chapel, The Plain and the winding Hudson River. Home games are sold out well in advance. People come from all over to see the cadets on parade, to enjoy tailgate picnics and to cheer Army on to victory. Tickets must be ordered months ahead of time from the Army Athletic Ticket Office at West Point (914/446-4996).

Michie Stadium is also the site of the Academy's graduation ceremonies. First Classmen march to the platform and receive their diplomas one by one. When the First Captain signals the end of the ceremony with the command, "Class Dismissed," newly commissioned second lieutenants toss their white caps

The joy of Graduation Day. *U.S.M.A. Archives*

into the air and celebrate the successful completion of their four
years at the Academy.

WEST POINT MUSEUM

Housed in Olmsted Hall next to the Visitors' Information Center, the West Point Museum holds the largest collection of military artifacts in the Western Hemisphere. Since the Revolutionary War, West Point has been a repository for trophies
surrendered and acquired in battle. A cannon captured at Saratoga, a musket from the Civil War, and a Viet Cong jacket are
reminders of battles Americans have fought over the past two
hundred years. Daggers and clubs from the Stone Age, medieval swords, and the casing from an atomic bomb show the
development of weapons over the centuries. Dioramas and
maps explain the strategies and tactics of war. One gallery
highlights the history of the Military Academy.

Only five per cent of the museum's 45,000 items are on display in Olmsted Hall at any one time, but a number of other pieces of the collection are exhibited throughout the Academy. In academic and administrative buildings, in reception and meeting rooms, paintings, statues and documents remind cadets and officers of West Point's rich heritage. In the museum itself, manuscripts, uniforms and other fragile pieces are rotated to protect them from deterioration. Both the public and the cadets for whom it serves as a museum of study can examine the weapons, uniforms, photographs, documents and artillery displayed in the six galleries.

History of Warfare Gallery

From the earliest times, man has resorted to armed conflict to resolve differences. Although the first man-made weapons were defensive in nature—shields and protective clothing—it was not long before men fashioned implements of battle and devised strategies to impose their will on the enemy. The History of Warfare Gallery traces the evolution of warfare from the ancient world through medieval times to the nuclear age.

The first half of the gallery is devoted to the strategies and accoutrements of war. Armor, weapons and campaign maps illustrate technological and tactical advances through the centuries. Four dioramas detail battles in which dramatic breakthroughs changed the way war was waged. The Battle of Cynoscephalae, 197 B.C., established the dominance of the Roman manipular infantry for over three hundred years. At Adrianople in 378 A.D., the Visigoths' cavalry triumphed over the Roman infantry in a battle that many historians identify as the beginning of the Middle Ages. The supremacy of the mounted warrior lasted for one thousand years until advances in weaponry enabled English foot soldiers armed with longbows to unseat the French knights at Crecy. The era of modern warfare was ushered in by the armies of the Swedish King Gustavus Adolphus in 1631 at the Battle of Breitenfeld. The flexibility of the Swedish troops and the mobility of their artillery proved superior to the textbook-perfect deployment of Count Tilly's massed formations. Other dioramas present the crucial historical conflicts at Avaricum, Leuthen, and Austerlitz among others.

The careers of Alexander the Great, one of the foremost military strategists of all times, and of Napoleon, whose campaigns altered the map of Europe, are highlighted. Also on view are numerous personal items of military figures both famous and infamous. Napoleon's campaign pistols are displayed along with his gold and silver sword presented in 1945 by Charles de Gaulle to General Eisenhower. In the World War II section is an ivory baton, given by Adolph Hitler to Hermann Göring as a symbol of his rank as Reichmarshal of Nazi Germany. Above the baton is Göring's Karinhall guest book containing signatures of Adolph Hitler, Benito Mussolini, Charles Lindbergh and Herbert Hoover.

Throughout the gallery, hundreds of items used and worn by soldiers reflect the changes in warfare from hand-to-hand combat to global engagement. The concluding panel with quotations from philosophers and statesmen reflects upon the role of war in society. It may be an inevitable consequence of human nature, as Thucydides and Plato see it, or it may be that dishonor and slavery are worse than war, as Winston Churchill states. But in Dwight D. Eisenhower's words, "Men acquainted with the battlefield will not be found among numbers that glibly talk of another war."

The American Wars Gallery

The American Wars Gallery presents America's history through its wars from colonial times through Vietnam. The causes and conduct of each war are described in a concise, clear text. Accompanying maps are color-coded to show sites of major engagements, terrain, troop movements and overall battle strategies. West Point's Department of History has designed each exhibit as a part of the cadet curriculum. Classes study battles of past wars, learning from the victories and mistakes of their predecessors. The Civil War Battle of Gettysburg, the turning point of the war, is diagrammed day by day, and the strategies leading to the decisive Union victory are analyzed in detail. Maps graphically depict the campaigns of both world wars, and time lines place major events in chronological order.

Soldiers' weapons, field equipment and uniforms personalize these moments in the nation's past. The service coat and cap of

World War I General John J. Pershing (Class of 1886) are displayed next to a Prussian officer's helmet. A Waffen SS uniform and an Italian Alpine (Mountain Troop) hat are shown along with General Eisenhower's (Class of 1915) personal sidearm and holster. Of special interest is the story behind the return of General Jonathan Wainwright's saber. Given to him by his mother on his graduation from West Point in 1906, the saber was stolen from General Wainwright's quarters during the Battle of Luzon in the Philippines in 1941. Discovered on the body of a Japanese officer in 1945, it was returned to General Wainwright and is featured in this section.

The coverage of the wars from the Revolution through World War II is extensive and full of interesting historical tidbits. For instance, the description of the 1777 Battle of Saratoga explains the reason British soldiers wore red coats. Because the smoky discharge from the weapons of the time often obscured the battlefield, officers could only identify their men by the bright color of their coats. In the Civil War section, the disparity in resources and fortunes of the North and South is poignantly apparent in the back-to-back figures of the Union and Confederate soldiers. The highly polished, well-equipped United States Infantryman stands in sharp contrast to the Southerner with his homespun uniform and worn boots. The World War II section contains the tattered socks, shaving gear and mess kits of Americans held prisoners by the Japanese. Unfortunately, only cursory coverage is given to Korea and Vietnam. While the museum has issued a call to veterans for artifacts of these conflicts, it seems that more attention could have been paid to these pivotal events. Still, the gallery is of great interest to the casual visitor as well as the serious student.

West Point Gallery

The history of West Point from its beginnings as a military post during the Revolutionary War to the modern day United States Military Academy is briefly chronicled in the West Point Gallery. Highlighting its phases of development, exhibits feature memorabilia of the institution and of well-known graduates. A portrait of Sylvanus Thayer, "Father of the Military Academy," is displayed along with his dress coat, dress sword and document box. Engineering tools of the pre-Civil War era recall West Point's preeminence as a scientific institution. Famous professors and superintendents are remembered through portraits and descriptions of their contributions to the Academy. Paintings by Robert W. Weir, legendary drawing master from 1834-1876, as well as one by James McNeill Whistler are on display. An unlikely cadet, Whistler excelled only in drawing class and was forced to leave in 1854.

1902 Army Baseball Team. Douglas MacArthur is seated on far right.
U.S.M.A. Archives

Cadet athletics receive extensive treatment. Fencing equipment and horsemanship medals testify to the importance of these sports in the Academy's history. There is a photograph of Army's first football team and a picture of Douglas MacArthur with his baseball teammates. The tradition of class rings was initiated in this country by the Corps of Cadets in 1835, and rings from the mid-1800s are on display. Scattered throughout the gallery are examples of cadet uniforms. Patterned after those worn by General Winfield Scott's soldiers at the Battle of Chippewa in 1814, they have changed little over the years. Thus, since 1816 when gray became the regulation color, the Long Gray Line has been the continuing symbol of the Academy.

The Small Weapons Gallery

The Small Weapons Gallery traces the evolution of small arms and personal weapons through the ages. An American Indian wooden club with carved spikes and a bird-like beak along with a Philippine Kalinga headhunter's axe are examples of the kinds of weapons used by early man. A fifteenth-century Swiss halberd, a nineteenth-century Japanese yari and Civil War lances represent the polearm, one of man's oldest weapons. Even before the use of stone and metal, prehistoric man sharpened wooden poles in the fire for the hunt.

Knives, too, have been used for thousands of years. Their shapes and sizes reflect their various purposes. The Nepalese Gurkha kukri is known as the best slashing knife in the world. The double-bladed bichwa, named for its resemblance to a scorpion, suggests its deadly function. The advent of protective armor brought about the development of flexible and accurate swords.

The invention of gunpowder brought a revolution in armsmaking. On display is a replica of a fourteenth-century handheld cannon. The original was found in the ruins of a German castle and is the earliest documented handgun. Case after case of rifles, pistols and assault weapons show the improvements made over the years in the speed, accuracy, range and power of small arms.

The Large Weapons Gallery

Even before the Military Academy was established, the nation's battle trophies were sent to West Point for safekeeping. On display in the Large Weapons Gallery is a British twelve-pound mortar which, together with other Revolutionary War artifacts, formed the basis of the museum's original collection. Through the years, over 45,000 items have been amassed, many of them large artillery pieces. With the opening of the new museum in 1989, space became available to display a number of these large trophies. A 1917 six-ton Renault tank, a World War II vintage Jeep and a World War I U.S. Army staff car stand under the huge murals of the Normandy landings on D-Day. Nearby is the casing of a "Fat Man" atomic bomb, the type of weapon detonated over Nagasaki on August 9, 1945.

The gallery also houses examples of guns, howitzers and mortars. There is a 1695 Chinese cannon captured from the walled city of Peking during the Boxer Rebellion at the turn of the century. A fifteen-meter field gun which fired the first American barrage at the Germans in World War I bears the hand-painted words, "First Shot at Huns 10-23-17 6:10 a.m."

A collection of hand grenades varying greatly in size and shape includes a Civil War "5 Pounder," a World War I French pinwheel, and one used in 1964 by the Viet Cong. In the artillery projectile case, several varieties of Civil War grapeshot are displayed. The clusters of small iron balls resemble the grapes for which these cannon charges were named.

Exhibits of hand-operated and automatic machine guns lead to examples of early military rocketry. Developed during the twelfth century in China, rockets were generally unpredictable and uncontrollable. Nevertheless, they were used extensively by the British in the War of 1812, and Francis Scott Key wrote of "the rockets red glare" in our national anthem. During World War II, the United States developed the accurate anti-tank, rocket-launched "bazooka," and German scientists pioneered the use of liquid fuel to power rockets, ushering in the age of modern missile technology. A time line recording 6,000 years of weapon development charts the relative importance of each type of armament.

History of the U.S. Army Gallery

For over two hundred years, men and women of the United States Army have made significant contributions to their country. In the course of performing their primary function—defending the nation—they have made important advances in the fields of medicine, engineering and transportation, among others. This gallery traces these contributions from the Revolutionary War to the present time, highlighting those made by West Point graduates.

During the Civil War, remarkable strides were made in surgical practices and the use of anesthetics. Further medical advances were made in the Spanish-American War. As a result of American deaths from yellow fever, Major Walter Reed undertook research which resulted in the virtual elimination of the disease in the United States and Cuba. Because of the Army's expertise, the Red Cross in World War II was able to establish an extensive blood donor system that continues even today.

Beginning with the Louisiana Purchase in 1803, men of the Army explored, surveyed and charted the country's expanding territories. For many years, most of the nation's trained engineers were West Pointers, and it was these men who designed and built America's roads, canals and bridges, opening the new areas and allowing for their development. In the mid-nineteenth century, William G. McNeill (Class of 1817) and George W. Whistler (Class of 1819) were the experts on railroad engineering, and in 1914, the Panama Canal was opened under the direction of George W. Goethals (Class of 1880). For four hundred years, a canal to connect the Atlantic and Pacific Oceans had been the dream of navigators and statesmen. Twice before, major efforts had failed. But the engineering and organizational skills learned at West Point enabled Goethals to make the dream a reality just seven years after his appointment to head the Canal Commission.

The Army also made considerable contributions in aviation. From the observation balloons used in the Civil War to the airplanes of the two world wars to the space technology of the twentieth century, the Army has been actively engaged in scientific research and development. As displays in this gallery illustrate, many technological advances necessitated by the exigencies of war have benefited Americans in times of peace.

HOTEL THAYER

Just inside Thayer Gate is the hotel named for the "Father of the Military Academy," Sylvanus Thayer. Built in 1926, it is owned by the Military Academy, and offers meals and lodging to both the West Point community and the public. The present hotel replaced a stuccoed, three-story structure built in 1829 on Trophy Point. Many famous guests, including Ulysses S. Grant,

William Tecumseh Sherman, "Stonewall" Jackson, Edgar Allan Poe and James McNeill Whistler, stayed at the hotel. Others were more permanent residents. General Winfield Scott, hero of the Mexican War, lived there in his retirement, and Pinky MacArthur moved in to oversee her son Douglas' four years at the Academy. When Robert E. Lee was West Point's Superintendent, wealthy Southern plantation owners often summered at the hotel. Its public rooms were the center of cadet social life, and hops were held in its ballroom. When the hotel was torn down, the lamp which once hung outside was taken to the Hotel Thayer and placed in the foyer leading to the dining room.

Today breakfast, lunch and dinner are served in a spacious, comfortable room overlooking the Hudson River. The courtesy that typifies West Point extends to the staff of the Thayer, and even the china with its gray-lined border reflects the Academy's traditions. A treat for children is the view of Osborne Castle from the windows of the dining room. In the movie *The Wizard of Oz* monkeys dressed in recut cadet uniforms circled the castle's turret.

OLD CADET CHAPEL

The classical simplicity of the Old Cadet Chapel reflects the faith of the founding fathers in the democratic ideals of ancient Greece and Rome. Its unadorned altar and highly polished wood floors suggest its military and masculine origins. West Point's oldest public building, the Chapel stood on the edge of The Plain across from the clock tower from 1838-1910. For over seventy years, cadets marched to worship services and received their diplomas at graduation exercises in the Chapel. It was here on Washington's birthday just before the outbreak of the Civil War that cadets gathered to hear a reading of Washington's 1796 farewell address pleading for national unity. With the growth of the Academy, a larger chapel was needed, and in 1911, when the New Cadet Chapel was dedicated, the Old Chapel was scheduled for demolition. Graduates banded together to preserve the beautiful old building which held their many memories. Stone by stone it was removed and reassembled at the

Interior of Old Cadet Chapel. *U.S.M.A. Special Collections*

Memorial to Benedict Arnold, Old Cadet Chapel, West Point.

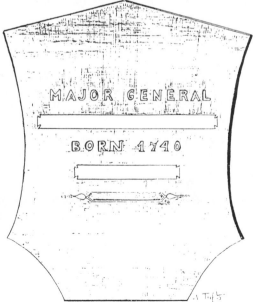

entrance to the West Point Cemetery where it still stands.

Lining the walls of the Old Chapel are black marble tablets which commemorate officers who served in America's early wars. On the east wall are memorials to Revolutionary War generals, and plaques on the west wall are dedicated to men who fought in the War of 1812, the Mexican War and the Spanish-American War among others. In the choir loft, Benedict Arnold's tablet lists only his rank and birthdate, not his name or date of death. Thus the Academy recognizes General Arnold for his bravery during the Battles of Quebec and Saratoga, but will not forgive him his treachery. Also in the Chapel are British cannon captured during the Revolutionary War.

Above the altar is a mural of "Peace and War" by nineteenth-century Academy drawing master Robert W. Weir. In the painting a bald eagle spreads his wings above a passage from Scripture invoking nations to righteousness. Weir, drawing master from 1834-1876, was a Hudson River School artist. His home in nearby Highland Falls was a gathering place for fellow artists as they set out to paint the countryside. In the back of the Chapel are brochures outlining a walking tour of the cemetery just outside and a file to help visitors locate specific graves.

THE WEST POINT CEMETERY

Soldiers who have served the nation from the Revolution to Vietnam are buried at West Point. Here in one of the nation's oldest military cemeteries are the graves of Major General George Armstrong Custer, Lieutenant General Winfield Scott and Colonel Edward H. White II, among others. Also honored are those who have contributed to the Academy. Colonel Sylvanus Thayer, Superintendent from 1817-1833, was known as the "Father of the Military Academy." The old tree that shades his grave bears initials carved by cadets over the years. Major General Daniel Butterfield, a Cold Spring resident and the officer who commissioned taps, has the cemetery's most elaborate monument. During the Civil War he fought in forty-three battles and skirmishes, and the names of these engagements are carved on the sixteen columns surrounding his tomb. Butterfield appears in Thomas Pritchard Rossiter's Hudson River School landscape "Pic-Nic on the Hudson" which hangs in the Julia L. Butterfield Memorial Library across the river in Cold Spring. Behind the Chapel lies Margaret "Molly" Corbin who took up her husband's arms as he fell in the Revolutionary War Battle of Fort Washington.

Ensign Dominic Trant's grave is the oldest in the cemetery. Born in Cork, Ireland, he came to fight for America's independence and died on November 7, 1782, at the age of eighteen. John Lillie, another soldier of the Revolution, lived to command the garrison at West Point after the war. He died in 1801, and his epitaph reads:

> Drew his sword for his country, 1775
> Sheathed it unsullied by dishonor while aide
> to General Knox 1783

Several markers indicate burial plots of unidentified eighteenth-century soldiers, many of whom fought in the Revolutionary War.

Major General George Washington Goethals (Class of 1880), appointed by Theodore Roosevelt to build the Panama Canal, is buried near astronaut Colonel Edward H. White II (Class of 1952) and General Lucius Clay (Class of 1918) who organized the Berlin airlift in 1948-49. In the northeast corner of the cemetery is the Cadet Monument, dedicated to cadets and professors who died while at West Point. The Cadet Monument and nearby Wood's Monument were once landmarks for ships navigating the treacherous S-curve of the Hudson. West Point has prepared a walking tour of the cemetery, and the tour leaflet is available in the Chapel.

OTHER WEST POINT SITES

Most sites described are open to the public. Those with restricted access are noted with (R).

FORT PUTNAM

"If the British had captured Fort Putnam, they would probably have neutralized 'Fortress West Point.' " (Fort Putnam Museum) Built in 1779 by the troops of General Rufus Putnam to protect Fort Clinton below, Fort Putnam, now restored to its eighteenth-century appearance, stands high above Michie Stadium. From its ramparts, Revolutionary War soldiers had a commanding veiw of ships attempting to navigate the treacherous S-curve of the Hudson. Visitors have the same magnificent view of the river today and can also see brightly polished cannon and casements (soldiers' living quarters). There is also a small museum on site. The displays in the museum are limited, and there is a lengthy (and at times tedious) sound and light show, "West Point and the Hudson Highlands 1775-1783." Dedicated students of the Revolution will find this show of interest. Cadet Dwight D. Eisenhower (Class of 1915), himself a Revolutionary War buff, loved to walk along the ramparts of Fort Putnam and think back on the nation's early military history.

FORT CLINTON

Only the ruins remain of Fort Clinton, which was designed by Thaddeus Kosciuszko during the Revolutionary War. Originally known as Fort Arnold, it was renamed when Benedict Arnold's treason was discovered. For years, cadet summer encampments were held on the northeast corner of The Plain near the old stonework of Fort Clinton. Dashing cadets parading in full-dress uniforms captured the imagination of daytrippers who traveled up the Hudson from New York City in the latter part of the nineteenth century. Cadet hops were held three times a week, and the very presence of young ladies on The Plain indicated that discipline was more relaxed in the summer. All this changed in the 1920s when Superintendent Douglas MacArthur moved the encampment to Fort Dix, New Jersey, to train the cadets with regular Army units.

CONSTITUTION ISLAND AND
THE WARNER HOUSE

A special treat available only in the summer is a trip to Constitution Island. From West Point's South Dock, a small 23-passenger

Summer encampment on the plain. *U.S.M.A. Special Collections*

boat makes the ten-minute trip to the island twice a day on Wednesday and Thursday afternoons. Constitution Island was fortified in 1775 because of its location at the S-curve of the Hudson, and it was from the island that the Great Chain was stretched to West Point during the Revolutionary War (see above, Trophy Point). After the British took the island and burned the fortifications in 1777, West Point was chosen as a more strategic position and has been garrisoned ever since.

Never again an important military position, the island passed into private hands and was purchased by Henry Warner in 1836. Warner's dream of an elegant summer retreat was dashed by the Depression of 1837, and instead Warner and his family took up permanent residence on the island. Warner's two daughters, Susan and Anna, wrote one hundred six books while living in the house. Susan's best seller *The Wide, Wide World* was second in sales only to *Uncle Tom's Cabin* in the nineteenth century. Anna is best remembered for her lyrics to "Jesus Loves Me."

What you see today is the house as it was when the sisters lived and worked there together. Guides tell the story of their daily life. Anna rose before dawn, prepared tea for her sister, and then, alr ays conscious of their dwindling resources, wrote by the ligh of a small oil lamp. Possessions had to be sold one by one to meet household expenses. When their father needed a winter coat, the sisters sold pieces of the family silver.

And yet, their life was not an unhappy one. They conducted Bible study classes for the cadets who rowed over from West Point to attend. Worried that grass stains would ruin the young men's white dress trousers, Susan and Anna wove straw mats for the cadets to sit upon as they studied. The house contains many mementos of the special relationship between the sisters and these young men. From the sisters, cadets received nosegays of island flowers, the only non-regulation items allowed in their rooms. On their tours of duty, the soldiers remembered the sisters with souvenirs and postcards from around the world.

Though impoverished, the sisters' special feeling for West Point would not allow them to accept the numerous offers to buy the island. One offer proposed turning the island into an amusement park, an idea they found ill-suited for land so near West Point. Mrs. Russell Sage bought the island late in Anna's life with the provision that Anna be allowed to live there and that the land be given to West Point on her death. Susan and Anna Warner are buried in West Point's cemetery on the grounds of the Academy they loved so well.

Constitution Island is the setting for Thomas Pritchard Rossiter's "Pic-Nic on the Hudson," a Hudson River School landscape that hangs in the Julia L. Butterfield Memorial Library across the river in Cold Spring. Today, it is cadets who picnic on the island. Since 1969, it has been set aside for cadet weekend activities, a use which would have greatly pleased the Warner sisters.

THE *COMMANDER*

The *Commander*, built in 1917, can take up to one hundred twenty-five passengers on its two-hour cruise up the Hudson. Departing from West Point's South Dock on weekdays from

May through October, it travels as far as Cornwall Bay just south of the Newburgh-Beacon Bridge. From its deck, sights off-limits or difficult to see from land—Flirtation Walk, Kissing Rock and "BEAT AIR FORCE" painted on the field house roof—are visible. A tour guide tells stories about the river and points out interesting spots along the way (914/446-7171).

Washington Hall, the 4500-seat Cadet Mess. *U.S.M.A. Archives*

WASHINGTON HALL

Although Washington Hall houses the chaplains' offices, class-rooms and Corps Headquarters, it is best known as the Cadet Mess. Three times a day cadets assemble here for meals. Form-ing up by company, cadets march into the hall, averting their eyes from the Foundation Eagle carved above the entrance. Tradition has it that any cadet who views the eagle during the school year will be found deficient in academics.

Washington Hall is enormous, able to accommodate all 4400 cadets at one time. Seated at tables for ten, cadets are served family style, and the entire Corps can be fed in twenty minutes. Special athletic and diet tables are set aside for those requiring variations from the 4000-calorie-a-day standard fare. Plebes at the foot of each table pour drinks and distribute desserts. So exacting is the Table Commandant, a First Classman, that Plebes carry paper templates to ensure that the portions they cut will be precisely equal and will pass inspection.

T. Loftin Johnson's famous mural depicting historic warriors and decisive battles covers one entire wall. In the north wing, a stained glass window traces the life of George Washington for whom the hall is named. From a balcony above the main entrance, known as the Poop-Deck, announcements are made. Many distinguished guests have addressed the assembled Corps from this platform. (R)

EISENHOWER HALL

Eisenhower Hall, the red brick building near Gillis Field House, is the center for cadet cultural activities. Its 4400-seat theater, designed to accommodate the entire Corps, is the second largest center for the performing arts in New York State. Only Radio City Music Hall in New York City is larger. Each season brings a wide range of offerings—symphonies, opera, Broadway shows, dance companies and celebrities—to "Ike" Hall's stage. Many of these productions are open to the public as are several art exhibitions scheduled throughout the year. The Cadet Fine Arts Forum and the Cadet Theater Arts Guild also sponsor many events at Eisenhower Hall, and dances are held in the Grand Ballroom overlooking the Hudson River. The Eisenhower Hall box office is located on the lower level of the building (914/938-4159).

TAYLOR HALL

Taylor Hall, the Administration Building, houses the offices of the Superintendent, the Academic Dean, the Directorate of Academy Relations and the Academic Board Room. Its 150-foot tower is an engineering feat. Built of stone without the support of girders, it is the tallest construction of its kind in the United States. On the second floor is the Superintendent's office. Surrounded by the portraits of all of his predecessors, the Superintendent looks out upon the Hudson River, a reminder of West Point's strategic importance during the Revolutionary War. A glass-front cabinet with objects that symbolize the three components of the Academy's program—academic, athletic, and military—makes clear to visitors the special nature of West Point.

The Academic Board Room with its vaulted ceiling, large stained glass window and dark wood paneling has the feel of a medieval hall. Carved on its massive stone mantel are nine figures of great warriors including the Biblical Joshua, Alexander the Great and Charlemagne. Several times a week the Board, composed of the Superintendent, Dean, Commandant and department heads, meets here to discuss academic policy. (R)

GRANT HALL

Grant Hall provides a relaxed setting in which cadets receive their guests. With overstuffed chairs, comfortable sofas, Oriental rugs and wood paneled walls, it resembles the living room of a gracious country home. Highly polished tables, leaded glass cabinets and flowers in porcelain vases decorate the room. Above the fireplace is a painting of Dwight D. Eisenhower (Class of 1915) in his World War II uniform. Portraits of other famous West Point graduates hang on the walls. At one end is the office of the cadet hostess, who plans social events for cadets. Grant Hall is reserved for upperclassmen, and Plebes must have special permission to use it. (R)

CHAPELS

Cadet Chapel (see page 23)

Old Cadet Chapel (see page 44)

Catholic Chapel

Built in 1899 in the Norman Gothic style, the Chapel of the

Most Holy Trinity was patterned after St. Ethelred's Carthusian Abbey Parish Church in Essex, England. Much of the interior was donated in honor of Academy graduates. Stained glass windows depict soldier saints and military orders of the Church. In 1960 when the Chapel was enlarged, the gilded figure of the Archangel Gabriel was added to the spire above the sanctuary. The Chapel holds daily Mass for the Roman Catholic population of West Point, and as the property of the Archdiocese of New York, is the only building on post not owned by the United States Government.

Jewish Chapel

Employing the same native gray granite as that of the Cadet Chapel, West Point's Jewish Chapel presents a contemporary interpretation of the military Gothic style. Completed in 1984, this house of worship includes a 250-seat sanctuary, classrooms, meeting rooms and a library. The gallery which connects the entrance and the sanctuary highlights significant Jewish contributions to West Point and the nation. Services are held each Friday night.

Post Chapel

Because of the expanded military demands placed upon West Point during World War II, a need arose for a Protestant worship facility in addition to the Cadet Chapel. Built in 1943 to serve soldiers and their families, the Post Chapel honors the four heroic Army chaplains who lost their lives in the sinking of the *Dorchester* on the third of February that year. Inside, a window entitled "The Four Chaplains" tells the story of these brave men who gave away their own life jackets so that others might live. Survivors tell how the four men, arms linked in prayer, went down with their ship. The Chapel is on Biddle Loop off Merritt Road.

ATHLETIC FACILITIES

Arvin Gymnasium

Emblazoned above the main entrance of the cadet gymnasium are Douglas MacArthur's immortal words:

Upon the fields of friendly strife
Are sown the seeds
That, upon other fields on other days
Will bear the fruits of victory.

With its five gyms, three swimming pools, basketball, handball and squash courts, weight room, facilities for boxing and wrestling, the cadet gymnasium ensures that every cadet can be an athlete. Named in memory of Captain Carl Robert Arvin (Class of 1965) who was awarded two Silver Stars for gallantry in Vietnam, the gym is an extensive complex composed of four sections. On the walls are Army "A's" recognizing cadets who have earned a varsity letter. Athletic trophies are on display in the north lobby which is open to the public. (R)

Gillis Field House

The slogans, "SINK NAVY" facing the post, and "BEAT AIR FORCE," visible from the river, make the Field House a West Point landmark. This facility, located near the North Dock, provides indoor space for varsity and intramural competitions. Its Carleton Crowell Memorial Track is named for the man who coached Army track and cross country teams from 1951 until his death in 1976. (R)

Holleder Center

The Holleder Center next to Michie Stadium houses the 2500-seat Tate Ice Hockey Rink and the 5000-seat Christl Basketball Arena. Since its completion in 1985, new cadets have reported for duty at this center on Reception Day (R-Day), their first day at the Academy. (R)

Army Athletic Ticket Office

Located near Eisenhower Hall, the Army Athletic Ticket Office handles all requests in person or by mail for Army athletic events. Tickets for many events—especially fall football games—must be reserved well in advance (914/446-4996).

Athletic Fields

Many outdoor fields are available for cadet athletic activities.

Buffalo Soldier Field across from the Hotel Thayer recalls the black troops who fought on the nineteenth-century frontier in the 9th and 10th Cavalry regiments. The Indians called them Buffalo Soldiers because they wore buffalo hides for warmth and embodied the courage of these animals of the Great Plains. The brick buildings behind the field once stabled the Academy's horses, and cadets took riding instruction in the area outside. Today, the horses are gone but the three mules—Ranger, Spartacus and Traveler—who serve as Army's mascots are housed in the Post Veterinary Clinic nearby.

The varsity football team practices on **Howze Field** near Michie Stadium. In the 1930s the cadets played polo there. Three additional fields are on The Plain: **Clinton, Daly** and **Doubleday Fields.** Doubleday Field, home of Army baseball, is named for Abner Doubleday (Class of 1842) who is credited with inventing the national pastime. North of Gillis Field House is **Shea Stadium**, West Point's outdoor track facility, dedicated to the memory of Lieutenant Richard T. Shea, Jr. (Class of 1952), who was posthumously awarded the Congressional Medal of Honor. While at the Academy, Shea set five long-distance track records and gave up his place on the United States Olympic Team to serve in Korea.

ACADEMIC HALLS

As an institution which concentrates on scientific, engineering and military training, West Point provides its cadets with state-of-the-art technological equipment and facilties. Nine-story **Mahan Hall** is the science and engineering building. **Bartlett, Washington** and **Lincoln Halls** contain additional classroom and laboratory space. **Thayer Hall,** once the Academy Riding Hall, is now divided into more than one hundred section rooms and houses West Point's central computers. Each cadet's personal computer is tied into this central system as well as into the library's computerized card catalog.

The **West Point Library** is recognized for its collections on military history, and preserves many records of West Point. Early in the nineteenth century Sylvanus Thayer convinced Congress of the need for textbooks on military history and strategy. He traveled to France and purchased a thousand volumes on behalf of the Academy. From this nucleus the library's collection has grown to almost 500,000 books along with numerous maps, prints, slides, newspapers, periodicals and tapes. While not open to the public, the collections are made accessible to researchers with special permission from the librarian. (R)

CADET BARRACKS

Cadet barracks are clustered around four quadrangles. **MacArthur Barracks** and **Eisenhower Barracks** on either side of Washington Hall are visible from The Plain. Other quarters also named for famous alumni include **Pershing, Lee, Grant, Bradley, Scott** and **Sherman Barracks.** Behind the Clock Tower in the **Central Area** is the one remaining section from the old Central Barracks built in 1851. Known as **First Division,** these barracks housed John J. Pershing (Class of 1886) and Douglas MacArthur (Class of 1903) as well as other First Captains from 1851-1918. Four rooms are set up to depict cadet quarters through time. In addition to Pershing's room and office, an 1853 room, a 1911 room and a 1960 room show how cadets lived in those years and may be viewed by the public on special occasions. First Division is also the site of the Treasurer's Office and of Honor Committee deliberations.

Just outside, in the Central Area, cadets walk off their demerits on Friday afternoons. In their dress grays, shouldering spotlessly cleaned rifles, they march back and forth from the guard room to the wall of Bradley Barracks. For every demerit received above the allowable limit, cadets must put in one hour of area time. Those who have gained much "walking experience" are called "area birds," and some even join the Century Club, once they have logged one hundred hours.

Also in the Central Area is the **French Monument** given in 1919 by the students of *L'École Polytechnique* to the cadets of the Academy. At one time cadets, upon completing their French studies, would hurl their French texts at the monument. The statue has four major flaws. As part of Plebe Knowledge, Fourth Classmen must know that the soldier's curved saber cannot be sheathed in his straight scabbard; that one of his jacket buttons is unbuttoned; that the bore of the cannon is too small to accommodate such large cannon balls and finally that wind cannot blow coattails in one direction and the flag in the other. (R)

THE AMPHITHEATRE

Below Trophy Point is the Amphitheatre, a small plateau on which the United States Military Academy Band gives Sunday concerts in the summer. Concertgoers enjoy musical programs which are enhanced by the lovely setting with its "million-dollar view of the Hudson." Fittingly, Tchaikovsky's *1812 Overture*, a work celebrating the French military victory, concludes every season. Performances are open to the public.

CADET HOSTESS HOUSE

Known as Marty Maher's house in the film *The Long Gray Line*, this fanciful gingerbread cottage, located near Eisenhower Hall, is actually the home of the Cadet Hostess. Traditionally a widow of an army officer, the hostess plans cadet social functions and instructs cadets in protocol and etiquette. Her house with its Victorian embellishments stands apart from the military Gothic buildings of the post. (R)

CLOCK TOWER

In 1857 a large clock was installed on the tower of the old Academic Building. On November 29, 1890, it struck the hour and signaled the start of the first Army-Navy game. When the old Academic Building was torn down in 1895 to make room for new barracks, the clock was moved, and its modern day replacement hangs on the tower of Pershing Barracks, guarded by granite gargoyles. The original clock was hand wound twice a week, and for forty-four years the task belonged to Sergeant Greenlief Winkelmann who forgot to wind it only once. In 1961 the old clock was replaced with a newer electrical model.

CULLUM HALL

General George W. Cullum (Class of 1833) was Academy Superintendent during the last years of the Civil War. In his will he provided funds for a hall at West Point to honor deceased graduates and those who had given distinguished service to the Academy. Portraits, statues and plaques pay tribute to these men, but Cullum stipulated that no one who had fought for the Confederacy would be memorialized here. Robert E. Lee and P.G.T. Beauregard are the exceptions since they also served as Academy Superintendents. Today, cadet hops are held in Cullum Hall which has been restored to its original 1898 Greco-Roman style. (R)

GENERALS' QUARTERS

Side-by-side facing The Plain are the homes of West Point's Superintendent and Commandant. Just across the road near Professors Row is the home of the Academic Dean. The Superintendent, a three-star general who heads the Academy, lives in the oldest building on post.

"Quarters 100," the Superintendent's house. *U.S.M.A. Special Collections*

"Quarters 100," first occupied by Sylvanus Thayer, was completed under his direction in 1820 and has been home to Academy Superintendents ever since. The first level is often used for Academy functions, and each year thousands of guests file through the rooms. The only official residence to receive more visitors than Quarters 100 is the White House in Washington, D.C. Many bequests have been left by previous Superintendents. A silver punch bowl belonged to Rene de Russy (1833-1838); a desk, to Henry Brewerton (1845-1852); and the Imari china was Douglas MacArthur's (1919-1922). Private living space is on the second floor, and in the basement, Thayer's old office has been restored to appear as it did in his time. It is said that the ghost of Thayer's cook, Molly, haunts the house. She supposedly rumples the coverlet in one of the bedrooms and leaves traces of blood on the cutting board in the basement kitchen.

The quarters next door belong to the Commandant of Cadets, a one-star general who is responsible for the military training of the Corps. The Dean of the Academic Board, another one-star general who oversees classroom instruction, traditionally lives in the brick, Victorian Gothic home facing Washington Road. (R)

LUSK RESERVOIR

Source of West Point's drinking water, Lusk Reservoir was constructed in 1898. This 78,000,000-gallon artificial lake lies just below Michie Stadium. At its south end is the Southeast Asia Memorial (see above) dedicated to those who lost their lives in Vietnam. The American Soldier Statue (see above) and the Air Cadet Memorial (see above) stand at the north end of the Reservoir.

OFFICERS CLUB

Located between Thayer and Cullum Halls, the Officers Club serves officers stationed on post and their families. First Class cadets may also use this facility. Moved to its present site in 1902, the Club has a restaurant, reception rooms and a semi-circular ballroom with panoramic veiws of the Hudson River. (R)

PROFESSORS ROW

Four homes built from 1821-1826 during the superintendency of Sylvanus Thayer face the river along Washington Road and form Professors Row. In these spacious homes, nineteenth-century professors lived with their families and conducted classes for cadets. Today, the dwellings have been divided to accommodate more families, and senior professors may request quarters there. (R)

SOUTH DOCK AND THE OLD TRAIN STATION

Along the river, off Williams Road, is the South Dock area. In the summer, the tour boat *Commander* leaves from this dock for its two-hour cruise of the Hudson (see above). In the marina are boats belonging to Academy personnel, and the waterfront serves as the base for cadet crew and sailing teams. The Superintendent's ferryboat also docks here. A large grassy field and picnic tables lining the river are available to the public.

Just across from the dock is the old West Point train station, now used by the West Point community for private social events. Until the late 1950s, incoming Plebes arriving by train were marched double time up the long, steep hill to The Plain. The fast-paced, strenuous climb was a harbinger of the demanding four years to come.

USMA INFORMATION

Army Athletic Association
West Point, NY 10996
(914) 938-2322

Army Athletic Ticket Office
(914) 446-4996

Hours to order tickets: Monday-Friday, 8:00 a.m. - 4:30 p.m.

Cadet Chapel

Daily, 8:00 a.m. - 4:15 p.m., Sunday morning worship service

10:30 a.m. during the academic year. Closed at times for special services.

Cadet Parades on The Plain

Late August to early November, April and May, football Saturdays. Call Visitors' Information Center for schedule (914) 938-2638.

Catholic Chapel

Daily, 8:00 a.m. - 4:15 p.m.

The *Commander*

Hudson Highlands Cruises
(914) 446-7171

May through October, by reservation. *Fee for cruise.*

Constitution Island and the Warner House
(914) 446-8676

Mid-June to October, Wednesday and Thursday afternoons, tours at 1:00 p.m. and 2:00 p.m., by reservation. *Admission fee.*

Eisenhower Hall Performing Arts Center
(914) 938-4159

Fort Putnam

May - last home football Saturday; Thursday - Monday, 10:30 a.m. - 4:00 p.m.

Gift and Book Shops

Visitors' Information Center (914) 938-2638
West Point Museum (914) 938-2203
Hotel Thayer (914) 446-4731
Association of Graduates (914) 446-5869

Hotel Thayer
(914) 446-4731

Restaurant open for breakfast, lunch and dinner. Hotel accommodations and conference facilities.

Jewish Chapel

Daily, 8:00 a.m. - 4:15 p.m.

Old Cadet Chapel and West Point Cemetery

Daily, 8:00 a.m. - 4:15 p.m.

Post Chapel

Daily, 8:00 a.m. - 4:15 p.m.

United States Military Academy Band Concerts

West Point Amphitheatre
(914) 938-2638

Visitors' Information Center
(914) 938-2638

Daily, 9:00 a.m. - 4:45 p.m. Guided bus tours of West Point (fee charged): April 1 - November, every 20 minutes, Monday - Saturday, 9:30 a.m. - 3:30 p.m., Sunday, 11:30 a.m. - 3:30 p.m.; December - March, Monday - Saturday, 11:00 a.m. and 1:00 p.m., Sunday, 2:00 p.m.

West Point Museum
(914) 938-2203

Daily, 10:30 a.m. - 4:15 p.m. Closed Christmas and New Year's Day.

CHAPTER 2

Guardian of the Nation: Two Centuries of Service

By 1780 the Revolution was floundering. The Continental Army had suffered calamitous defeats in the South. Soldiers were deserting and enlistments were running out. After five long years of fighting, George Washington was struggling to hold his battered army together. The British under Sir Henry Clinton knew that capturing Fortress West Point could be the turning point of the war. Major General Benedict Arnold, snubbed by Congress and deeply in debt, arranged to surrender West Point to the British. At a secret meeting with the enemy, he handed over his records of West Point's fortifications and troop strength and returned to his command. Shortly afterward while meeting with General Washington's aides, Arnold received word that the spy carrying his information had been taken. He fled down the Hudson on the frigate H.M.S. *Vulture,* and the name Benedict Arnold was forevermore linked to treachery.

Had West Point fallen, the colonies might never have gained their independence. George Washington knew that this rocky promontory overlooking the narrow S-curve of the Hudson was of utmost strategic importance and called it "the key to the Continent." From the beginning of the war, the British sought control of the narrows to divide the Americans and cut supply and communication routes between New England and the other colonies. After the American victory at Saratoga, Washington ordered his troops to fortify West Point and to control navigation along the river. In order to obstruct British ships, a Great Chain was stretched from an island in the middle of the channel to the shore below the fortifications. Twelve hundred links weighing 150 tons were floated on logs and successfully deterred enemy shipping. No British vessel ever attempted to test the barrier.

Garrisoned since January 20, 1778, West Point is the oldest military post in continuous service in the United States. When the Continental Army was disbanded at the end of the war, it was one of only two outposts maintained by Congress. Here the battle trophies, reminders of the new nation's victory, were stored, and here General Washington urged the country to establish a military academy to train its future officers. Despite the reverence Americans felt for their leader, they were suspicious of standing armies and an elite officer corps so reminiscent of the society they had just overthrown. For the rest of his life, Washington sought approval for an academy. In his last letter written two days before his death, he stressed once again the need for such a school. Ironically, it was Thomas Jefferson, egalitarian and champion of the citizen soldier, who in 1802 finally persuaded Congress to charter the United States Military Academy at West Point.

THE FIRST YEARS

When classes began in April 1802, the entire Academy consisted of seven officers and ten cadets. Unlike other educational institutions of the time, West Point was exclusively devoted to the study of engineering and science. As directed by Congress, the Chief Engineer of the Army Corps of Engineers, Jonathan Williams, was appointed Superintendent. No admission requirements were set—a twelve-year-old boy and a married man were two of the first cadets. There were no textbooks, no fixed school term and no military service mandatory upon graduation. The Academy struggled along, ignored by Congress and the nation until the War of 1812 when West Point all but emptied, sending faculty and students off to fight. At one point only one cadet and one instructor, Alden Partridge, remained on post.

When Partridge became Superintendent, he brought many changes to the Academy. Known as "Old Pewter" or "Old Pewt," Partridge had a hard, unyielding nature and felt he must be personally involved in every detail of cadet life. He planned the mess hall meals, inspected rooms and drilled the Corps on The Plain. He regimented the cadets' day from reveille to lights out, virtually eliminating any free time. He even designed the gray uniforms, patterned after those of General Winfield Scott's troops at the Battle of Chippewa in 1814, and still worn by cadets today. Although Partridge brought necessary structure, he was in constant conflict with his faculty. In 1817, President James Monroe removed him from office, provoking Partridge's lifelong vendetta against the Academy he had served so diligently.

THE THAYER ERA

It was with the appointment of Sylvanus Thayer as Superintendent in 1817 that the true history of the Academy begins. After receiving his degree from Dartmouth, Thayer graduated from West Point in 1808 and taught mathematics there from 1810 until called into active service during the War of 1812. Recognizing how poorly prepared the American troops were, Thayer requested permission to visit the military training schools of Europe to study their methods. President Madison sent him to *L'École Polytechnique* in France and authorized him to purchase books, maps and tactical guides on the art of warfare. These materials, sent back to West Point, formed the basis of the first

Sylvanus Thayer, "Father of the Military Academy."
West Point Museum

military library in the United States.

Using the knowledge he had gained abroad, Thayer reorganized the Academy. He standardized the school year and set firm graduation requirements. He instituted daily recitations by every cadet in every subject. Class size was limited to no more than fifteen men. He doubled curriculum offerings and made West Point the premiere scientific institution of its day. In addition, he held cadets to the standards expected of gentlemen, thus laying the foundation for West Point's venerable Honor Code. Cadets were evaluated regularly on their deportment as well as their academic skills. This objective system based on performance rather than family influence determined their military postings after graduation. Thayer took a personal interest in the progress of each cadet and had the reputation for knowing every detail of each cadet's life. In his early morning conferences, he amazed cadets with his up-to-the-minute knowledge of their debts, demerits and deficiencies. Not until years later was the secret of Thayer's omniscience revealed. His clerk, Timothy O'Maher, cut up the weekly academic and disciplinary reports and assembled the pieces of each cadet's record within the pigeonholes of Thayer's desk. With a quick downward glance, Thayer had all relevant information available to him.

Thayer was well aware that many Americans still viewed the Academy with distrust. During the summer encampments, he marched his well-turned-out troops to Boston, New York and Philadelphia, inspiring the crowds and winning their admiration. He hosted dignitaries from around the world and impressed his influential visitors with the high quality of the program at West Point. Never forgetting that it was the President and Congress far away in Washington who controlled the purse strings, he kept them constantly informed of the Academy's operations. Even so, various political factions attempted to undermine his authority. In 1831, in a dispute with President Andrew Jackson over the reinstatement of a cadet he had dismissed, Thayer resigned. Leaving from the South Dock, Thayer boarded a steamboat for New York. Although he lived until 1872 and became the first president of the Association of Graduates, he never again returned to West Point. He left an academy viable and strong and is revered as the "Father of the Military Academy."

FROM THAYER TO ROBERT E. LEE

Part of Thayer's legacy was a superb faculty who continued to train expert civil engineers so necessary to the growth and expansion of the country. He had gathered men who were the best in their fields to teach engineering, geometry and mathematics. As Professor of Engineering for forty years, Dennis Hart Mahan (Class of 1824) wrote the texts and taught the men who built America's canals, railroads and bridges throughout the nineteenth century. He never fought a battle, but his text *Advanced Guard, Outpost, and Detachment of Troops, with the Essential Principles of Strategy and Grand Tactics (Outpost)* greatly influenced how the Civil War was fought.

In spite of the contributions made by so many West Pointers, Americans were not yet convinced of the Academy's worth. They saw it as a breeding ground for a military aristocracy, ill-prepared to lead troops in battle. The Mexican War proved otherwise. After Santa Anna's troops crossed the Rio Grande in April 1846, President Polk asked Congress for a declaration of war.

West Pointers performed brilliantly, helping to win every battle from Monterrey to Mexico City. These junior officers, tried for the first time on the battlefields of Mexico, became the legendary figures of the Civil War. Fighting side by side at Vera Cruz and Chapultepec, they gained practical experience and strengthened the ties of friendship that crossed the lines of battle in that later conflict. In April 1847, the American army, marching to Mexico City, was halted at a mountain pass by Santa Anna's forces. Captain Robert E. Lee (Class of 1829), in a daring feat of reconnaissance, discovered a route to outflank the enemy, and troops under Captain George B. McClellan (Class of 1846), Lieutenant Ulysses S. Grant (Class of 1843) and others took the pass of Cerro Gordo. At Buena Vista, Colonel Jefferson Davis (Class of 1828) and his Mississippi Rifles came to the rescue of vastly outnumbered American troops and turned a near defeat into victory. General Winfield Scott had the highest praise for these young West Pointers. He declared, ". . . but for our graduated cadets, the war between the United States and Mexico might, and probably would, have lasted some four or five years, with, in its first half, more defeats than victories falling to our share; whereas in less than two campaigns, we conquered a great country and a peace, without the loss of a single battle or skirmish."

In 1852, Robert E. Lee became West Point's ninth Superintendent. As a cadet Lee never received a single demerit and graduated second in the Class of 1829. (Charles Mason of New York was first in the class. He resigned his commission after two years, and eventually became Chief Justice of the Iowa Supreme

Robert E. Lee as Superintendent (1852-1855).
U.S.M.A. Archives

Court.) Known as the "marble model" for his always perfect deportment and appearance, Lee was nevertheless beloved by his classmates. As Superintendent, his compassion and understanding endeared him to the cadets. He felt the Academy's course of study should include more liberal arts subjects and military fieldwork as well as engineering. He effected the first major curriculum changes since the days of Sylvanus Thayer. Robert E. Lee cherished West Point and his service in the United States Army, but as the differences between North and South came to a head in the 1860s, he, along with other Southern West Pointers, was forced to make a wrenching personal decision. Lee's devotion to the Academy made his one of the most poignant.

THE CIVIL WAR YEARS

The question of slavery and the right of states to determine their own destinies had always been issues of debate among Americans. By the late 1850s, these differences had become so entrenched and emotions so inflamed that there was little hope for the country to remain undivided. Echoes of this discord reached even West Point, as isolated as it was from the mainstream of public affairs. Cadets came from every state in the nation and brought with them their sectional beliefs and loyalties. When the fanatic abolitionist John Brown raided Harper's Ferry in 1859, his body was hanged in effigy from the window of Pierce Young, a cadet from Georgia. When Abraham Lincoln won the presidential election in 1860, Cadet Henry Farley of South Carolina resigned, the first of seventy-six cadets to leave West Point and join the army of the Confederate States of America (CSA). But it was the surrender of Ft. Sumter on April 12, 1861, that forced cadets to choose between the North and the South. Torn between loyalty to their individual states and the flag of the nation to which they had sworn allegiance, these young men suffered the added anguish of knowing that whatever their choice, they would face friends and classmates in battle.

From the first volley, West Pointers confronted each other across the lines. Major Robert Anderson (Class of 1826) held Ft. Sumter against the South Carolinians commanded by his former artillery student P.G.T. Beauregard (Class of 1838). General Beauregard had been Superintendent for only five days when he resigned to heed the call of his home state of Louisiana. He ordered Wade Hampton Gibbes (Class of 1860) to fire upon the fort. Gibbes' shot was returned by Abner Doubleday (Class of 1842), who is better remembered for his connection with baseball. Thus began the war.

Academy leadership proved crucial. Commanders on both sides followed the precepts of Professor Mahan, and in fifty-five of the sixty major battles, West Pointers led both the North and the South. Jefferson Davis (Class of 1828), President of the Confederacy, recognized that West Point–trained officers were a great asset to the South and would help compensate for its limited resources. He immediately appointed them to high ranking positions in the CSA, and their resounding victories early in the war counterbalanced the North's advantages in numbers and industrial production. All told, 306 West Point graduates fought for the Confederacy. Members of Congress were incensed. Realizing that the federal government had financed the training of men who were now leading the enemy, many senators supported an unsuccessful motion to abolish West Point rather than fund it. Not only did they question the appropriation, they also wondered if the solidarity Union officers felt toward their former classmates might affect their conduct of the war.

Five U.S.M.A. graduates, Union army commanders in the Civil War: (left to right) Wesley Merritt, Philip Sheridan, George Crook, John Gregg or James Forsyth, and George Armstrong Custer. *U.S.M.A. Special Collections*

Many friendships did transcend the years of strife. Union General George Armstrong Custer and Major General Thomas Lafayette Rosser, CSA, both Class of 1861, were Academy roommates who encountered each other in several battles. Early in the war Custer was amazed to spot Rosser riding before his troops, an easy target in his cape with bright red lining. The next day Rosser received a message saying, "Tam, do not expose yourself so. Yesterday I could have killed you." At Gettysburg, twelve of the thirteen top Confederate officers were West Pointers, and many had served at the army cavalry school in nearby Carlisle, Pennsylvania. Gerard A. Patterson recounts in *Rebels from West Point* that as the Southern leaders passed through this familiar territory on their way to the encounter, several stopped to pay formal calls on families with whom they had been on social terms while stationed there. In 1864 during the siege of Petersburg, Virginia, George Pickett (Class of 1846), CSA, ordered bonfires lit in celebration of the birth of his son. U.S. Grant on the other side responded by lighting bonfires along his lines and sent the baby a silver service from his father's old comrades and friends.

The enduring friendships which enabled the West Pointers to rejoice in each other's happiness also made the inevitable losses in war even more poignant. In October 1864, Southern General Dodson Ramseur (Class of 1860) was mortally wounded in the battle at Cedar Creek. Recognized by George Custer, he was taken to Sheridan's (Class of 1853) Union headquarters, where doctors from both sides tried to save his life. He died surrounded by his old classmates, and his friends assured safe passage for his body back to his home in North Carolina. For Ramseur's young wife and the new baby he would never see, Custer sent along a lock of the general's hair. In the war's final hour, it was Lee's faith and trust in the honor of a fellow West Pointer that allowed him to surrender to Grant at Appomattox. Though his army was shattered and its fighting days over, Lee knew he would receive honorable terms. In fact, at Lee's request Grant wrote, "Let all the men who claim to own a horse or mule take the animals home with them to work their little farms." As Lee rode back to his troops, Grant was quick to stop the Union cheers of victory. "The war is over; the rebels are our countrymen again."

RECONSTRUCTION THROUGH WORLD WAR I

By 1868, Southerners were once again accepted as cadets at

West Point. Quick to move toward reconciliation, the Academy did little to assimilate the war's enormous military advances and social changes. While the nation entered a period of great development, the Academy stagnated. Its Academic Board, composed of the permanent professors and the Superintendent, rigidly adhered to the established curriculum and refused to incorporate the educational innovations of other colleges and universities. West Point was no longer the archetype by which scientific institutions were judged. Cadet behavior was regulated to excessive standards. Infractions were punished to the maximum degree, and there was little room for flexibility. Hazing took on extreme proportions. Where once it was no more serious than boyish pranks, it became destructive, vindictive and dangerous. Cadets were required to maintain unnatural physical positions and were forced to eat and drink potentially lethal substances. Plebes were frequently made to swallow large quantities of tabasco sauce. Oscar Booz, who entered the Academy with a pre-existing throat condition, became ill and resigned during his Plebe year. His family attributed his death less than a year later to the additional damage caused by this hot, spicy liquid.

Some of the worst hazing occurred during Plebes' first three weeks at the Academy. Designed to introduce the new recruits to military conduct, this orientation often got out of hand. Upperclassmen tormented their charges unmercifully, screaming commands, marching them at double time and depriving them of food and sleep. Not surprisingly, this conditioning became known as "Beast Barracks."

It was during the Reconstruction era that the first black cadets attended West Point. Of thirteen admitted, only three graduated. The first was Henry O. Flipper, Class of 1877. Tolerated but not accepted by others, black cadets were isolated. It was not until recent decades that blacks became truly valued members of the Corps.

Two positive outlets for cadet energy became part of Academy life in this period. Baseball, played by Yankee soldiers during the Civil War, was popularized on The Plain by returning veterans. Dennis Mahan Michie (Class of 1892), who had played football in prep school at Lawrenceville, introduced the game to cadets. In 1890, the first Army-Navy football game was played, a tradition which has continued to the present day. West Point's football stadium, named in Michie's honor, was built in 1924. (Michie died fighting in the Spanish-American War.)

On February 15, 1898, the American battleship *Maine* was sunk in Havana harbor with great loss of life and property. "Remember the *Maine*" became the cry that rallied the country and took us to war with Spain. The war lasted only a few months, but once again Academy men played an important role. John J. Pershing (Class of 1886) saw action in both Cuba and the Philippines and served as a provincial military governor in the Far East. Hugh Scott (Class of 1876) also held administrative posts which prepared him to assume the superintendency of West Point in 1906. For the first time since the Civil War, West Pointers who had fought for the Confederacy once again wore Army blue. Fitzhugh Lee, Joseph Wheeler and Thomas Rosser commanded units of volunteers under their country's banner. Newspaper reports of battles recounted the daring exploits of American soldiers, glorified the military and unified the country. With vast new territories to administer and protect, the Army was expanded. The Corps of Cadets at West Point was expanded as well. The influx of new men and the upcoming centennial of its founding prompted an examination of the Academy's obsolete facilities. A massive building program was undertaken, creating the imposing Gothic structures seen today.

West Point's one hundredth birthday was celebrated in style. June Week 1902 brought President Theodore Roosevelt and other dignitaries to the graduation ceremonies. The president handed out diplomas and delivered a stirring address praising the contributions Academy men had made to their country. At long last, Southern graduates returned to join their Northern brothers, unified in their devotion to the Academy that had nurtured them all.

In its second century, West Point continued to send forth men of great ability. The roll call of graduates in the first decade and a half of the twentieth century is filled with names of men who became the heroes of the two world wars. Douglas MacArthur was Class of 1903; George S. Patton, Jr. graduated in 1909; and the Class of 1915, which included Dwight D. Eisenhower and

Cadet John J. Pershing (Class of 1886).
U.S.M.A. Special Collections

Omar Bradley, was called the "Class the Stars Fell On." Fifty-nine of its 164 members attained the rank of brigadier general or higher. These were the junior officers of World War I, all serving under General John J. Pershing (Class of 1886), Commander-in-Chief of the American Expeditionary Force (AEF).

Mobilizing millions of American men to fight for the first time on European soil was a monumental task. Conscription, unnecessary since the Civil War, was reinstituted in 1917. West Point itself was again almost emptied. Four classes were graduated early to provide leadership for the 2.2 million draftees. The National Guard was activated, and Douglas MacArthur molded units from twenty-six states into his famous Rainbow Division.

Fiercely loyal to their flamboyant colonel, they followed MacArthur into the trenches, proudly wearing the red, yellow and blue patch of their division. It was General Pershing who ensured that American troops would fight together as a distinct force under their own officers. The pressure from foreign allies to feed the vigorous doughboys, fresh from America, into their decimated ranks was intense. French and British forces had been fighting since the German march through Belgium in 1914, and three long years of bitter combat throughout France had exhausted their resources. Had Pershing acquiesced, the AEF would have lost its identity, and its crucial impact would have been diluted.

We as a nation entered the Great War full of idealism and sent our troops "over there" to fight the war to end all wars. President Woodrow Wilson was hailed in France as a conquering hero come to make the world safe for democracy. But the idealistic hopes for a peaceful world were shattered by the petty infighting and demands for vengeance of our victorious allies. The American people were disillusioned and felt betrayed again by the corrupt Old World. Isolationist and antimilitary sentiment prevailed at home, and West Point did not escape the backlash.

THE MacARTHUR YEARS

Into the postwar confusion of West Point came Douglas MacArthur. Appointed Superintendent in June 1919, MacArthur found veterans returning to resume their studies and the class organization in disarray. Recognizing that warfare had undergone a revolution on the battlefields of France, he was appalled that cadets were still being taught the tactics of the nineteenth century. He embarked upon a program of extensive reorganization. To break down the insularity of West Point's outlook, he required all cadets to read two newspapers a day, and he sent faculty members to visit other educational institutions. The first and third classes no longer enjoyed relaxed summer encampments at West Point. Instead, they traveled to Fort Dix, New Jersey, to train with the regular army. Realizing that the modern soldier needed an understanding of the men he would lead as well as knowledge of the new technology, MacArthur pressed for the inclusion of psychology, sociology and political science courses. He had observed that in combat situations men who were athletes performed exceptionally well and readily won the respect and admiration of their troops. Therefore, he made athletics a keystone of the curriculum. All cadets were required to participate in the expanded intramural sports program, and a full travel schedule was set up for interscholastic games.

Believing that some of the regulations which governed cadet life were unduly rigid, MacArthur allowed his charges more free time, additional furloughs and more spending money. He also took a firm stand against hazing. Working through a committee of cadets, he attempted to limit the indignities and physical punishments to which Plebes were subject. The committee ruled that Plebes could no longer be deprived of food on the whim of an upperclassman or forced to perform physically dangerous acts. Yet by no means was MacArthur an indulgent superintendent. He ordered reveille sounded earlier, depriving cadets of a precious hour of sleep; he compelled them to march to and from their summer training in New Jersey, wearing heavy field packs on their backs; and he required cadets to live by the gentlemanly code of conduct he himself embodied. Implicit since the Thayer years, the Honor Code was formalized under MacArthur's direction, and a cadet committee was charged with its enforcement.

All these changes met with great resistance. Partly because of MacArthur's autocratic style and partly because the innovations represented such a break with tradition, faculty members, disgruntled old graduates (DOGS) and even some cadets opposed them. His hazing reforms drew special fire from the DOGS. Having survived their own Plebe year, they pointed to the unity, the self-confidence and the pride of achievement engendered in classes which had weathered hazing together. Besides, they felt that if they had had to endure it, others should too. The Academic Board obstructed almost every change in the curriculum. With the support of many DOGS, board members bombarded Army Chief of Staff Pershing, himself not a great fan of MacArthur, with criticisms of the Superintendent's changes to their beloved Academy. On January 20, 1922, Pershing reas-

Douglas MacArthur as Superintendent,
1919-1922. *U.S.M.A. Archives*

signed MacArthur to the Philippines, relieving him of his command.

Some say that Pershing had other, more personal, reasons for banishing MacArthur. Both he and MacArthur had been suitors for the hand of Louise Brooks, a Philadelphia divorcée who had been Pershing's official hostess in Washington. It was only fifteen days after MacArthur's engagement to Mrs. Brooks was reported in *The New York Times* that Pershing issued orders sending the new couple to the Far East.

Despite his reassignment, MacArthur never lost his abiding devotion to West Point and its future. Almost all his reforms were eventually adopted, establishing the framework for the modern Academy. Unlike Thayer, he did return to the citadel high above the Hudson. In 1962, two years before his death, MacArthur proudly accepted West Point's highest honor, the Sylvanus Thayer Medal. He told cadets, "But in the evening of my memory, I always come back to West Point. Always there echoes and re-echoes in my ears—Duty, Honor, Country. Today marks my final roll call with you. But I want you to know that when I cross the river my last conscious thoughts will be of the Corps; and the Corps; and the Corps. I bid you farewell."

WORLD WAR II

In the years preceding World War II, many of MacArthur's ideas were put into practice. Congress increased the number of cadets in the Corps, and for the first time, Academy graduates received a bachelor of science degree. New Army postgraduate schools were established to offer specialized military training, enabling West Point to concentrate on what it had always done so well—sending forth men of character ready to lead citizen soldiers in the nation's defense. Robert Eichelberger (Class of 1909), who would hold Pacific commands in World War II, became Superintendent in 1940. During his tenure, additional acreage around West Point was acquired for infantry training, and the airfield outside nearby Newburgh, New York, was enlarged for Academy use. When Francis Wilby (Class of 1905) took over in 1942, he was thus able to offer flight training for the cadets. Wilby and his commandant Philip Gallagher (Class of 1918) developed a rigorous program to prepare cadets for combat and compressed the four-year program into three. Rumors that the War Department might shut down the Academy during the war and convert it to an officers training school never materialized, probably because of Wilby's foresight.

As in every previous war, West Point again fulfilled its mission. Its sons distinguished themselves in Europe and the South Pacific. Dwight D. Eisenhower from the legendary Class of 1915 was named commander of all Allied forces in Europe. After coordinating the largest amphibious landings in history—North Africa in 1942 and Sicily in 1943—Eisenhower was directed to ". . . enter the continent of Europe and . . . undertake operations aimed at the heart of Germany and the destruction of her armed forces." To do so, he had to transport hundreds of thousands of men across the formidable barrier of the English Channel. No invading force had successfully crossed it since 1066. On D-Day, June 6, 1944, American and British forces stormed the beaches of Normandy and began the long march to Berlin. On that very day, three thousand miles away, Eisenhower's son John was graduating from West Point.

General Anthony "Tony" McAuliffe (Class of 1919) and his 101st Airborne Division were besieged at Bastogne during the last German counteroffensive of the war in December 1944. They were outnumbered by more than two to one; supplies were desperately low; and weather conditions made aerial reinforcement impossible. When the Germans sent a formal demand for surrender, McAuliffe made his now famous reply: "Nuts!" In one word he affirmed both the indefatigable American fighting spirit and the stalwart courage of West Point men.

Still the Americans were trapped. After conferring with Omar Bradley (Class of 1915) at his headquarters in Luxembourg, George Patton (Class of 1909) met with General Eisenhower (Class of 1915) in Verdun to plan the relief of Bastogne. The only one to have anticipated the German advance, Patton astonished Eisenhower with his bold, daring counterstrategy. As always, he was prepared to press forward. He stood immediately ready to turn three divisions ninety degrees northward toward the German bulge. Risky under the best of conditions, this operation was especially dangerous in the ice and snow of winter. On the day after Christmas, Patton's Fourth Armored Division pushed through enemy lines to rescue McAuliffe's 101st. This was Patton at his best—maneuvering with speed and decisiveness, always on the attack. Despite his flaws he was the general most feared and admired by the enemy. According to Martin Blumenson, the authoritative biographer of Patton, a German senior officer captured in March 1945, stated, "General Patton is always the main topic of military discussion. Where is he? When will he attack? Where . . . ? How? With what? . . . General Patton is the most feared General on all fronts."

Whereas victory was close at hand in Europe, it seemed as though fighting in the Pacific would go on as it had for years. On December 27, 1941, the Japanese captured the Philippines. General Douglas MacArthur (Class of 1903) and General Jonathan M. Wainwright (Class of 1906) evacuated American and Filipino troops to Bataan and Corregidor. Ordered by President Roosevelt to escape to Australia and plan Allied strategy in the Pacific, MacArthur was incensed at having to abandon his men. Vowing to return, he left the defense of Corregidor to General Wainwright. Wainwright held out until May 6, 1942, against the enemy's overwhelming air power and naval blockade. His stalwart defense diverted Japanese resources and saved Australia from attack.

With the decisive Battle of Midway in June 1942, American forces gained the offensive, but the Japanese were not about to surrender. During the six months of terrible fighting at Guadalcanal, Japanese soldiers fought relentlessly to the bitter end. In Papua, New Guinea, troops under General Robert Eichelberger (Class of 1909) and Australia's Sir Edmund Herring met with unyielding resistance. Holding tenaciously each inch of occupied territory, the Japanese forced American commanders to wage a three-year, island-by-island campaign. The price was enormous. In capturing Iwo Jima alone, over 6800 men lost their lives, and 21,000 more were counted as casualties. Leading the Tenth Army in an amphibious assault on Okinawa, Lieutenant General Simon Bolivar Buckner, Jr. (Class of 1908) was killed in action. Okinawa was an essential base for the planned Allied invasion of Japan and for postwar Pacific strategy.

However, an all-out invasion of the Japanese home islands proved unnecessary. The horror of the first atomic bomb explosions over Hiroshima and Nagasaki convinced the Japanese to capitulate. Douglas MacArthur, having redeemed his promise to return to the Philippines, received the Japanese surrender on the deck of the battleship *Missouri* in Tokyo Bay on September 2, 1945.

THE MODERN ACADEMY

Atomic weapons forever changed the way wars would be fought. No longer would the strength of America's troops and vast natural resources .ensure victory. With the possibility of total annihilation and the proliferation of nuclear weapons, mankind could be held hostage by anyone with a bomb. The new dimension of destruction shattered many of the underlying assumptions by which governments dealt with one another. Repercussions of this upheaval were felt at West Point. The times demanded a new kind of military leader. Taking MacArthur's reforms a step further, the Academy revised its curriculum to train leaders who would be effective at the conference table as well as on the battlefield. Psychology, economics and world affairs became valued parts of West Point's course of study. An expanded elective program was introduced, and cadets were permitted to choose a field of concentration. In addition, the Corps of Cadets was greatly enlarged.

The limited conflicts of Korea and Vietnam changed military strategy as well. Under the auspices of the United Nations, American forces attempted to repel the North Korean incursion into South Korean territory in June 1950. Fighting continued for three long years. Although in theory the United Nations forces had unlimited men and materiel at their command, in fact they were inhibited from waging all-out war not just by political restraints, but by the fear of nuclear escalation.

The same constraints applied in Vietnam, where United States troops encountered the guerrilla tactics of the North Vietnamese Regular Army and the Viet Cong. Without the moral authority of a United Nations directive, public support for the war was limited. The 1960s saw antiwar demonstrations, draft card burnings and revolts against all forms of accepted standards. The military establishment came under intense criticism, and Americans once again questioned the need for an academy to educate an elite corps of professional officers. And yet, officers trained at West Point demonstrated dedicated leadership and extraordinary heroism on the battlefields of Korea and Vietnam.

General Garrison H. Davidson (Class of 1927), who served under George Patton (Class of 1909) in World War II, was assigned to Eighth Army Headquarters in Korea. In an attempt to prevent the Chinese from retaking Seoul in the spring of 1951, Davidson conceived a defensive strategy that stopped the enemy north of the city. So effective was his plan that it became known as the Davidson perimeter defense. In July 1953, Lieutenant Richard T. Shea, Jr. (Class of 1952) led his troops in a series of attacks against enemy forces during the bloody fighting at Porkchop Hill. Hopelessly outnumbered, his company fought in close hand-to-hand combat, and Shea himself was seriously wounded in the neck and body. Refusing evacuation five times, he fought on to the death, a symbol of courage and true leadership for his men.

Because of the nature of the war in Vietnam, it was individual acts of bravery that demonstrated the leadership and character of the men who fought there. Both Major Donald W. Holleder (Class of 1956) and Captain Robert F. Foley (Class of 1963) evacuated wounded soldiers at great risk to their own safety. Holleder, an operations officer with the 11th Infantry Brigade, left the safety of a base camp to run into the midst of enemy fire and died attempting to rescue the wounded. Captain Foley, caught with his men in dense jungle terrain, singlehandedly carried out a counterattack and provided cover until the injured could be withdrawn. He continued on despite his own wounds, and destroyed three enemy gun emplacements. Lieutenant Colonel Andre Lucas (Class of 1954), supervising a ground attack from a helicopter already heavily damaged by enemy fire, flew within enemy range to resupply his troops with ammunition. He was later killed directing the withdrawal of his men. When Captain Paul W. Bucha (Class of 1965) was dropped by helicopter behind enemy lines with a small reconnaissance party, he and his men encountered a battalion-size force. Pinned down by machine gun fire, Bucha crawled toward the gun emplacement and singlehandedly demolished the bunker with grenades.

All these acts of gallantry embody ideals and standards long cherished at West Point. It has always been the mission of the Academy to prepare military leaders whose service will bring honor to themselves and their country. Yet despite the moral courage of many individuals, the Vietnam experience altered the way Americans viewed the military and led many to question the role of authority. Balancing the changes in American society with the standards and high expectations traditional at the Academy, West Point reexamined cadet life. Cadets were granted greater freedom. Even Plebes were allowed leave at Christmas, and all cadets were given one month off in the summer. Permitted to choose among a variety of courses, cadets were given the opportunity to express opinions which did not always agree with those of their instructors. More and more members of minority groups were admitted to West Point. And in 1976, the Corps was revolutionized by the admission of women who today account for ten per cent of its strength. In 1989, for the first time in its history, a woman, Kristin Baker, was appointed First Captain of the Corps of Cadets.

As in the past, West Point stands in sharp contrast to other American colleges. Cadets are held to the highest of standards in both their academic and personal lives. Physical conditioning is given high priority. Military regimentation governs each hour of the day, and as future officers, cadets are trained to make quick, informed decisions under pressure. Putting into practice leadership principles emphasized in the classroom, upperclassmen assume junior officer positions. Above all, West Point strives to develop character. Imbuing cadets with the strength to represent their country and to lead their armies in its defense, the Academy also seeks to send forth men and women to contribute to America's progress in times of peace. In its long and illustrious history, the United States Military Academy at West Point has more than fulfilled George Washington's vision. For almost two hundred years, the Long Gray Line has served our nation, ever faithful to "Duty, Honor, Country."

CHAPTER 3

Duty, Honor, Country: Life As a Cadet

Hidden somewhere in the Sixth Division barracks was a billiard room. Night after night cadets disappeared into a secret hideout where they played for hours on end. The tactical officers (Tacs) were perplexed. They knew the table existed, but all attempts to unearth it had been in vain. Having purchased the table in New York, cadets transported it across the frozen Hudson under the cover of darkness on a bitter winter's night in 1865. They installed it in a coal room which was fitted out as a gentlemen's club of the day. They offered memberships to their fellows at ten dollars each, and for nearly a year the club flourished. But at long last, the game was up; the cadets, however, had the last laugh. When the Tacs burst through the coal room door, they found an empty room, a roaring fire, barrels of crackers and cheddar cheese, and a note of welcome from the club members.

The Tactical Officers on duty at the Academy:

We, the members of the Billiard Club, . . . desire to present this
billiard table, . . . to the Officers on Duty at West Point, as a slight
token of our gratitude to them, for the generous courtesy displayed by them towards us, in allowing us for so long a time to
enjoy the privilege of the Club. . . . Hoping that you will be
pleased to accept this little token of our regard, we are,

Very respectfully yours.

By Order of the Committee

Cadets have always met the challenge. Whether it is outwit-
ting Tacs with their ingenious pranks or facing the rigors of their
eighteen-hour days, cadets have found the resources within
themselves to surmount almost any obstacle. The Academy
program is designed with one purpose: to educate young men
and women to assume leadership roles in their country's service. It demands total commitment to four years of arduous
military, physical and academic training which emphasizes the
need to perform well under stress. Character is the key, and it is
the integrity inculcated by the Honor Code that becomes the
guiding principle for these future officers.

As members of the Regular Army, cadets receive an annual
salary from which they must buy their uniforms, textbooks and
computers, and pay for their meals and laundry. Housing, tu-
ition and medical care are provided as is the opportunity for a
comprehensive and excellent undergraduate education leading
to a Bachelor of Science degree. In return, cadets agree to serve
in the United States Army for five years upon graduation. Their
daily life is far different from that of students at other American
colleges. Upon entering the Academy, cadets take an oath of
allegiance to the United States government and accept the Uniform Code of Military Justice. Recognizing that the profession of
arms requires regimentation, they subject themselves to military
discipline which requires considerable limitations on their personal freedom. The challenges and opportunities are many for
these young men and women dedicated to the pursuit of excel-
lence. They find their rewards in the Academy's ideals of "Duty,
Honor, Country" and in the service they will render their nation.

Daily recitation. *U.S.M.A. Special Collections*

ACADEMICS

The West Point experience concentrates on three major areas—academics, military training and athletics. The academic program consists of a prescribed thirty-two course core, eight physical education courses and twelve electives. After Plebe year, cadets select either the humanities and public affairs track or the mathematics-science-engineering track. Electives, chosen from over four hundred offerings, lead to a concentration in a field of study or an optional major. Specialization beyond the professional major—the education of a military officer—is relatively new in the Academy's history. Founded as a school of military engineering, West Point originally came under the jurisdiction of the Army Corps of Engineers. In fact, it was Thomas Jefferson's intent that West Point graduates use their engineering skills to help build America's bridges and canals as well as its batteries and redoubts. Engineering is still a major emphasis with such sub-specialities offered as engineering physics and systems engineering as well as mechanical and civil engineering.

Still the core curriculum is the heart of the academic program. Schooling cadets in the arts and sciences, it provides them with the tools and knowledge necessary to be future officers in the United States Army. Training cadets to analyze problems in search of workable solutions, it instills in them confidence in their abilities and in those of other West Pointers on the battlefield or at the conference table.

As in the days of Sylvanus Thayer, the "Father of the Military Academy," classes are small. With only twelve to sixteen students in a section, there is maximum opportunity for student/ teacher interaction, and instructors closely monitor each cadet's progress. Thayer believed that every cadet should recite every day in every class. While today recitation is no longer the sole means by which instructors judge mastery of subject matter, they will not tolerate anything less that total preparation and never have. The legendary Professor Dennis Hart Mahan, who taught at West Point from 1830-1871, seemed to know instinctively which cadet had not studied and called on him immediately. Today's cadets ascribe the same power to their instructors.

Not surprisingly, cadets feel pressured and enjoy any opportunity to break the tension. West Point annals are filled with accounts of classroom capers. In a class on weaponry, Jefferson Davis (Class of 1828), future president of the Confederacy, terrified his artillery instructor, Zebina Kinsley ("Old Zeb"), when he presented him with a lighted hand grenade. As everyone fled the room, Davis calmly threw the grenade out the window. In another famous story, Ulysses S. Grant (Class of 1843) was at the blackboard in engineering class. In his breast pocket was a classmate's large silver watch which the cadets had been examining prior to class. At the entrance of the instructor, Zealous B. Tower, Grant had deftly concealed the timepiece. Unbeknownst to the other cadets, the watch's owner had set it to go off during the class. In the midst of Grant's recitation, it began to strike the hour. Tower ordered the door closed to shut out the noise, but the bonging grew louder. Grant continued unruffled to the amazement of his fellows while the professor madly searched the room for the source of the disturbance. Grant's composure under pressure presaged the steadiness he would later display in battle.

The Academy has always viewed the classroom as a testing ground. Science class was especial torture for James McNeill Whistler. Asked to define "silicon," Whistler described it as a gas, thus hastening the end of his Academy career. Years later, he said that had he answered correctly, he would have been a major general rather than an artist.

Today, grade point average is still a major component of the cadet ranking system instituted by Thayer. Since 1818, names of the First Five in each class have been reported annually in the official Army Register. For many graduates, distinguished military careers have fulfilled the promise of their high academic achievements. Robert E. Lee (Class of 1829) graduated second in his class, and Douglas MacArthur, first in the Class of 1903, achieved an astonishing average of 98.14%, a mark unsurpassed for twenty-three years. On the other hand, George S. Patton, Jr. (Class of 1909) did not shine in his studies. Turned back after his first year, it took him five years to complete the Academy program, and he still ranked low in his class. His intellect, however, was superb as evidenced by his brilliant tactics on the battlefield. It is probable that his low grade point average resulted from a reading disorder, now known as dyslexia.

Certain words describing academic abilities and learning styles have become part of cadet slang. Patton was a "goat," near the bottom of his class. "Engineers" are at the top. To be "hivey" is to learn easily, and to be a "file boner" is to get ahead at the expense of classmates. To be "found," found deficient, results in dismissal from the Academy. The goal is to be "pro," proficient in studies, but the Academy's program emphasizes other areas as well. Affirming Thayer's ideal of educating the whole man, the West Point experience balances academic instruction with military and athletic training.

MILITARY TRAINING

From high school senior to cadet in one day—a dramatic transformation takes place on The Plain. Early in the summer, incom-

Military training. *U.S.M.A. Archives*

ing Fourth Classmen arrive at West Point for their six-week Cadet Basic Training (CBT). On their very first day, they learn to stand, walk, sit and respond in a military manner. They are issued uniforms; their hair is cut; they learn to salute and march in unison. Their military training has begun, and it will continue for four years, permeating every aspect of cadet life. Regulations specify how beds must be made, how uniforms must be arranged in closets, and even prescribe how many items may be on desks. Under the direction of the Commandant, the Corps is organized as a brigade and subdivided into regiments, then battalions and finally companies. Cadets live on military time, awakened at 0600 by reveille. In company formation they march to meals and put into practice their training in military maneuvers and drills.

"New cadets" are introduced to military life in Cadet Basic Training. This intensive six-week trial, once known as Beast Barracks, forces cadets to call upon every ounce of physical strength and mental resolution within them. Not everyone makes it. Long days are spent on marches, on the rifle range and negotiating steep terrain. Drilling for hours on end, new cadets are taught to respond to commands with immediacy and precision. They learn about West Point's long, tradition-filled past and embrace its ideals of duty, honor and service. On maneuvers, in athletic competition and in a week-long bivouac at the end of CBT, they develop the reliance on one another and the comraderie that will carry them through their exacting Plebe year.

The two weeks between Christmas leave and the beginning of the second semester are set aside for military instruction. Field training takes place in the summer. Cadets spend their second summer at West Point's Camp Buckner where they work in small combat units and are exposed to everything from infantry to artillery to air defense operations. In their third and fourth summers, cadets are assigned to lead regular Army units and to supervise CBT and Third Class Training. They also participate in such military specialty courses as jungle warfare, arctic operations, and escape and survival techniques. Throughout their years at the Academy, cadets assume leadership roles and take on more and more responsibility as they move up through the ranks. They gain the discipline, self-confidence and skills they will need as commissioned officers in the United States Army.

ATHLETICS

Every cadet is an athlete, not just a spectator but a participant. Cadets are instructed to arrive at West Point in good physical condition, ready for the rigors of Cadet Basic Training. For the next four years, cadets hone their physical skills and develop their athletic talents. They must take eight semesters of physical education classes, and all participate in either interscholastic or intramural sports. Twenty-eight sports are offered on the intercollegiate level, ranging from football and baseball to swimming, track and volleyball. Twenty-four club teams compete against other colleges and universities in such areas as cycling, fencing and skiing. Every year some twenty-five cadets from the marathon team run the Boston Marathon. Cadet companies field intramural teams which play each other for the regimental and brigade championships. The Academy designs its program to develop leadership and teamwork and to encourage physical activity throughout life.

Athletics have not always played such a major role in cadet life. For its first fourteen years, the Academy had no formal athletic program. In 1816 Pierre Thomas was appointed Master of the Sword to instruct cadets in the gentlemanly sport of fencing. (Since World War II, the position of Master of the Sword has been retitled Director of Physical Education.) Fencing, military calisthenics and, later, horsemanship were the only authorized physical activities until the Civil War. Riding, introduced in 1839, served a military purpose. On the frontier, cavalry officers fought Indian campaigns on horseback. Ulysses S. Grant (Class of 1843) was celebrated for his horsemanship. In his last year at West Point, he jumped his horse York five feet, six inches, setting a record that stood for twenty-five years. In fact, one of the last vestiges of the nineteenth-century Academy was the horsemanship required of cadets. Until 1947, they took instruction in the Riding Hall, and officers frequently kept their own horses at government expense.

It was Douglas MacArthur, Superintendent from 1919-1922, who recognized the need for an intensive athletic program in cadet training. As a commander in World War I, he had observed that officers who were athletes performed well in combat and easily won the respect and admiration of their men. He instituted the intramural program and made sure each cadet participated in at least one sport ever year. An outfielder during his own days at the Academy, MacArthur was especially interested in baseball. Each week he reviewed the team's performance and planned future strategy with the coach. In his short jacket, carrying his riding crop, he was a familiar figure on the sidelines at football practice as well. Thirty-seven years after his superintendency, as Supreme Commander for the Allied powers in Japan, MacArthur exhorted cadets before the 1949 Army-Navy game. "From the Far East I send you one single thought, one sole idea—written in red in every beachhead from Australia to Tokyo—there is no substitute for victory!"

West Point's program has produced a number of nationally acclaimed athletes. Doc Blanchard and Glenn Davis, the famous "touchdown twins," each earned the Heisman Trophy in the 1940s, as did Pete Dawkins in 1958. Dick Shea received the Army Athletic Association's award as the outstanding athlete in

Class of 1915 wearers of the Army "A": Omar Bradley (third row, third from right), Dwight D. Eisenhower (second row, third from left), and James Van Fleet (third row, extreme left). *U.S.M.A. Archives*

the Class of 1952. Setting five long-distance track records, he gave up his chance to compete in the Olympics that year in order to serve in Korea. Shea was killed in action at Porkchop Hill, and West Point's track and field facility was named in his honor. A number of famous generals excelled in athletics during their days at the Academy. Omar Bradley (Class of 1915) was known for his baseball throwing arm, and Dwight D. Eisenhower (Class of 1915) was called the "Kansas Cyclone" on the football field and "Daredevil Dwight" for his bold horsemanship. Injuries cut short the football careers of both Eisenhower and George S. Patton, Jr. (Class of 1909). Patton went on to earn his Army "A" in the 220-yard low hurdles.

Recognizing the important role of athletics in the training of military leaders, West Point challenges cadets to realize their full athletic potential. The strength, discipline and endurance acquired in athletic competition will stand them in good stead in future years. In Douglas MacArthur's words, emblazoned above the gymnasium door:

> Upon the fields of friendly strife
> Are sown the seeds
> That, upon other fields on other days
> Will bear the fruits of victory.

Early Army-Navy football game. *U.S.M.A. Special Collections*

THE ARMY-NAVY RIVALRY

In 1890, Annapolis issued a challenge: Play us in football on November 29th. Only two people at West Point had ever played football before. One was Dennis Mahan Michie who had instigated the whole plan. Michie had played at Lawrenceville prep school and was eager to introduce the game to the Corps. Knowing the Academy could never resist, he convinced his midshipmen friends to challenge the cadets. Since his father, Peter Smith Michie, was head of West Point's Academic Board, permission to play the game was granted. Unfortunately, the cadets were only allowed to practice when weather was unsuitable for Saturday afternoon parades, and they were beaten 24-0. Army units everywhere rallied to redress this humiliation. They sent money for uniforms and training, and Harry Williams, a former Yale gridiron star, volunteered to coach without pay. The next year, a better prepared group of cadets traveled to Annapolis and soundly beat Navy 32-16.

Not only did football begin a new chapter in Army sports history, it also radically changed the life of cadets. The Academy was no longer as isolated as it had been. Cadets traveled to other campuses, and visiting teams brought the outside world to West Point. The Army-Navy rivalry became the focus of the fall season, and cadets yelled themselves hoarse every year. The rivalry became so intense that these contests had to be suspended twice. At the Army-Navy Club in New York City, a brigadier general and a rear admiral challenged each other to a duel after the 1893 game. The duel was averted, but the Secretary of War and the Secretary of the Navy halted future contests. No games were played between 1894 and 1898. Reinstated in 1899, they were once again suspended in 1928 and 1929 because of a dispute about player eligibility. In 1930, however, the Academies were called upon to play a game for charity. Since the country was deep in the Depression, neither could refuse. The games resumed and have been played every year since. Even in the midst of World War II, soldiers fighting in Europe and the Pacific enthusiastically supported their service teams and followed the scores. In 1944 when Army beat Navy 23-7, Douglas MacArthur telegraphed head coach Earl "Red" Blaik, the most successful coach in West Point history, "The greatest of all Army teams Stop We have stopped the war to celebrate your magnificent success." The war years brought a twist in the old rivalry. Today when Plebes are asked in which year cadets cheered for Navy, they must answer, "1943." Since gasoline shortages prohibited midshipmen from traveling to West Point for the game, one cadet regiment learned Navy songs and rooted Navy on to their 13-0 victory.

The Army-Navy game is a highlight of the Academy year. "Beat Navy" is almost a second motto at West Point, and the words "SINK NAVY," painted on the field house roof, are a year-round reminder of the rivalry. The blanket worn by Army's mascot, the mule, carries a star for every Army victory over Navy. A mule may seem a strange mascot for the fierce Army team. However, the animals were extremely important to the nineteenth–century Army. Mules transported weapons and supplies, and their strength and endurance represent qualities necessary not only to football teams but to every soldier.

At West Point football is viewed as battle. The day before every home game, cadets dress in fatigues, ready to take on the enemy. Those in the stands consider themselves the twelfth man on the field and remain on their feet throughout the entire contest. The high spirits and enthusiasm of both cadets and midshipmen are contagious. Millions of fans across the nation join servicemen in cheering on the teams, and at the Academy itself, the results of this game can make or break the season.

PLEBE YEAR

Plebe year is the toughest at West Point. As the lowest class,

The transformation begins. *U.S.M.A. Archives*

Plebes spend their entire first year earning the right to be accepted as equals by upperclassmen. The key word is survival. Through hours of demanding physical conditioning, of drills and parades on The Plain, and of exacting academic classes, Plebes struggle to gain the knowledge and bearing expected of West Point cadets. Their days are long and structured minute by minute. Plebe year is meant to be hard. The program is designed to identify those who are suited to life at the Academy and those who are not. As Plebes say, "You're not supposed to like it, just put up with it." Approximately fifteen percent of the new cadets who enter in July resign or are dismissed before the end of the year. However, Plebe year molds the survivors into highly skilled young men and women, ready to take their place in the Long Gray Line.

The day they arrive, new cadets and their parents assemble at the Holleder Center. While their parents tour the post, new cadets plunge into a frenzy of activity. First they receive regulation T-shirts and shorts and *Bugle Notes,* the Plebe Bible. Following a checklist pinned to their shorts, they rush from station to station to acquire uniforms, equipment, military haircuts and I.D.'s. In several drill periods, they learn rudimentary formations in preparation for the afternoon ceremonies. From the beginning, they learn to obey orders instantaneously and to accept their lowly status in the Corps. As *Bugle Notes* states, Plebes outrank only "the Superintendent's dog, the Commandant's cat, the waiters in the Mess Hall, the Hell Cats, the Generals in the Air Force, and all the Admirals in the whole damned Navy." In the late afternoon, newly formed companies march in precise formation to The Plain. There, as their parents look on, new cadets take the Oath of Allegiance and officially begin life at the Academy.

At the end of the six-week grueling trial of Cadet Basic Training, new cadets pass in review before the entire Corps and become Fourth Classmen. Their trial continues as the academic year begins. A full schedule of classes is added to their military and physical conditioning. The upperclassmen, who have returned from summer tactical training, put further pressures on the Plebes. Fourth Classmen must respond immediately to commands from their superiors. Although bracing, an exaggerated, stiff-backed, chin-down posture is no longer allowed, Plebes must stand rigidly straight when so ordered. They must walk at a minimum of one hundred twenty paces per minute, must hug the walls of building corridors and make all turns at right angles.

At meals, Plebes serve upperclassmen and must sit upright with their feet flat on the floor and their backs one fist's distance from the back of the chair. Their vision must be confined to the physical boundaries of the table. Plebes may not speak unless addressed by an upperclassman, and when so addressed, must cease eating, come to attention, look the speaker in the eye and answer all questions appropriately. They must also be able to recite verbatim Plebe Knowledge, set questions and answers about the heritage of the Corps. Questions range from details about facilities on post—"How many lights in Cullum Hall?" Answer: "340 lights, Sir."—to obscure references to the Academy's past. "How is the cow?" Answer: "Sir, she walks, she talks, she's full of chalk, lacteal fluid extracted from the female of the bovine species is highly prolific to the nth degree." This seemingly absurd response has its origin in the old mess hall where the Plebe water corporal was asked how much milk was left in the pitcher.

Plebes must also be prepared to sing the Corps songs and cheers on demand. Each morning they memorize the menus for breakfast, lunch and dinner as well as the articles on the front page and sports page of *The New York Times*. Those who are assigned as Minute Callers stand at designated posts and count down the minutes to various formations. "Attention all cadets, there are ___ minutes until assembly for _____ formation. The uniform is _____. The menu for (breakfast, lunch, dinner) is (main dish, side dish, dessert, and beverage). ___ minutes remaining." At the beck and call of upperclassmen, they may never initiate conversation with their superiors. When spoken to, they must respond in full sentences, addressing upperclassmen as "Sir." While exacting, this intiation is a far cry from the hazing of the past.

Hazing was extreme in the days immediately following the Civil War. Originally limited to boyish pranks and tricks devised at summer encampments, harrassments escalated to at times life-threatening proportions. Plebes were constantly told to brace, to perform endless sets of push-ups and deep-knee bends, and to eat potentially dangerous substances. Those who had unusual names, who came from famous military families or had distinguishing physical characteristics were designated for special torment. The names MacArthur, Sheridan and Long-street on the incoming Plebe lists targeted these new cadets for abuse even before they arrived at West Point. The tallest and the shortest were singled out, and those who showed signs of independent spirits received harsh treament as well. Dwight D. Eisenhower (Class of 1915) was older than most when he entered the Academy, and his unshakable self-assurance proved frustrating to upperclassmen. Born to lead, he gathered fellow Plebes in midnight sessions to plot revenge against the most vicious upperclassmen.

Sometimes being singled out had humorous results. When Hiram Ulysses Grant received his appointment to the Academy,

President Ulysses S. Grant (Class of 1843) and family. His wife, Julia Dent Grant, was the sister of Grant's roommate at West Point. *U.S.M.A. Special Collections*

official documents listed him as U.S. Grant. The "S" may have stood for Simpson, his mother's maiden name, or it may have simply have been an error. Upperclassmen eagerly awaited the arrival of the new cadet they had already nicknamed "United States" or "Uncle Sam." Unlike the lean, lanky caricature, Grant was barely five feet tall at the time. Nevertheless, he became Sam Grant for his entire four years at West Point and went down in history as Ulysses S. Grant.

Decades later Douglas MacArthur (Class of 1903) was singled out for especially intensive hazing because of his father's prominence in the Civil War. In the midst of performing series after series of spread eagles (brutal deep knee bends), he collapsed in convulsions. Denying that he had succumbed, he refused to name those responsible. Later as West Point Superintendent, MacArthur took a strong stand against hazing. In modern times, the excesses of hazing have come under control, and the Academy urges upperclassmen to direct their energies in positive ways. Still many feel the best policy is to remain unnoticed. Robert Baker (Class of 1966) told his daughter Kristin (Class of 1990) as she entered the Academy, "Try to stay in the background so you can stay out of trouble." Her outstanding leadership qualities, however, won Kristin Baker national attention when she was appointed the first woman First Captain of the Corps in 1989. Another father gave different advice. "Do your damnedest in an ostentatious manner all the time." Not surprisingly, these words of wisdom came from the flamboyant George S. Patton, Jr. (Class of 1909).

Plebe year is long and intense. After Christmas leave when the excitement of new experiences wanes, cadets enter what used to be called the Gloom Period. No longer can they anticipate Saturday afternoon Army football games. Days are bitterly cold and short. Sometimes the demanding routine becomes too much to bear. The foundlings (those found deficient in academics or conduct) are dismissed, and others resign. Edgar Allan Poe left in March 1831. An unlikely cadet, he entered West Point to win the support and good will of his guardian John Allan. When Allan disowned him, Poe stopped attending classes and refused to fulfill his duties. He was court-martialed and dismissed before completing his plebe year. Superintendent Sylvanus Thayer recognized Poe's genius and encouraged him in his writing. He even allowed Poe's fellow cadets to contribute to the publication of his next volume of poetry.

Most cadets manage to survive these dark days. For a long time the Gloom Period officially came to an end with 100th Night. Cadets performed plays and skits which lampooned their instructors and officers on the spring night exactly 100 days before graduation. Even today, 100th Night and the arrival of spring signal Plebes that the end is in sight. For a brief time, they experience what it's like to be upperclassmen. For the two hours preceding dinner on 100th Night, Plebes and First Classmen exchange positions, and during the meal, First Classmen serve the Plebes. This role reversal comes to an end with Attention to Orders, announcements at the end of dinner.

After 100th Night, activities intensify, and Plebes attack their demanding schedules with renewed energy. Their year culminates in Recognition, a ceremony which immediately follows the Graduation Parade. With the entire Corps in formation, upperclassmen "about face" and shake hands with the Plebes in friendship. As full-fledged West Pointers, these new Third Classmen take their place as equals. They have passed the test.

HONOR CODE

"A cadet will not lie, cheat or steal nor tolerate those who do." West Point's Honor Code is a simple statement expressing the minimum ethical standards expected of cadets. For four years, cadets must live these words both on post and off. In an atmosphere where high moral principles are understood, they come to expect integrity from themselves and their fellows. As cadets move forward in their careers as officers, the Honor Code forms the foundation of their professional conduct as well. Integrity is crucial. Officers must be able to rely on the word of other officers, especially in times of battle, and must keep the faith of the men who follow them. As representatives of the nation, they must be upright and trustworthy. An officer's honor must be inviolable, and the purpose of West Point's entire program is to provide the nation with leaders of character.

In the early nineteenth century under Sylvanus Thayer, the unwritten code of gentlemanly behavior was West Point's standard. No formal rules were necessary since a gentleman's word was his bond, and cadets were expected to be truthful in all their dealings. In later years, first cheating and then stealing were expressly prohibited. Not until 1970 were cadets explicitly forbidden to tolerate these offenses. The nontoleration clause may be the most difficult tenet for cadets. In today's society, there is not a high value placed on accountability, especially at the expense of a friend. And yet, cover-ups are abhorred, and individuals are expected to live by the standards of their profession. At West Point, it is clear that each cadet is responsible not only for his actions, but also for the integrity of the entire Corps.

Although its present wording differs from its first codification in 1921 under Superintendent Douglas MacArthur, the Honor Code has always embodied the Academy's high expectations for its cadets. The cadets themselves are responsible for its enforcement. Each company elects one First Classman and one Second Classman to represent it on the Cadet Honor Committee. The committee is charged with educating the Corps, promoting an atmosphere in which the code will flourish and setting an example of integrity for others to emulate. Should a violation occur, the committee hears evidence and passes its findings on to the Superintendent who reviews the case. If he determines that the violation justifies separation from the Academy, he forwards his recommendation to the Secretary of the Army for final disposition.

It can be difficult to live up to the standards of the Honor Code. Each year some cadets fail and leave West Point. In 1951, a cheating scandal erupted resulting in the dismissal of ninety cadets, fifty-one of whom were members of Red Blaik's famed football team. The nation as well as the Academy reeled as these cadets with such promise and talent fell in disgrace. The most devastating breach of the Honor Code occured in 1976, when 152 cadets were charged with cheating on an electrical engineering exam. The overwhelming magnitude of this incident prompted calls for a reevaluation of the entire system. As a result, the hearing process was revamped to include due process safeguards for cadets. In addition, the Academy rededicated itself to the ideals of the code.

Most cadets succeed in living by the principles of the Honor Code. While their academic, physical and military training are of the highest quality, it is character which sets West Point graduates apart. They carry with them the confidence in themselves and their colleagues engendered by these high ethical standards, and integrity governs their every act.

HOW TO BECOME A CADET

It is an honor to be appointed to the United States Military Academy. Exceptional candidates from every state in the nation compete for the available slots. Each must present high academic credentials and must be in superb physical condition. In addition, each candidate must secure a Department of the Army or Congressional nomination. From a pool of nearly 15,000 applicants, 1300-1400 young men and women are chosen annually to enter the new Plebe class. Most have been leaders in high school—on the athletic fields, in the classrooms and in their communities. At West Point they will find new challenges and develop capabilities far beyond what they ever dreamed possible.

Applicants must be between the ages of seventeen and twenty-two and citizens of the United States. (Under a special provision, West Point may accept up to forty students from friendly foreign nations.) Applicants must be unmarried and pledge to remain so throughout their Academy years. Furthermore, each must be academically proficient and pass West Point's rigorous medical and physical qualifying exams.

Congress, the Vice President and territorial governors are each allotted a specific number of nominations. Each Senator and Representative may recommend up to five candidates from his district. Additionally, children of Army officers and enlisted men as well as honor graduates of military, naval and ROTC training schools are eligible for Department of the Army nominations. Approximately twenty percent of all those nominated eventually win appointments to the Academy. Moreover, all sons and daughters of those awarded the Medal of Honor are granted admission if qualified. Applicants receive notification of acceptance by April and must report for duty early in the summer.

Most cadets:
—graduated in the top fifth of their high school classes
—were National Honor Society members
—scored 500-600 in the verbal section of the SAT exam and
600-700 in the math section
—were leaders in high school student government
—captained varsity athletic teams

A CADET'S DAY: MEETING THE CHALLENGE

From reveille at 0600 to the strains of taps at night, cadets are on
the go. West Point challenges them to perform an incredible
number of tasks each day. At 120 paces per minute, Plebes rush
from class to parade ground to athletic field, and even expe-
rienced upperclassmen can barely complete the assigned work.
They are all in training for times when they will have to respond
under pressure and make sound, instantaneous decisions. They
learn to use each minute and to accomplish more in one day
than they ever thought possible.

A TYPICAL DAY

Morning:
0600	Reveille
0630-0710	Breakfast
0715-0720	Morning Day Formation
0720-1130	Class or Study

Afternoon:
1145-1230	Lunch
1230-1325	Commandant's Time
1335-1535	Class or Study
1535-1800	Intramural, Club or Intercollegiate Athlet-ics; Parades; Extracurricular Activities; or Free Time

Evening:
1825-1900	Dinner
1900-1930	Cadet Duties

1930-2030	Study Conditions; Extracurricular Activities
2030-2330	Study Time
2330	Taps
2400	Lights Out

Cadet life has always been strictly regimented. As early as 1816 under Superintendent Alden Partridge, cadets put in sixteen-hour days filled with study, military drills and maneuvers. No free time was allotted. Yet young men, isolated for four years in the fortress on the Hudson, needed outlets for their enthusiasm and high spirits. Amidst the seriousness of their training, they have always found ways to play pranks on each other and to outwit authority. Heavy equipment has been dismantled, and pieces have found their way to strange places. Cadets have hidden pets—birds, fish, gerbils, and even a monkey—knowing full well they were not officially sanctioned roommates. Fireworks have always been irresistible to cadets. After a New Year's Eve display ushering in the year 1880, the entire Corps was confined to quarters.

Other needs proved overwhelming as well. Men at this age are always hungry, and in the early days, only two meals a day were served. Jefferson Davis (Class of 1828), William Tecumseh Sherman (Class of 1840) and George Armstrong Custer (Class of 1861) received many demerits for supplementing their meager rations with forbidden feasts prepared in their rooms. Whenever they could escape detection, cadets would "run it" to Benny Havens' Tavern in Buttermilk Falls. There they would find roasts and fowl turning on the spit, pots of soup, and pies freshly baked by Mrs. Havens. The pride of the house was Havens' own flip, known throughout the countryside. Only Benny could brew this mixture of cider or ale and eggs, sweetened and spiced and heated with a hot iron "flip dog." Cadets would risk court-martial to partake of Benny's specialty and the convivial atmosphere of his establishment. Benny would keep a watchful eye out for Academy officers and warn cadets of their approach. On one midnight run, Jefferson Davis fell off a cliff trying to evade the Tacs who had raided the tavern. Had a tree not broken his fall, the Confederacy would have had a different

Evening at Benny Havens. Benny is in the center with a pitcher of his famous "Flip." Cadets conceal themselves in the doorway. *U.S.M.A. Special Collections*

president. For over fifty years, Benny Havens befriended cadets—Edgar Allan Poe called him "the only congenial soul in this God-forsaken place." His tavern is immortalized in the song still sung today, "Benny Havens, Oh!" (see page 119).

Early on, recreation was limited. Through the mid-1800s, debating was the only extracurricular activity allowed. Today more than ninety activities are offered. Cadets ski, sail, and golf and participate in scuba diving, mountain climbing and white-water rafting. In addition to the traditional 100th Night show, cadets stage at least two major drama productions every year. Interest in the arts is high. Symphony orchestras, dance groups and Broadway casts perform at Eisenhower Hall. Cadets run their own radio station and publish *Bugle Notes,* the *Pointer,* and the yearbook, *Howitzer.* There are five chapels on post, and cadets are active in religious fellowships. Plebes gather in the Grand Ballroom of Cullum Hall on Saturday nights; upperclassmen use Grant Hall. Benny's Lounge is exclusively for the use of First Classmen while Boodlers and the Cadet Restaurant are open to all cadets. The Cadet Social Programs Branch sponsors weekly hops, dances to which students from other colleges are invited. Cadets have always looked forward to West Point hops as a welcome break from their daily routine.

From the early days dancing was a required activity. Part of a gentleman's training, this skill was necessary for future officers who would attend military balls and diplomatic receptions. Beginning in 1823, each cadet had to take dance classes during his first two summers. In the absence of women, cadets partnered one another and practiced for hops to which ladies were invited.

Cadet Hop. Harper's Weekly, September 3, 1859. *U.S.M.A. Special Collections*

Cadet hops were splendid affairs. Young women from surrounding towns, and even some from New York City, Boston and Philadelphia, waltzed away the evenings in the arms of handsome cadets. Their dance cards were filled with names of men who would one day become famous in their country's service. Treasured mementos, these cards were often saved for

Cadet Hop dance card, 1908. George S. Patton (Class of 1909) listed on line 5.

years and passed on to daughters and granddaughters. Throughout the nineteenth century and up until World War II, dancing classes continued, and many believe that movements learned on the dance floor made for graceful precision on the parade ground.

With classes, sports and military training, cadets' days seem impossibly full. Because they learn to make the most of each minute, they are able to meet the demands of the curriculum and participate in a wide variety of activities as well. After four years, they are ready to take their places as officers. The Army knows it can count on West Pointers to get the job done.

CHAPTER 4

Traditions of the Corps: Cadet Slang, Songs and Cheers

CADET SLANG

Cadets have always had a language of their own. Certain words have meaning only to those who have spent four years at the Academy. The West Point experience is a unique one, and it takes a special vocabulary to describe it. Cadet slang incorporates vestiges of the Academy's past, and is another tie that binds graduates together.

ASAP	as soon as possible
Area Bird, n.	cadet who is serving punishment by being obliged to walk on the area
Army Brat, n.	son or daughter of a career Army soldier
Beanhead, n.	Fourth Class cadet (also SMACK)
Beast, n.	"Old Corps" slang for Cadet Basic Training
B.J.	fresh; lacking in respect. "Bold before June," (when graduation was in June)
blow off, v.	to not worry about something. To not complete an assignment/homework ("I blew it off")
bogus, adj.	uncalled for; audacity
bolo, v.	to fail a test or qualification
boodle, n.	cake, candy ice cream, etc.
Boodler's, n.	the cadet snack store
boot, v.	to revoke the appointment of a cadet, commissioned or non-commissioned officer
butt, n.	the remains of anything; as the part (butt) of a month, also the butt of a cigarette
Butter Bar, n.	a new Second Lieutenant
circular file, n.	trashcan
civvies, n.	civilian clothing
cold, adj.	absolutely without error, as "a cold max"
Com., n.	the Commandant of Cadets
Cow, n.	member of the Second Class
Crab, n.	one who attends the Naval Academy
D., adj.	deficient; below average, as in academics
dick, n.	cadet who makes life difficult for peers

dick on, v. verb form of **dick;** as in smudging another's shoes or taking too much food at table

D.M.I., n. Department of Military Instruction

D.P.E., n. Department of Physical Education

Engineer, n. one well up in his studies; a cadet in the upper sections in academic work

F.C.D.T. or **D.T.** Fourth Class Development Time

F.C.P, n. First Class Privileges

F.D., n. full dress uniform

File Boner, n. one who gets ahead at the expense of class-mates

Firstie, n. member of the First Class

find, v. to discharge a cadet for deficiency in studies or conduct

Foundling, n. one who is dismissed from the Academy for deficiency in academics or deportment

fried egg, n. insignia of the USMA worn on the hat or tarbucket

Gray Hog, n. an extremely USMA-oriented cadet

G.I. a government issue (not to be used when referring to enlisted personnel)

Ghost, n. a Fourth Class cadet who hides in his/her room to avoid the upperclass or to shirk duties; also refers to an upperclass cadet who is rarely seen around a cadet company

Goat, n. a cadet in the lower sections; a cadet near the bottom of his/her class

green girl, n. comforter, blanket

Green Suiter, n. Army officer

gross, adj. blundering; disgusting

held report, n.   explanation of report

Hell Cats, n.   musicians who sound reveille and the calls

hive, v.   to understand, to comprehend. n. an intelligent person or one who learns quickly

hop, n.   cadet dance

hotel night, n.   one night a week when sheets are broken down due to laundry send out

Ikette, n.   girl who frequents Eisenhower Hall for the sole purpose or picking up a helpless male cadet; impressed only by the "man in a uniform" image

IRP   immediate response, please!

juice, n.   electricity, electrical engineering

limits, n.   limits on the reservation to which cadets are restricted

make, v.   to appoint a cadet as officer or non-commissioned officer in the Corps of Cadets

max, n.   complete success, a maximum. v. to make a perfect mark in academic recitation; to do a thing perfectly

O.A.O., n.   one and only

O.C., n.   Officer in Charge

O.D., n.   olive drab

Odin, n.   Norse god to whom cadets appeal for rain before parades, inspection, etc.

P., n.   professor; an instructor

PDA, n.   public display of affection

ping, n.   agitated state of haste

Plebe, n.   cadet of the Fourth Class, a freshman

Plebe Bible, n. *Bugle Notes;* the handbook of the Corps of Cadets

PMI, n. afternoon inspection, a state less than AMI

police, v. to throw away, to discard; to clean up

poop, n. information to be memorized

poop-deck, n. balcony in the Mess Hall from which orders are published

poop-sheet, n. page of information

pop off, v. sound off in a military manner

pro, adj. proficient, above passing in studies or looks

pull out, v. to complete an assignment barely on time, meeting only minimum standards (also **slug stopper,** n.)

quill, n. (2-1) report for a delinquency. v. to report a cadet for breach of regulations

rack, n. cadet bed, also sack. v. to sleep

recognize, v. to place a Fourth Class cadet on upperclass status

R.H.I.P. Rank Hath Its Privileges (as well as its obligations)

roger I understand

room con, n. confinement to quarters, as a punishment for breach of discipline

SAMI, n. Saturday Morning Inspection

sham, v. to try to get out of doing something that is one's responsibility; take the easy way out

slug, n. special punishment for a serious offense; also SLAM. v. to impose a special punishment on someone

Snake, n.	one who will cut-in at hops. v. to cut-in
S.O.D., n.	Senior Officer of the Day
S.O.G., n.	Senior Officer of the Guard
solids, n.	engineering mechanics
sound off, n.	powerful voice. v. to use the voice so as to be heard, shout
S.O.P.	Standard Operating Procedure
spaz, v.	to function improperly. n. someone who functions improperly
spec (speck), v.	to memorize verbatim, as: "to spec blind." (Also **spec and dump**)
Squid, n.	one who attends the Naval Academy
Star Man, n.	distinguished cadet
Striper, n.	Cadet Captain
Supe, n.	the Superintendent
Tac, n.	Tactical Officer
Ted, n.	intelligent person or one who learns quickly (also **geek**)
T.E.E., n.	term end examination
tie up, v.	to make a gross error
tour, n.	one hour's walk on the area (punishment); a period of duty, as a "guard tour"
trou, n.	trousers
Turnback, n.	re-admitted cadet
unsat, adj.	unsatisfactory performance
walking experience, n.	time spent walking off demerits
went-off, n.	special attention from an upperclass student

woo-poo-u, n.   where you're at!; also **woops!**

woops, n.   sounds **Squids** make when they see West Point cadets

wopper,
W.O.P.R., n.   Written Oral Partial Review

W.P.R., n.   Written Partial Review

writ, n.   written recitation, an examination

Yearling, n.   member of the Third Class; (also **Yuk**)

You fly, I buy   You pick up the food and I'll pay for it.

Zoomie, n.   one who attends the Air Force Academy

SONGS AND CHEERS

West Point is an Academy rich in tradition. Over the years, many of its stories and legends have been commemorated in song and verse. Some have endured, passed down from class to class. Even though their origins may be obscure, these songs and cheers serve to unite the cadets of today with those of the past.

THE ALMA MATER

Hail, Alma Mater dear,
  To us be ever near.
Help us thy motto bear
Through all the years.
  Let Duty be well performed.
  Honor be e'er untarned.
Country be ever armed.
West Point, by thee.

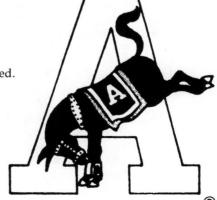

Guide us, thy sons, aright,
Teach us by day, by night,
To keep thine honor bright,
  For thee to fight.
When we depart from thee,
Serving on land or sea,
May we still loyal be,
  West Point, to thee.

And when our work is done,
Our course on earth is run,
May it be said, "Well done;
  Be thou at peace."
E'er may that line of gray
Increase from day to day
Live, serve, and die, we pray,
  West Point, for thee.

THE CORPS! THE CORPS! THE CORPS!

The Corps, bareheaded, salute it,
  With eyes up, thanking our God—

That we of the Corps are treading
  Where they of the Corps have trod—

They are here in ghostly assemblage,
  The men of the Corps long dead.

And our hearts are standing attention
  While we wait for their passing tread.

We sons of to-day, we salute you—
  You, sons of an earlier day;

We follow, close order, behind you,
  Where you have pointed the way;

The long gray line of us stretches
  Thro' the years of a century told,

And the last man feels to his marrow
  The grip of your far off hold.

Grip hands with us now though we see not,
  Grip hands with us, strengthen our hearts—

As the long line stiffens and straightens
  With the thrill that your presence imparts.

Grip hands tho' it be from the shadows.—
  While we swear, as you did of yore,

Or living, or dying, to honor
  The Corps, and the Corps, and the Corps.

BENNY HAVENS, OH!

Come fill your glasses, fellows, and stand
  up
  in a row.
To singing sentimentally we're going for to
  go;
In the Army there's sobriety, promotion's
  very slow.
So we'll sing our reminiscences of Benny
  Havens, Oh!
CHORUS:
Oh! Benny Havens, Oh! Oh! Benny Havens,
  Oh!
We'll sing our reminiscences of Benny
  Havens, Oh!

To our kind old Alma Mater, our rockbound
  highland home
We'll cast back many a fond regret as o'er
  life's sea we roam;
Until on our last battlefield the light of
  heaven shall glow.
We'll never fail to drink to her and Benny
  Havens, Oh!   —Chorus

May the army be augmented, promotion be
  less slow.
May our country in the hour of need be
  ready for the foe;
May we find a soldier's resting place
  beneath a soldier's blow.
  With room enough beside our graves for
  Benny Havens, Oh!   —Chorus

ARMY BLUE

We've not much longer here to stay,
  For in a month or two,
We'll bid farewell to "Kaydet Gray,"
  And don the "Army Blue."
CHORUS:
Army Blue, Army Blue,
  Hurrah for the Army Blue,
We'll bid farewell to "Kaydet Gray,"
  And don the "Army Blue."

With pipe and song we'll jog along,
  Till this short time is through,
And all among our jovial throng,
  Have donned the Army Blue.   —Chorus

'Twas the song we sang in old plebe camp,
  When first our Gray was new.
The song we sang on summer nights,
  That song of Army Blue.   —Chorus

Now, fellows, we must say good-bye,
  We've stuck our four years thru,
Our future is a cloudless sky,
  We'll don the Army Blue.   —Chorus

To the men and women of the Corps
  Who've seen their four years thru
The work was hard, they did their part
  and all for Army Blue.   —Chorus

OFFICIAL WEST POINT MARCH

West Point, at the call,
Thy sons arise in honor to thee,
May thy light shine ever bright,
Guide thy sons aright,
In far-off lands or distant seas.

Thy name first above all,
Through all the years thy motto we will bear;
We, thy sons as we fight,
May we strike for the right,
Alma Mater, ever for thee.

ON BRAVE OLD ARMY TEAM

The Army team's the pride and dream
    Of every heart in gray,

The Army line you'll ever find
    A terror in the fray;

And when the team is fighting
    For the Black and Gray and Gold,

We're always near with song and cheer
    And this is the tale we're told:

The Army team
    (Band accompaniment)
    (Whistle)

                                    Rah Rah Rah BOOM!

CHORUS:
On, brave old Army team,
On to the fray;
Fight on to victory,
For that's the fearless Army way.
    (Whistle chorus)

AWAY WE GO

Away, away, away we go,
What care we for any foe?
Up and down the field we go,
Just to beat the Navy.
A-R-M-Y! T-E-A-M!
    (Repeat three times)

SLUM AND GRAVY

Sons of slum and gravy
Will you let the Navy
Take from us a victory? Hell No!
Hear a warrior's chorus,
Sweep that line before us,
Carry on the victory! Let's Go!
Onward! Onward! Charge against the foe,
Forward! Forward! The Army banners go!
Sons of Mars and Thunder,
Rip that line asunder,
Carry on to victory

BLACK, GOLD, GRAY

Black, Gold, Gray, as sons we salute you,
Ready to battle, and your honor defend,
    We love you.
At your call the Corps true responds.
And we will fight to defend your name.
    Our dear Old Alma Mater to the end.

WHISPER, TALK, SHOUT*

C — C — C — A — D
E — E — E — T — S
C — A — D — E — T — S
West Point, West Point,
FIGHT!

*repeat three times

LONG CORPS YELL

Rah! Rah! Rah! — Rah! Rah! Rah!
West Point — West Point
Arr . . . . May!
Ray! Ray! Ray!
Rah! Rah! Rah! Rah! Rah! Rah! Rah!
West Point — Team! Team! Team!
  BEAT NAVY!

LOCOMOTIVE YELL

Rah! Rah!—Ray! Ray!—U.—S.—M.—A.
Rah! Rah!—Ray! Ray!—U.—S.—M.—A.
Rah! Rah!—Ray! Ray!—U.—S.—M.—A.
Rah! Rah!—Ray! Ray!—U.—S.—M.—A.
Rah! Rah!—Ray! Ray!—U.—S.—M.—A.
Arrr . . . . May!
Team! FIGHT!

RIPPER

A — Rrr — M-Y
T - Eee — A-M
(Spell) A-R-M-Y-T-E-A-M
ARrrr — May —
— Team FIGHT!

ROCKET YELL

(Whistle) — BOOM! — Ahhh
USMA Rah! Rah!
USMA Rah! Rah!
Hoo — Rah! Hoo — Rah!
AR — MAY! Rah!
Team! Team! Team!

USMA CHEER

U — S — M — A
U — S — M — A
USMA
Go! Fight! Win!

GRIDIRON GRENADIERS

Eyes Right! Watch us fight! Army's going to
    score.
We're the boys who make the noise,
We've licked this gang before.
We have never known defeat,
We would rather fight than eat,
We're the heroes of the Gridiron
    Grenadiers.

CHORUS:
Roll that score. ---------------- Way up!
Roll that score. ---------------- Way up!
They will never want to play us any mo-or-
    or-ore.
Ya-ha-ha-ha-ha! Ha- ha- ha- ha- ha!
We're the heroes of the Gridiron
    Grenadiers.

THE OFFICIAL U.S. ARMY SONG

March along, sing our song
with the Army of the free.
Count the brave, count the true
who have fought to victory.
We're the Army and proud of our name;
We're the Army and proudly proclaim:
First to fight for the right,
and to build the Nation's might,
and the Army goes rolling along.
Proud of all we have done,
fighting till the battle's won,
and the Army goes rolling along.

Then it's Hi! Hi! Hey!
the Army's on its way.
Count off the cadence loud and strong!
For where'er we go,
you will always know
that the Army goes rolling along.

Valley Forge, Custer's ranks, San Juan Hill
    and
Patton's tanks,
and the Army went rolling along.
Minutemen from the start,
always fighting from the heart,
and the Army keeps rolling along.

Then it's Hi! Hi! Hey!
the Army's on its way.
Count off the cadence loud and strong!
For where'er we go,
you will always know
that the Army goes rolling along.

Men in rags, men who froze,
still that Army met its foes,
and we'll fight with all our might
as the Army keeps rolling along.

Then it's Hi! Hi! Hey!
the Army's on its way.
Count off the cadence loud and strong!
For where'er we go you will always know
that the Army goes rolling along.

Keep it rolling!
And the Army goes rolling along, along.

CADET PRAYER

O God, our Father, Thou Searcher of human hearts, help us draw near to Thee in sincerity and truth. May our religion be filled with gladness and may our worship of Thee be natural.

Strengthen and increase our admiration for honest dealing and clean thinking, and suffer not our hatred of hypocrisy and pretense ever to diminish. Encourage us in our endeavor to live above the common level of life. Make us to choose the harder right instead of the easier wrong, and never to be content with a half truth when the whole can be won. Endow us with courage that is born of loyalty to all that is noble and worthy, that scorns to compromise with vice and injustice and knows no fear when truth and right are in jeopardy. Guard us against flippancy and irreverence in the sacred things of life. Grant us new ties of friendship and new opportunities of service. Kindle our hearts in fellowship with those of a cheerful countenance, and soften our hearts with sympathy for those who sorrow and suffer. Help us to maintain the honor of the Corps untarnished and unsullied, and to show forth in our lives the ideals of West Point in doing our duty to Thee and to our Country. All of which we ask in the name of the Great Friend and Master of all.
—Amen.

PART II

The Hudson Valley

Great Estates with lawns sweeping down to the Hudson River; formal gardens abloom with roses; Revolutionary War stronghold and symbol of hope in the dark days of World War II—the Hudson Valley is all this and more. During the Revolutionary War, George Washington had headquarters in Newburgh, and his Continental Army spent a winter in New Windsor nearby. General "Mad Anthony" Wayne took the British by surprise with a lightning strike at Stony Point, and Fortress West Point guarded the waterway that united the colonies. It was West Point that Benedict Arnold tried to betray to the British, and it was three Tarrytown militiamen who captured his accomplice and saved the country.

Great river families built manor houses on the banks of the Hudson. From Clermont, Montgomery Place and Van Cortlandt Manor, they established their preeminence in politics and society. In the nineteenth century, wealthy industrialists made the Valley a summer retreat. Their Gothic castles and Beaux-Arts mansions were symbols of America's Gilded Age. For twelve years, Franklin Delano Roosevelt's home in Hyde Park was the Summer White House. At Springwood, F.D.R. greeted world

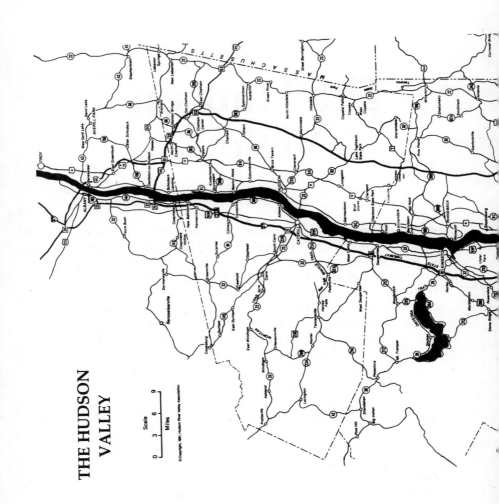

THE HUDSON
VALLEY

Scale

Miles

© Copyright, 1981, Hudson River Valley Association

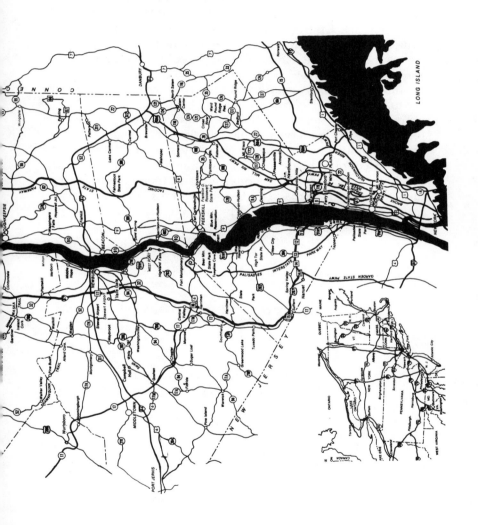

leaders, and from this, his boyhood home, he drew the strength to rally the nation.

The majestic river, winding its way through the granite cliffs of the Hudson Highlands, inspired landscape artists who founded America's first native school of painting. Thomas Cole and Frederick Church, Albert Bierstadt and Thomas Rossiter painted the waterfalls, sunsets, mountain peaks and autumn scenes that made the Hudson River School famous at home and abroad. The Valley's wooded glens and country hamlets kindled the imagination of Washington Irving who wrote of the legendary folk of Sleepy Hollow.

Today, stately mansions still command the heights, and the region's past is preserved at historic sites and small museums. Antique shops line the streets of picturesque river towns, and winding country lanes lead to working farms and orchards. Small wineries flourish and offer tours of their cellars and picnics in their vineyards. The beauty of the Hudson Valley remains undiminished, and its rich traditions reflect its more than three hundred fifty years of history.

CHAPTER 5

Historic Orange County

HIGHLIGHTS...

—Washington's Headquarters during the Revolutionary War

—The Last Encampment of the Continental Army

—America's Oldest Winery

—Home of America's First Sports Heroes—The Trotting Horse Museum

Established in 1683, Orange County was named in honor of William, Prince of Orange, and settled by the Dutch and the English. During the Revolutionary War, several important battles and skirmishes were fought in the county, and in 1782-83

George Washington made his headquarters in Newburgh. Nearby New Windsor was the site of his troops' last encampment, and Henry Knox and other generals were billeted in county homes. Sports history was made in Goshen where the Historic Track hosted harness racing's most famous event, the Hambletonian Stake, named for the horse whose progeny still dominates the racing world today. America's oldest winery, Brotherhood, founded in 1839, is in Washingtonville, and Hill-Hold Farm in Montgomery recalls the important role agriculture has played in the county's economy. Storm King Art Center and Sugar Loaf Crafts Village showcase local art and artists. All these sights, easily accessible from the United States Military Academy, reveal the rich heritage of West Point's county.

REVOLUTIONARY WAR SITES

WASHINGTON'S HEADQUARTERS

Once the "Queen of the Hudson," the city of Newburgh suffered economic depression when the railroad displaced the river as the main artery for transportation of goods and services. It has never recovered. Yet the Broadway, lined with boarded-up shops and dilapidated houses, leads to Washington's Headquarters, an eighteenth-century oasis at river's edge. In 1782, General Washington ordered his aides to search out a location along the Hudson. His requirements were simple. He needed a house that commanded a view of river traffic; that was spacious enough to accommodate his large staff; and that had fireplaces which did not smoke. His aides selected the house of Jonathan Hasbrouck who had billeted troops and served the patriot cause until his death in 1780. Here Washington spent the last sixteen months of the war, planning Continental Army strategy while awaiting news of peace negotiations in Paris.

Purchased by the State of New York in 1850 from the Hasbrouck family, Washington's Headquarters was the first publicly owned historic site in the country. Because of the great reverence felt for George Washington, the State Legislature approved the acquisition and set a precedent for preservation of other historic sites. From the beginning, the site drew many visitors including such prominent men as Robert E. Lee, then Superintendent of nearby West Point. As the first publicly owned historic site, the house has reflected changing theories in historical interpretation. At one time, it contained a hodgepodge of furnishings and artifacts acquired with the house or donated by county residents. Today, curators have furnished the house as it was when Washington lived and worked there.

Washington moved into the house just as peace negotiations commenced in Paris in April 1782. Uncertain that Britain and the colonies would agree on terms, Washington drilled his troops and planned for future battles, even training them for a possible amphibious assault on New York City. In addition, he upheld the authority of the Continental Congress by refusing an offer to become king of the new country and by eliminating the threat posed by the Newburgh Letters (see below).

Nevertheless, his months at Newburgh were relatively calm, and Washington's days took on a steady, regular pattern. Each room in the house is set up to suggest a part of his daily routine. In his bedroom is the table at which he breakfasted each morning with his wife Martha, who spent twelve of the sixteen months in Newburgh with her husband. Much of the General's day was spent in his office, reading dispatches and receiving couriers who had ridden in from the New Windsor Cantonment (see below) or from West Point. At 2 P.M., long wooden planks were set up on sawhorses in the visitors' waiting room for the formal, two-to-three hour midday meal. Those awaiting interviews with the General were invited to join the Washingtons, the officers of the day and important guests. Washington's aides-de-camp, taking a break from their clerical work, served at table until returning to their afternoon duties. These young men had a separate office where they wrote letters for Washington, filed and processed his paperwork and often met with people in his stead. Washington thought of them as his sons, and each evening, they joined him and Martha for a light supper at 9 P.M. The boxes of documents tied up in red tape, the fold-away campaign beds, and the military maps and charts suggest the bustling activity that surrounded Washington even in the closing months of the war.

On the grounds, a tower and a monument commemorate the Continental Army's victory and Washington's proclamation of peace. The museum building features exhibits detailing the defense of the Hudson Highlands and the life of the Revolutionary War soldier. A large, three-dimensional map traces the course of the war up and down the Hudson and shows the strategic importance of the river to both the British and the colonists. A huge log boom, on display in this room, indicates the massive proportions of the Great Chain which the Americans stretched across the Hudson at West Point (see Chapter 1). Other rooms hold memorabilia relating to Washington as well as other items of historic interest acquired over the years. A library and archives room, accessible only to scholars, contains a set of Washington's published papers, a few of his letters, and much material relating to the Revolutionary War. Every February, Washington's birthday is celebrated with three days of lectures, concerts and special activities on the museum grounds. The staff is extremely knowledgeable and welcomes the opportunity to share with visitors the little-known details of this period of Washington's life.

84 Liberty Street
Newburgh, N.Y.
(914) 562-1195

DIRECTIONS:
From West Point: Route 9W north to Newburgh. Right onto Broadway. Right onto Liberty Street to #84.

From New York City: New York State Thruway (87) north to Exit 17 Newburgh. Take Route 17K east which becomes Broadway. Right onto Liberty Street to #84.

NEW WINDSOR CANTONMENT

Eight thousand Continental Army soldiers camped at the New Windsor Cantonment in the winter of 1782-1783, the last winter of the Revolutionary War. General George Washington ordered his troops to construct seven hundred log huts with *"regularity, convenience* and even some degree of *elegance"* to protect themselves from what turned out to be one of the coldest seasons on record. Mindful of the need to maintain order and give his men purpose during the winter's lull in fighting, Washington created work projects including the building of a meetinghouse for the troops called the Temple.

Though only five miles from Washington's Headquarters in Newburgh, soldiers at the Cantonment felt far removed from their commander. Moreover, they were tired of the war, which had already dragged on for seven long years, and angry with their treatment by Congress. Discontent grew, and in the late winter of 1783, the anonymous Newburgh Letters circulated among the troops, threatening Congress and demanding back pay and pensions.

New Windsor Cantonment, last encampment of the Continental Army, Vails Gate.

Catching wind of the conspiracy, Washington rode to the Cantonment and addressed the officers gathered at the Temple. In a dramatic appeal, the General entreated his men to remain loyal to him and to the fight for freedom. Humbling himself before them, he put on the glasses he seldom wore in public and said, "Forgive me for putting on spectacles. I've grown gray in your service, now I grow blind." The officers responded with tears in their eyes and renewed their pledges of fealty. On April 19, 1783, the eighth anniversary of the Battles of Lexington and Concord, Washington announced the Cessation of Hostilities with Great Britain. The troops celebrated the end of the war by burning thirteen candles in each hut, one for each colony. By June, most of the army was disbanded, and a small corps traveled to West Point to man the garrison there.

Today, uniformed guides demonstrate eighteenth-century camp life and work in buildings that are reproductions of those once on the site. The interpretive program demonstrates Revolutionary War camp life. While the summer reenactments cannot duplicate the cold, harsh conditions of winter, they do give a glimpse of what life was like at the Cantonment. Soldiers drill on the parade field with Revolutionary War weapons; the blacksmith works in his shop; and men cook their meals and ready equipment for inspection. A small museum supplements the outdoor activities with exhibits on artillery, uniforms and implements. Of special interest is an original Badge of Military Merit. Created by George Washington to honor deeds of valor by enlisted men, it was the forerunner of the Purple Heart.

Temple Hill Road
Vails Gate, N.Y.
(914) 561-5073

DIRECTIONS:
From West Point: Route 9W north to Route 94 south to Vails Gate. Right onto Temple Hill Road. Proceed one mile.

From New York City: New York State Thruway (87) north to Exit 17 Newburgh. Route 17K east to Route 300 south. Watch for signs to New Windsor Cantonment.

KNOX'S HEADQUARTERS

Major General Henry Knox, artillery commander under George Washington, took up quarters in the Ellison house four different times from 1779-1782. From this house, he directed several campaigns in defense of the Hudson Highlands during the Revolutionary War. In days of relative calm, he was joined by his wife Lucy, a large, jolly woman who weighed 240 pounds. Together they hosted balls that were famous throughout the county. Three young women who attended one of their dances—Sally Janson, Gitty Winkoop and Maria Colden—etched their names in a pane of glass still on view in the house. Other generals, including Nathanael Greene and Horatio Gates, also used the house as headquarters. Gates lived here from November 1782 to April 1783 while in command of the troops at the New Windsor Cantonment. One of his aides-de-camp, John Armstrong, was later identified as an author of the mutinous Newburgh Letters (see above).

The Ellisons, owners of the house, were prosperous farmers and traders who held property in both colonial and British controlled areas. They wisely accommodated both sides and kept their wealth and lands intact throughout the war. Today their home, which was built in 1754, is furnished as the generals would have found it during the Revolutionary War. The dining room is set with Wedgwood creamware, an eighteenth-century pattern still produced today. During the war, George Washington carried seventeen cases of this china with him for use at his various headquarters. In the room set aside for the generals are Revolutionary War uniforms and an alliance cockade. The cockade, a symbol of American and French unity against the British, combined a black feather representing the United States with a white feather for France. There is also a small museum room with displays of restoration work done on the house. Periodically, concerts and special events are held on the grounds.

Vails Gate, N.Y.
(914) 561-5498

DIRECTIONS:

From West Point: Route 9W north to Route 94 south. Knox's Headquarters is on the left, just before Vails Gate.

From New York City: New York State Thruway (87) north to Exit 17 Newburgh. Take Route 17K east to Route 300 south to Vails Gate. East on Route 94. Knox's Headquarters is on the right.

STONY POINT BATTLEFIELD

Only twelve miles south of West Point in Rockland County is the site of a decisive battle of the Revolutionary War. The British held Stony Point, the southern entrance to the Hudson Highlands, and thereby controlled river communication and supply routes between New England and the other colonies. So confident were they of its impregnability that the British at one time offered American engineers an opportunity to study the fortifications.

In hopes of countering George Washington's defensive strategy and luring him into a pitched battle, British General Sir Henry Clinton dispatched 6000 troops to Stony Point in 1779 and tightened the stranglehold on the northern colonies. Refusing to fall into the trap, Washington ordered General "Mad Anthony" Wayne to employ guerrilla tactics in an attack on the stronghold. From their camp at Fort Montgomery, Wayne led his troops on an eight-hour forced march over the mountains. Not even his men knew the destination, and to maintain secrecy, Wayne took into custody everyone he met along the way. The soldiers were armed only with bayonets, their muskets unloaded for fear that the sound of gunfire would alert the enemy. Just after midnight on July 16, 1779, Wayne attacked, and in fifteen minutes of fierce hand-to-hand fighting, his forces routed the British. With this victory, the colonists turned the British away from the Hudson and the North. The remainder of the war was fought in the South.

Each year on the weekend in July closest to the anniversary of the battle, uniformed soldiers reenact the encounter for the public. The ruins of the fortifications still exist, and throughout the summer, visitors can walk the battleground and follow the footsteps of Mad Anthony's men. At the Visitors' Center, an excellent ten-minute audio-visual presentation sets the stage for the self-guided tour. The small museum contains artifacts from the battle.

Stony Point, N.Y.
(914) 786-2521

DIRECTIONS:
From West Point: 12 miles south on Route 9W to signs for Stony Point Battlefield.

From New York City: Route 9W north to Stony Point Battlefield just north of Haverstraw.

OTHER SITES

TROTTING HORSE MUSEUM AND HISTORIC TRACK

In the nineteenth century, horse racing was the national pastime, and trotters were the first sports heroes. Chewing gum, tobacco, washing machines, a popular Two Step—even children—were named for the famous horse Dan Patch. When Dan Patch died in 1916, the nation mourned, and his devoted owner died only thirty-two hours later. So intense was the interest in racing that Currier & Ives issued prints of winning horses only days after their record-breaking runs.

Two carved stone horse heads flank the entrance of the old Good Time Stable, now the Trotting Horse Museum. In the wooden stalls that once held horses, exhibits tell the story of the trotter's place in American sports history. Old hay chutes and cabinets showcase bits, horseshoes, bridles and other horse gear. Photographs conjure up images of the early days of racing. An entire exhibit is dedicated to Hambletonian, "the daddy of 'em all." Born in nearby Chester, New York, in 1848, Hambletonian sired over thirteen hundred foals. His offspring prevailed over all others, and even today his bloodline dominates the world of harness racing. The most famous harness race of all, the Hambletonian Stake, is named for him. Run in Goshen from 1930-1956, it is now held at the Meadowlands in New Jersey with prize money totaling over one million dollars.

Upstairs in the old hayloft, a collection of sulkies shows how these light, two-wheeled carriages have developed over the years. Improvements were made in weight, axle construction and wheel size, giving the driver more control over speed and stability. Also on display is an original mobile starting gate, built onto a 1932 Model-A Ford. In a first floor addition, two rooms are devoted to those who have made major contributions to harness racing. Lifelike statuettes capture the individuality and personalities of these drivers, owners, traders and breeders.

The Club House Room replicates the original Club which stood to the rear of the Historic Track. In the comfort and ease of the Club, men who followed the sport gathered to greet one another and consult on racing matters. Today, the drawings of

Trotting Horse Museum, Goshen.

Frederic Remington hanging on the walls recall the heyday of harness racing. Few people realize that Remington first made a name for himself rendering racing scenes, long before he became famous for his Western paintings and bronzes. Just outside is the Historic Track, the only sporting site in the country to be designated a Registered Historic Landmark. Races are still held here for two weeks every summer, and throughout the year drivers may be seen exercising their horses as trainers look on. A well-stocked gift shop, the Weathervane, carries books, jewelry, games, prints, shirts—all manner of horse-related items. Whether or not you love horses, the museum, track and gift ship are well worth a trip.

240 Main Street
Goshen, N.Y.
(914) 294-6330

DIRECTIONS:
From West Point: Route 9W north to Route 293 south; Route 6 west to Route 17 west to Exit 124B Goshen; Route 207 north to Main Street, Goshen.

From New York City: New York State Thruway (87) north to Exit 16 Harriman. Route 17 west to Exit 124B Goshen; Route 207 north to Main Street, Goshen.

BROTHERHOOD WINERY, WASHINGTONVILLE

In operation since 1839, Brotherhood Winery offers visitors tours through America's oldest winery and explains the winemaking process. Tastings are available at the conclusion of the tour. (See Chapter 14 for further information and directions.)

BEAR MOUNTAIN STATE PARK

A rural Central Park just moments away from West Point, Bear Mountain State Park has over 5000 acres of woods and playing fields and 140 miles of walking trails. The very first section of the Appalachian Trail was opened in 1922 on this land. The park offers a variety of recreational activities and educational displays. Boat rentals on Hessian Lake, picnic facilities and a swimming pool are available in summer, and ice skating, cross-country skiing and sledding areas are open in the winter. Bear Mountain and nearby Harriman State Park were begun in 1927 with a gift of 10,000 acres and one million dollars from Mary Williamson Harriman. The Palisades Interstate Park Commission working with the American Museum of Natural History designed nature trails which became models for state parks throughout the country. These well-maintained trails reflect the innovative ecological and environmental thinking of the 1920s, yet still provide interesting, relevant information today.

There are small trailside museums along the way, each devoted to a particular aspect of the natural surroundings or local history. The Geology Museum details local minerals and rock formations and contains bones from the Gordon Mastodon found fourteen miles north of the museum. The Nature Museum features local animals and describes those that may be found in the park. Of special interest is the History Museum where a large map traces the course of the Revolutionary War along the Hudson. Various sections light up to illustrate battle sites and fortifications dating from April 1775 to October 1777. A diorama shows how the Great Chain (see Chapter 1) was floated across the river to disrupt British navigation. Other exhibits present camp life, uniforms and weaponry of the war.

Like the park's other facilities, Bear Mountain Zoo is from an earlier era. Cages seem small and bare in comparison to modern zoos where attempts are made to place animals in natural habitats. However, signs reassure visitors that the animals in captivity are being nursed back to health or cannot otherwise survive outside on their own, and the animals do seem content and healthy. Also typical of its time is the Bear Mountain Inn. Food and lodging are unexceptional, but serviceable and convenient.

Bear Mountain, N.Y.
(914) 786-2731

DIRECTIONS:
From West Point: Route 9W south to traffic rotary; follow signs to Bear Mountain State Park.

From New York City: Palisades Interstate Parkway north to Route 6.
Follow signs to Bear Mountain State Park.

HILL-HOLD FARM

Thomas Bull was a Tory sympathizer, and two of his three sons
actually fought for the British. Held in custody by the American
forces for two years, Bull was nevertheless able to retain his
holdings, and for the next two hundred years, his descendants
lived in the house he built in 1769. Today Hill-Hold has been
restored as an 1830s country home and farm, emphasizing the
self-sufficiency of rural households of the period.

Inside are many items owned by generations of the Bull family. A mourning picture worked on silk by Martha Bull hangs in
the entry hall. With typical Victorian sentimentality, it shows a
family grieving near a weeping willow tree as doves fly off to the
Great Beyond.

What was probably the best parlor is now the dining room.
Parlors in the late 1700s were multi-purpose rooms. Until about
1790, this one probably contained a tilt-top dining table and a
canopy bed for the master and mistress of the house. When it
was no longer proper for a family of position to entertain, eat
and sleep in the same room, this became a formal dining room.
Across the hall is the room that became the main sitting room.
Above the Burling mahogany desk is a portrait of Sally Bull,
who married her cousin James. Sally, the first child to be born in
the house, was "full of jokes and fun all the day long." Her
mischievous sense of humor is evident despite the sombre dress
and formal pose of the time. A photograph of her at eighty is
said to catch the same fun-loving twinkle in her eyes.

Upstairs are two large rooms. In the principal bedroom is a
wing chair commode on loan from the Metropolitan Museum of
Art in New York City. In the workroom is an unusual fold-away
rope bed and a prized early eighteenth-century Dutch kas with
rare half-ball feet. To show the interior wall construction, portions of plaster have been removed.

In the 1790s, an above-ground kitchen was built. Equipped
with the implements of its time, it features a huge cooking
hearth and a beehive oven. Copper pots, pewter dishes and a

tinware collection fill the wooden shelves. The butter churn and tub are reminders of how highly Goshen butter was regarded in the early 1800s. Occasionally, a costumed volunteer gives open-hearth cooking demonstrations.

Outbuildings so necessary to a farm household include a wooden smokehouse, a large barn with earthen floor and wooden stalls, a woodshed and an outhouse. Fences and enclosures keep the pigs, cows, sheep and fowl away from the herb and vegetable gardens. There is also an old copper still, recalling Orange County's reputation for superb applejack whiskey.

Goosetown Schoolhouse

Also on the property is the Goosetown School, used until 1939 and later moved to this spot. Amy Bull Crist, retired Orange County Superintendent of Schools and descendant of Thomas Bull, began her career here, and guides tell stories of her days in this one-room schoolhouse. Teaching grades one through eight, she often had several children from the same family, and if one forgot to do his homework another was sure to tell their mother and father. Children brought vegetables or pieces of meat to add to the pot of soup bubbling on the wood stove. The wooden blackboard had written assignments for each grade, and while one class recited on the bench near the teacher's desk, others worked at their lessons. The old piano and table filled with games provided welcome breaks for both teacher and students. Then as now, being chosen to help with the chores was an honor. Students were allowed to fill the inkwells, to fetch the water for the bucket and dipper or to raise the flag. The teacher's day did not end when class was dismissed. She often was required to clean the schoolhouse and keep it in good repair. The Goosetown School gives a feel for what schooling was like for most of our country's history.

Campbell Hall, N.Y.
(914) 294-7661

DIRECTIONS:
From West Point: Route 293 south to Route 6 west to Route 17 west. Take Goshen Exit 124 to Greenwich Avenue and North Main Street through village to Route 207 north. Left onto Route 416. Proceed one mile; look

for signs. Hill-Hold is on the right.

From New York City: New York State Thruway (87) north to Exit 16 Harriman. Take Route 17 west. Take Goshen Exit 124 to Greenwich Avenue and North Main Street through village to Route 207 north. Left onto Route 416. Proceed one mile; look for signs. Hill-Hold is on the right.

BRICK HOUSE

Using bricks imported from England rather than local field-stone, Nathaniel Hill built a classic Georgian home for his family in 1768. For seven generations the Hills lived in this house. Neither a period restoration nor a home representative of its last inhabitants, Brick House has been decorated to reflect the different periods in which it was occupied. The Georgian Parlor represents its earliest era. The 1768 paneling on the fireplace wall features fluted pilasters and dentil molding, and the cabinets on either side of the hearth display the family's collection of "flow blue" china. The pair of ribbonback Chippendale-style chairs are said to have been part of George and Martha Washington's set at Mount Vernon. In 1830, a wing was added which included a separate formal dining room and several rooms upstairs.

Another parlor is decorated in the Victorian style of the 1860s. Stripes in the door and window moldings, part of the 1830 remodeling, pick up the rose and burgundy colors of the upholstery and Turkey carpet. The wooden fireplace mantel has been marbleized in the popular mode of the day. Daguerreotypes sit atop tables throughout the room, and a family album with posed portraits is typical of the period.

Upstairs are several bedrooms furnished with pieces dating from the early to mid-1800s. In the housekeeper's room an ironing board, candlesticks and a dress form suggest the duties of this important servant. Also in the room is a table set with books and slates, ready for the children's lessons. In the dressing room off the master bedroom are the musket and sword used by Nathaniel's son Peter in the Revolutionary War.

Montgomery, N.Y.
(914) 457-5951

DIRECTIONS:
From West Point: Route 9W north to Route 17K west; go approximately 8 miles to Montgomery, N.Y. Watch for Brick House signs. Enter from Berea Road.

From New York City: New York State Thruway (87) north to Exit 17 Newburgh. Take Route 17K west for approximately 8 miles to Montgomery, N.Y. Watch for Brick House signs. Enter from Berea Road.

SUGAR LOAF CRAFTS VILLAGE

Over fifty shops, clustered along the main street of Sugar Loaf Crafts Village, offer local handcrafts for sale. Woodcarvers, jewelers, sculptors, cabinetmakers and potters live and work in these eighteenth- and nineteenth-century buildings. Often they may be seen in their shops, hard at work on their creations. Sugar Loaf has been a center for craftsmen since its early days as a stagecoach stop and supply center for local horse traders and dairy farmers. In the 1960s, there was a new influx of artisans, drawn by the town's traditional commitment to craftsmen. All shops are open on Saturdays and Sundays, while only some have midweek hours. Opening times tend to be late, and few stores begin business before 11 A.M.

Before or after shopping, the Sugar Loaf Inn is a pleasant place for lunch or dinner. The circa 1854 building, once a Grange Hall and then a country store, still has its wooden floors, hand-hewn beams and coat hooks on the walls. Mixed sets of chairs surround antique tables, and fresh flowers in crocks and soup tureens add to the bright, country atmosphere. Entrees range from simple cheese and paté in a basket to seafood, chicken and steaks lightly prepared with creative ingredients. The kitchen is partially open to the dining room, and guests can watch the chef at work. Other restaurants are available in Sugar Loaf Village, including the Barnsider, a nice place for hamburgers and other sandwiches. In summer, several ice cream stores are open.

Sugar Loaf, N.Y.
(914) 469-4963

DIRECTIONS:
From West Point: Route 293 south to Route 6 west. Route 17 west to Exit

127. Follow signs to Sugar Loaf.

From New York City: New York State Thruway (87) north to Exit 16 Harriman; Route 17 west to Exit 127. Follow signs to Sugar Loaf.

STORM KING ART CENTER

The four hundred acres of Storm King Art Center provide a huge outdoor park for modern sculpture. Over one hundred thirty works by Alexander Calder, Louise Nevelson and other masters are displayed in the Woodland, Terrace, Hilltop and Fields Galleries as well as in the museum building with its nine exhibit rooms. The drive from West Point is spectacular and the setting magnificent. A must-see for those who love modern sculpture, the rolling hills and expansive grounds make for an enjoyable outing even for those not interested in this type of art. Picnic facilities are available to visitors.

Mountainville, N.Y.
(914) 534-3115

DIRECTIONS:
From West Point: Route 9W north to Route 94 south to Route 32 south. Follow signs to Storm King Art Center.

From New York City: New York State Thruway (87) north to Exit 16 Harriman. North on Route 32 for 10 miles. Follow signs to Storm King Art Center.

MUSEUM VILLAGE

Museum Village introduces visitors to the crafts, professions and services necessary to life in pre-industrial, rural America. Thirty-five buildings, many brought from nearby towns, are clustered in a village-like setting with each building devoted to a specific task. Here you will find Belknap and McCann Candle and Soap Makers, the J.C. Merritt General Store, and the Monroe Journal and Printing Office. Other buildings house exhibits of nineteenth-century farm tools, collections of firefighting apparatus and cast-iron stoves dating from 1820-1910.

Of particular interest is the Vernon Drug Store. The original rounded glass display cases hold assortments of soaps and potions of the time as well as dozens of prescription lenses for eyeglass fittings. The old marble Seneca soda fountain has spigots for lemon, pineapple, orange, chocolate, strawberry, raspberry, vanilla and sasparilla syrups. A reminder of the store's primary purpose is the druggist's mortar and pestle on his table behind the counter.

In the Natural History building is a twelve foot by twenty-three foot skeleton of a mastodont discovered in a meadow in Harriman, N.Y., only two miles away. These creatures lived 12,000-20,000 years ago, and the remains of more than one hundred have been found in New York State, mostly in Orange County. Cabinets of curiosities contain arrangements of insects, birds, butterflies and shells, documenting the Victorian craze for collecting and displaying nature's bounty.

Although Museum Village's literature promises costumed craftsmen demonstrating their tasks, often only a few are on hand. On one peak summer weekend, only a weaver, broom-maker and log cabin guide were in evidence. The cooperage, the harness maker's and the smithy are full of interesting items, but without roaring fires, sounds of hammer on anvil or apprentices, exhibits are strangely lifeless.

Monroe, N.Y.
(914) 782-8247

DIRECTIONS:
From West Point: Route 293 south to Route 6 west to Route 17 west. Take Exit 129 and follow signs to Museum Village.

From New York City: New York State Thruway (87) north to Exit 16 Harriman. Route 17 west to Exit 129. Follow signs to Museum Village.

WOODBURY COMMON

Over seventy outlet shops make up the Woodbury Common Shopping Village, located at the intersection of the New York State Thruway (Exit 16) and Route 17. These shops feature upscale merchandise from such manufacturers as Anne Klein,

Liz Claiborne, Van Heusen, Adidas, Royal Doulton and Dansk. Clothing stores carry a large selection of current styles in a wide range of sizes. On average, there is a 20-25% savings over department store prices, but sale items may offer savings up to 70%. In a center courtyard are fast food restaurants and a three-theater cinema, usually showing at least one movie for general audiences. Woodbury Common is not enclosed, but its layout provides convenient, comfortable shopping in an attractive setting.

Harriman, N.Y.
(914) 928-7467

DIRECTIONS:
From West Point: Route 9W north to Route 293; Route 6 west to intersection of New York State Thruway (87) at Exit 16 Harriman.

From New York City: New York State Thruway (87) north to Exit 16 Harriman.

CHAPTER 6

New Paltz

HIGHLIGHTS . . .

—Seventeenth century stone houses along the oldest street in America
—The last of the great Victorian mountain resorts

With the Hudson River to the east and the Shawangunk Mountains to the west, New Paltz sits amidst the farmlands of the Wallkill Valley. Site of the State University of New York (SUNY) at New Paltz, this bustling college town offers lectures, concerts and athletic events to students, townspeople and visitors. Yet just off Main Street is Huguenot Street, the "oldest street in America," where French Protestants established a village in the seventeenth century. Fleeing the persecution of Catholic King Louis XIV, the Huguenots traveled first to Germany then to Holland and finally to the New World in search of a place where they could worship freely. Settling in the Dutch towns of

Wiltwyck (now Kingston) and Hurley, they found the freedom they sought, but were concerned that their children were becoming too Dutch. In 1677 twelve men, known as the Duzine, bought a large tract from the Esopus Indians and received a patent for their land from Colonial Governor Edmund Andros. Naming their village "die Pfalz" after the province of Pfalz in the Palatinate where they had first found refuge, the Patentees built small, wooden houses along the Wallkill River. As they prospered, they replaced the original structures with the stone houses that line Huguenot Street today.

HUGUENOT STREET

Unusual as it is to find one seventeenth-century house in an area, it is even more unusual to find five of them along one street. Built by the Patentees who settled New Paltz, the houses on Huguenot Street reflect the influence of the Dutch among whom they had lived. The original structures consisted of three rooms, one on top of the other—a kitchen below, sleeping quarters above and an attic loft. All were warmed by a large jambless fireplace, traditional in their former homes in northern France as well as in the homes of the Dutch. Inefficient and smoky, jambless fireplaces had no sides or dampers, making it almost impossible to maintain a steady temperature. Most were replaced in the eighteenth century by the more popular English style, leaving Huguenot Street with some of the finest remaining examples in this country. Because these houses were occupied by the descendants of the Patentees for over two hundred fifty years, many architectural features characteristic of the early days have been retained. Today, family associations preserve and maintain the dwellings as examples of Huguenot life in the New World. Visitors may tour the houses along with the reconstructed French Church and the 1799 LeFevre House.

Jean Hasbrouck House

Built and enlarged by Jean Hasbrouck from 1692-1712, the Jean Hasbrouck House was a general store as well as family home. The center hall with its forty-two-foot beam, hewn from a single tulip tree, separates the family living quarters on the left from the store on the right. Like most of the furnishings in the house, the country Queen Anne chairs in the sitting room belonged to the family. Carved into the chair legs are the letters "HB", signifying that they were specially made for the Hasbroucks. In typical Dutch fashion, a carpet covers the table. Carpets were considered works of art and far too valuable to be used on floors. Sitting rooms were unusual at the time since in most, less prosperous homes, family life centered around the kitchen.

Jambless Fireplace, Old Stone House, New Paltz.

The kitchen of the Jean Hasbrouck house is in the original 1692 section. Relocated from the cellar around 1712, it contains an exceptional jambless fireplace which covers almost an entire wall. Its huge hearth, open to the room, provides no protection from sparks or flame. Black cast iron pots, heavy Dutch ovens and a skillet with a five-foot-long handle attest to the backbreaking, dangerous nature of cooking in colonial times. The blue and white Cantonware displayed in the room was the family's everyday china. Costly antiques today, they were merely ballast for the English and Dutch trading ships.

The room to the right of the center hall was the store run by Jacob Hasbrouck, son of Jean, and carried on by his descendants. Supplying the community with cloth, equipment and staples, the store was also a tavern for men who came to purchase household necessities. Above the original bar hangs Jacob's scales, engraved with his initials and the date 1746. At the end of the hallway, an original staircase leads to the loft with an exhibit of spinning wheels and looms.

Abraham Hasbrouck House

Another Hasbrouck, Abraham, who was the town's military leader, also began building a house in 1692. Abraham's kitchen was the social center of the town where the men gathered on Saturday nights to watch cock fights. In typical Dutch-Huguenot style, the cellar kitchen was warmed by a huge jambless fireplace and was paved with stone. The small trap door in the ceiling was left open at night to provide heat for the bedroom above. Women of the town, forbidden to attend the cock fights, would peer through the trap door to watch the activity in the kitchen below.

Two other rooms, the living room with seven doors and the smaller side room, were added by 1712. In the living room is a tilt-top table which the family placed against the windows at night to keep in the heat and to provide privacy and security. The Dutch wall bed was reserved for those who were ill or elderly. Because of its position near the fire and because its doors could be shut, it was the warmest bed in the house. Also in the room is a night lantern. Each of the original families had its own pattern cut into the tin, and each lamp cast a distinctive shadow. Thus at night, townspeople could identify one another by the lanterns they carried.

Seams on the outside walls indicate where the additions were made to the house. Because it was difficult to construct new rooms exactly even with the original structure, old stone houses often had different levels. The herb garden to the east of the house contains plants that were vital to the early settlers who used herbs to flavor their food and to treat various illnesses.

Bevier-Elting House

Patentee Louis Bevier built this house in 1694. By the 1720s, his son Samuel had rented the front room to the Elting family for use as a general store. This store, in competition with Jean Hasbrouck's across the road, continued in operation until 1800. When Samuel Bevier died in 1767, the house was purchased by the Eltings, and their descendants continued to live there until 1963 when the Huguenot Historical Society acquired it.

The house has several distinctive features. Its covered porch, which provided outdoor workspace, is unusual for such an early house. The extensive use of glass is also unusual. Glass was heavily taxed by the English and was therefore used sparingly in colonial times. Only prosperous families could afford the luxury of large windows. The Bevier-Elting House has a front room window with thirty panes of glass as well as a ten-paned transom over the front door. There is an exceptional amount of storage space. A subcellar running the full width of the house held family provisions and the shopkeeper's supplies. The ladder steps leading from the center room to the attic above is almost three hundred years old and the only original stairway of its type on the street.

Hugo Freer House

Not the most spectacular example of Huguenot architecture on the street, the Hugo Freer House shows how an old stone house was adapted for use through the years. Although the exterior remains much as it was in the early days, the interior has gone through many changes. Modern appliances in a 1950s kitchen, central heating and fitted carpets seem incongruous in an old stone house. Yet, one of the joys of Huguenot Street is to see how these houses were handed down from family member to family member and lived in year after year. The Reverend John Follette, a descendant of Hugo Freer and the last inhabitant, sold the house to the Huguenot Historical Society in 1955.

As in most of the houses on the street, many of the furnishings once belonged to family members and have been collected by the various family associations to display in the houses that bear their names. The chest which carried Hugo Freer's belongings to the New World is in the living room, and a linsey-woolsey spread woven for Jane Freer is in the bedroom. An old rope bed recalls the days when ropes strung across bed frames had to be kept taut to support the mattress. Sagging ropes meant an uncomfortable night and thus the good night wish, "Sleep tight." One room is set up as a vender's supply room. Itinerant peddlars boarded with families in town while they sold their goods and mended used items. They provided needed services which the town could not support year round.

Deyo House

Dramatically altered both inside and out, the Deyo House is a Victorian family home built upon the foundations of the original 1692 stone house. Completely remodeled in 1894 by the Brodheads, descendants of Patentee Pierre Deyo, the house contains the most up-to-date conveniences of the time—electricity, indoor plumbing, radiators and even an electric sink complete with agitator-washer. Mr. Brodhead was a New York banker who used the house as a summer retreat and often entertained his clients here. Parquet flooring, elegant, tiled fireplaces and a bridal-cake plaster ceiling are evidence of the Victorian love of ornamentation.

The parlor and dining room are part of the original 1692 structure. The window sills, two-to-three-feet deep, hint at the thick stone beneath the smoothly plastered walls. The painting over the mantel in the parlor recalls the early days of New Paltz. A small child is strapped into a walker to prevent her from toppling into a jambless fireplace. Upstairs is a display of family quilts and coverlets and a sewing room with clothing of the period. In the front solarium is an exhibit of Victorian toys and children's furniture.

LeFevre House

From the street, the Federal brick LeFevre House seems to have no kinship with the other houses on Huguenot Street. The classical symmetry of this elegant, spacious home separates it from the rough-hewn stone dwellings of the Patentees and identifies it as the residence of a family which had prospered over the years. However, the original hipped roof, long since replaced, and the stone sides still in evidence attest to the family's Dutch-Huguenot heritage. The house was built by Ezekiel Elting in 1799. Several of his daughters married LeFevre men, and today, the home is owned by the LeFevre Family Association.

The long center hallway, the high ceilings and neoclassical detailing are characteristic of Federal houses. Rooms were large and set aside for specific purposes. No longer did the family cook, eat and sleep in the same room. The LeFevre dining room has eighteenth-century shield back chairs and an elaborately carved mantel. The fireback, from the Elting family's old stone house, came from the Sterling Forest Foundry, the foundry that forged the Great Chain that was stretched across the Hudson at West Point during the Revolutionary War (see Chapter 1). The room across the hall was Ezekiel Elting's store. It is now decorated as a parlor with furniture pushed back against the walls in typical Federal fashion.

Upstairs, the Doctors' Room holds nineteenth-century medical instruments, record books and personal belongings of doctors who practiced in New Paltz. Another bedroom contains an exhibit devoted to lacemaking. The Huguenots were expert lacemakers in France, and when they fled to seek religious freedom, they wore their wealth in lace about their waists. Unfortunately, in the New World, the flax used to make linen thread was of such poor quality that the art of lacemaking, once handed down from mother to daughter, died out.

French Church and Huguenot Cemetery

The French Church was built in 1972 by the Crispell Family Association to honor Patentee Antoine Crispell. It is a reproduction of the Huguenot French Reformed Church constructed in

1717. The Crispell family spent seven years researching architectural designs and details of the period, since no accurate drawings of the first stone church remained.

To build this church, wide plank flooring, pews and beams were carved and planed by hand. Hinges, door handles and other hardware were fashioned after those found in the stone houses along the street. In accordance with Church doctrine, the building was constructed as a square rather than in the shape of a cross. The square shape derives from the Huguenot belief that all were equal in the eyes of God and that no one should take precedence over another. Each family rented a pew, and because the church was unheated, brought footwarmers filled with bricks or coals to keep warm in the winter. The church's old Bible was used in the early days when services were conducted in French. When Dutch and then English replaced French, the Bible was sold at auction to Jacob Hasbrouck, whose descendants donated it to the Hugenot Historical Society.

The church is topped by a cupola from which a man summoned villagers to worship by blowing a horn. The horn was also used to sound the alarm in times of danger. Ten of the Patentees are buried in the cemetery just outside the church. Since many of the original grave markers no longer exist, memorial tablets honor these men. The oldest remaining tombstone is inscribed with the name of Andries LeFevre who died in 1714. The graveyard was in use until 1864.

DuBois Fort

According to the terms of the patent granted by Governor Andros, the Huguenots had to build a secure fortress for the protection of the community. DuBois Fort was built by Daniel DuBois in 1705, and it served as his family home as well as a gathering place for the townspeople. The thick stone walls were designed with open rifle holes at intervals, and the basement was large enough to quarter troops in an emergency. Since the Patentees had a good relationship with the Esopus Indians, the fort was never needed for defense, and in later years, the rifle holes were filled in. Today, DuBois Fort is a restaurant serving lunch and dinner in the summer.

Seventeenth century stone house, Huguenot Street, New Paltz.

(914) 255-1889 (tours)
(914) 255-1660 (office)

DIRECTIONS:
From West Point and New York City: New York State Thruway (87) north
to Exit 18 New Paltz. Turn left onto Route 299 and follow Main Street
through New Paltz. Make a right turn onto Huguenot Street immediately before the bridge over the Wallkill River. Tours begin at Deyo Hall
on Brodhead Street.

OTHER HISTORIC SITES

MOHONK MOUNTAIN HOUSE

Only six miles west of the town of New Paltz is Mohonk Mountain House, a resort designated a National Historic Landmark.

Founded by the Smiley family in 1869, Mohonk has always been a place where families vacation amidst the majesty and splendor of the Shawangunk Mountains. Set on the northwest corner of a glacial lake, surrounded by 7500 acres of unspoiled terrain, the 300-room Victorian hotel offers year-round activities. In summer, canoeing, fishing, swimming, horseback riding, tennis and golf are available, while in winter, guests may ice skate and cross-country ski. Throughout the year, miles of hiking trails and carriage roads are open, and special theme weekends, children's programs and afternoon teas are offered. The last of the great mountain resorts that dotted New York State at the turn of the century, the hotel has begun to show its age. Nevertheless, it remains a quiet, conservative retreat in the Quaker tradition. Operating on the full American Plan (room and three meals a day), Mohonk also welcomes day guests. A pass available at the gatehouse entitles visitors to use the facilities and to enjoy a meal at Mohonk.

(914) 255-1000

DIRECTIONS:
From West Point and New York City: New York State Thruway (87) north to Exit 18 New Paltz. Turn left onto Route 299 and follow Main Street through New Paltz. Cross the bridge over the Wallkill River; take the first right. After approximately one-quarter mile, bear left at the fork, and continue up Mountain Rest Road to the Mohonk gate.

ADAIR VINEYARDS

A small, family winery, Adair Vineyards is located just outside New Paltz in a 200-year-old Dutch barn. Jim Adair explains how he makes his wine and offers samples for tasting. (See Chapter 14 for further information and directions.)

CHAPTER 7

High Falls, Stone Ridge and Hurley

HIGHLIGHTS. . .

—DePuy Canal House—an extraordinary restaurant in a 1797
  stone tavern
—Antique shops down country lanes
—The largest concentration of seventeenth-century stone
  houses in America

The three small villages of High Falls, Stone Ridge and Hurley
offer a quiet contrast to the hectic pace of everyday life. The area
has remained rural and out of the mainstream of development

in the Hudson Valley. While rich in the history of New York State, this is not a region with an abundance of museums and historic sites. Rather, it invites visitors to explore country lanes, old stone houses and antique shops in barns and carriage houses. Spend the day, or stay the night in one of the area's bed and breakfast inns. But the main reason to visit this area is dinner at the DePuy Canal House.

HIGH FALLS

DePUY CANAL HOUSE

Steamed cheese spiral pasta with shiitake mushroom sauce; red swiss chard cilantro Florentine with poached pheasant egg; prawns *rouille* on a timbal of sea scallop mousse—each dish is a

DePuy Canal House, High Falls.

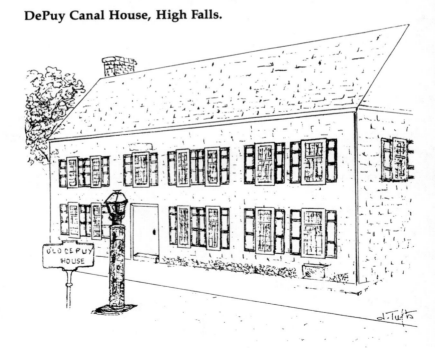

masterpiece. The creative energy necessary to perfect such offerings would satisfy most other restaurants for years, but chef/owner John Novi at DePuy Canal House enthusiastically develops an entire new menu each week.

Fresh local produce complements meat and fowl purchased from nearby farms. Venison from Lucky Star Ranch across the Hudson in Rhinebeck and goat cheese from Coach Farms in Gallatin are frequently incorporated into his special dishes. Desserts at the Canal House are outstanding as well. Novi's parents once ran a bakery down the street, and Mrs. Novi still bakes her famous chocolate cake (no wonder chocolate is John Novi's passion) as well as vanilla and chocolate biscotti. Wines from Europe, California and such Hudson Valley vineyards as Benmarl, West Park, Clinton and Millbrook (see Chapter 14) stock the 1000-bottle wine cellar.

The restaurant is housed in an eighteenth-century stone building. From 1797 to 1836, it was a tavern run by Simeon DePuy. When work began on the Delaware and Hudson Canal in 1825, his Stone House Tavern prospered because of its location on the canal's bank. After DePuy's death in 1836, the house passed through a series of owners and at one time was the lock tender's home. Around the turn of the century, the canal was closed, its function superceded by the railroads, and the house fell into disrepair. In 1964 when he was only twenty-one, even though he had no plans for its use, John Novi borrowed money to buy the run-down, boarded-up old canal house. Five years later, after schooling in Italy and extensive work on the building, he opened the DePuy Canal House Restaurant.

With fires burning in the fireplaces, with dark wood beams and wide plank floors, with fresh flowers and candlelight, the restaurant has the feel of an eighteenth-century tavern and the comfortable elegance of today. It is tempting to linger over the intriguing descriptions of all the dishes offered and difficult to choose among them. The remarkable creativity of John Novi is evident in each course, and an evening at DePuy Canal House can be an extraordinary event.

Route 213
(914) 687-7700

DELAWARE AND HUDSON CANAL MUSEUM, CANAL WALK AND THE FALLS

The D & H Canal Museum

This small but surprisingly comprehensive museum tells the fascinating story of the D & H Canal. A large map at the entrance traces the course of the 108-mile-long canal from Honesdale, Pennsylvania, to its terminus at Eddyville, New York, near Kingston. The D & H Canal, designed by Benjamin Wright, chief engineer of the Erie Canal, was the result of a business venture undertaken by two brothers, Maurice and William Wurts. When the War of 1812 cut off America's supply of English coal, native coal reserves had to be found and mined. The Wurtses purchased anthracite coal fields in Pennsylvania and sought an alternative to the expensive overland route to the lucrative New York City market. They envisioned a man-made canal stretching from the Pennsylvania mines to the Hudson River. The brothers had to convince skeptical prospective backers that their coal would be commercially successful. At that time, Americans burned only bituminous (soft) coal.

Accordingly, in January of 1825, they staged a dramatic demonstration outside the Tontine Coffee House in lower Manhattan. They set fire to a pile of their coal, and the resulting blaze convinced onlookers that anthracite coal was indeed superior to bituminous. People rushed to invest in the Wurtses' Delaware and Hudson Canal Company, and within a few short hours all stock had been sold. The building of the D & H Canal became the first million-dollar private venture in the United States.

An enormous undertaking, the canal, begun in 1825, was not completed until 1828. Because of the differences in elevation along the canal's route, 108 locks were needed to raise and lower barges to the correct water level. At some points, height variations were so great that engineers had to build a series of locks close together. It took about twenty minutes to transverse each lock, and bargemen often waited several hours at locations where locks were clustered. Small communities grew up at these places to supply and service the barge families. These towns were considered ports along the waterway, and stores took names such as Seaside Supply, seemingly incongruous so far inland.

In the museum is a working model which demonstrates how locks functioned. Another exhibit is a life-size reproduction of a barge cabin. Entire families lived in this cramped space because the barge was their home as well as their livelihood. A major expenditure, barges were often bought on an installment plan, and by the time the barge was fully paid for, it was worn out and needed to be replaced. Young children walked along the tow path, guiding the horses and mules which pulled the barges along the canal. Hours were long—at the height of the canal's operation, the channel was open from 4 A.M. to 10 P.M., or for as long as there was enough light to see. Even so, since barges crawled along at three miles per hour, the entire trip from Honesdale to Eddyville took ten days. By the end of the nineteenth century, railroads provided a faster, more efficient means of transport, and in 1898 the D & H was closed. Many of the towns along the canal ceased to exist.

Mohonk Road
(914) 687-9311

The Canal Walk

Five of the D & H Canal locks were located in High Falls, and although the town suffered when the canal was closed, it managed to survive. The abandoned locks, Numbers 16 to 20, were designated a National Historic Site in 1969. Today, a brochure is available at the museum for a self-guided tour of what remains of these structures. The tour begins at Lock 16 next to the DePuy Canal House. One corner of this old stone tavern was beveled to prevent the tow ropes from fraying as they were pulled taut to to secure barges unloading supplies. A little further along is a slip where bluestone and locally made cement were loaded onto the boats.

A thriving cement industry was a by-product of the canal's construction. Huge quantities of cement needed to build the locks had to be shipped all the way from Syracuse. By chance, engineers at High Falls noticed rocks of the type that usually made good cement. The stone exceeded their expectations. It made the stongest natural cement known in the world, and this local cement was used in the base of the Statue of Liberty, the Brooklyn Bridge and the U.S. Capitol.

Two of the locks, Numbers 18 and 20, retain their four snubbing posts. As a barge entered the lock, it was snubbed—tied by ropes around the post to secure it—as the water level was raised or lowered. Few walls remain intact. Water pressure was needed to support the sides, and the Canal is now dry. The aqueduct that spanned the Canal at High Falls is also gone. This water channel was one of four built along the Canal by John Roebling, who later designed the Brooklyn Bridge. Only the supports are left of the aqueduct, which with its cable suspension construction was considered an engineering wonder of the day. The entire canal walk takes about forty-five minutes and requires hiking through some rather rough terrain. Since there are no descriptive markers, it is very helpful to have the Canal Walk brochure. Insect repellant is also recommended.

The Falls

Just across Route 213 from DePuy Canal House, a road leads through the woods to the falls for which the town was named. At the falls, markers describe the history of the D & H Canal, the ruins of the old stone mill and Roebling's aqueduct. Picnic tables are available above the falls, and the flat rocky outcroppings below are also great perches for picnickers.

DIRECTIONS:
From West Point and New York City: New York State Thruway (87) north to Exit 18 New Paltz; Route 299 west through New Paltz; right turn onto Route 32 north toward Rosendale; left onto Route 213 west to High Falls.

STONE RIDGE

A sunny day, the Old King's Highway, Dutch stone houses— Stone Ridge is the perfect setting for a day of antiquing. Shops in old houses, barns and even a schoolhouse offer furniture, glassware, paintings and estate jewelry. Collections of country pine, oak, Empire and Art Deco range from the exceptional to the eccentric. The excitement of the hunt leads from room to room within a shop and from store to store along Route 209.

The Bankers' Daughter, an antique shop in an 1840 classic brick colonial, is filled with wooden cabinets, tinware, wardrobes, washstands, baskets and silver spilling over into a barn and carriage house out back. The house itself, built by Dr. Levi Lounsberry, was the only brick house in the village of Stone Ridge—a testament to the owner's wealth and good taste. Acorn Antiques in the center of the village specializes in Mission Oak and period arts and crafts. The owners are extremely knowledgeable about local history and are eager to share information with their customers. At Elm Rock Antiques, several dealers share an eighteenth-century house. There are many other shops both in Stone Ridge and the surrounding towns. Most have copies of "Antiques: A Treasure Hunter's Guide," published by the Antiques Dealers Association of Ulster County. The brochure describes over fifty shops and locates them on an easy to follow map.

Stone Ridge is part of the area settled by English soldiers in the late 1600s. When the British gained control of New Netherlands in 1664, they brought in soldiers to maintain order in the Dutch settlement of Kingston. By 1668, the authorities decided that the soldiers were no longer needed and offered them farmland a few miles inland. Joined by Dutch settlers, they built log houses clustered together for protection against the Indians. Later, when the Indians were no longer a threat, the farmers built more permanent dwellings on their own holdings.

Others settled along Route 209, an old Indian trail, known at one time as The Old Mine Road and later as the King's Highway. One of the longest early roads in America, it was built by the Dutch to transport copper ore 104 miles from the Delaware Valley to Kingston. The ore was discovered by prospectors who had heard Henry Hudson's reports of Indians smoking copper tobacco pipes and wearing copper necklaces. Today, seventeenth-century copper pieces from these early Dutch mines can be seen in the Rijksmuseum in Amsterdam.

During the Revolutionary War, the citizens of Stone Ridge and the surrounding towns strongly supported the rebellion. Fleeing the British, the State Senate abandoned Kingston on October 6, 1777 (see Chapter 8), and met as a Council of Safety just north of Stone Ridge in the Andrew Oliver house which, unfortunately, no longer exists. This house served as the capitol of New York State from October 19 to November 18 when the Council moved to Hurley. Five years later as the war drew to a close, George Washington spent the night at the Wynkoop-Lounsberry House on his way from West Point to Kingston. His troops lodged at the Tack Tavern which had served as the Ulster County Courthouse when Kingston had been burned earlier in the war.

Today, historic markers identify the old Tack Tavern in the center of town and the Wynkoop-Lounsberry House across the street. The Dutch heritage is evident. Ulster County has the largest concentration of stone houses in the country, and those in and around Stone Ridge are unusual stone buildings of the post-Revolutionary War period. Unlike the small stone dwellings of the original Dutch settlers, these two-story homes are spacious, attesting to their builders' prosperity. Ulster County abounds with antique shops filled with mementos from the area's past, and detours down country lanes elicit thoughts of an earlier day.

DIRECTIONS:
From West Point and New York City: New York State Thruway (87) north to Exit 18 New Paltz; Route 299 west through New Paltz; right turn onto Route 32 north toward Rosendale; left onto Route 213 west through High Falls; right onto Route 209 to the Village of Stone Ridge.

HURLEY

The small village of Hurley has more early stone houses than any other town in America. Nine of the twenty-six stone houses, built between the late 1600s and 1818, line the quiet residential Main Street. Only once a year, on Stone House Day, the second Saturday in July, do these privately owned homes open their doors to the public. But even when the houses are not open, a walk down Main Street envelops visitors in the history of this 300-year-old village. Halfway down the street is a large framed map with descriptions of the historic houses, and a self-guided walking tour compiled by the Hurley Heritage

Society is available at the post office. Historical markers and plaques on houses give additional information.

Settled in 1661 by Dutch and Huguenot families from nearby Kingston (see Chapter 8), the town then called Niew Dorp (New Village) was burned by the Indians two years later. Three men were killed and thirty-five settlers were taken captive in retaliation against the Dutch, who sold Indians into slavery in Manhattan. Search parties combed the surrounding areas and within a year, all of the captives had been recovered. On one of these expeditions, Louis DuBois noticed the fertile lands along the Wallkill River to the south, and fifteen years later he returned with eleven other Huguenots to found the town of New Paltz (see Chapter 6).

When the territory came under English rule, Niew Dorp was rebuilt and named Hurley after Colonial Governor Francis Lovelace's estate in Ireland. Fiercely patriotic during the Revolutionary War, Hurley was the temporary home of New York State's Council of Safety in 1777, and later welcomed George Washington on his way from West Point to Kingston in November 1782.

Washington was received at the **Houghtaling House,** then a tavern and gathering place for the town (corner of Hurley Avenue and Main Street). Mattys Ten Eyck offered the good wishes of the community to the General. According to village legend, Ten Eyck delivered a long speech from the doorway while Washington remained on his horse and listened patiently in the rain. Just down Main Street is the **Van Dusen House,** capitol of New York State from November 18 to December 17, 1777. Meeting in the dining room, the Council of Safety hid the papers they brought with them from Kingston in the secret room above the kitchen. This house is unusually large for its 1723 date of construction. The L-shape structure is believed to be original since there are no seams indicating later additions. The hardware on the front door is unique to Hurley. The latch and knocker, as well as the pancake hinges, were made in the town's early blacksmith shop.

The **Elmendorf House** is thought to be the oldest in town. Once known as the Half-Moon Tavern, its shutters still bear crescent shapes cut into the wood. The **Polly Crispell Cottage** next door was a blacksmith shop. Iron spikes hidden inside the fireplace were designed to keep out witches and demons who were believed to invade homes through their chimneys. A path between the Crispell Cottage and the Elmendorf House leads to the **Old Burial Ground.** On a lovely hill, amid tall birch trees, are graves of the early settlers. Bluestone markers date back to 1715, but the gravestone of Captain Mattys Ten Eyck (1658-1741) is the oldest that can be read in its entirety.

The **DuMond House** came to be known as the Spy House or Guard House. Lieutenant Daniel Taylor, convicted of treason at

Dutch Reformed Church, Hurley.

a court-martial in New Windsor, was imprisoned in the Du-Mond House and hanged from an apple tree across the street on October 19, 1777. Just across from the church is the **Dr. Richard Ten Eyck House.** A station on the underground railroad in Civil War times, the house was a hiding place for escaped slaves making their way to freedom in Canada. A tunnel near the barn connected the Ten Eyck house to the church which provided sanctuary for the runaways. A shutter on the northwest side of the house has a hole made by an Esopus Indian bullet, and arrowheads have been found on the property. On the outskirts of town is the **Wynkoop House.** The original house, built before 1676, forms the core of the current house. For over three hundred years, 1663-1971, the property was held by one family. One of the early owners, Revolutionary War Colonel Cornelius Wynkoop, was killed in this house by a slave in the early 1790s. The Wynkoop House was the country farmhouse used in the 1982 movie *Tootsie.*

In Hurley, community life has always centered around the church. In the early days, settlers had to travel to the Dutch Reformed Church in Kingston (see Chapter 8). Not until 1801 were they granted permission to build their own church. The present church, built upon the stones of the old in 1853, stands at the entrance to Main Street, and its towering spire is a landmark for miles around. Inside, the old pews bear name plates of families who once owned them. It is the church that sponsors Stone House Day each July. In addition to organizing tours of the stone houses, parishioners hold a country fair and sponsor demonstrations of Revolutionary War camp life.

DIRECTIONS:
From West Point and New York City: New York State Thruway (87) north to Exit 18 New Paltz; Route 299 west through New Paltz; right turn onto Route 32 north toward Rosendale; left onto Route 213 west through High Falls; right onto Route 209 through Stone Ridge to Hurley; follow signs to village.

CHAPTER 8

Kingston

HIGHLIGHTS...

—The Old Stone House where New York State's first Senate met

—The Old Dutch Church, the site where George Washington spoke in November 1782

—The graveyard where New York's first Governor is buried

The third oldest Dutch settlement in the New World, Kingston retains many of its old stone houses and historic buildings. Settled in 1652 near the confluence of Rondout Creek and the Hudson River, the town was originally known as Esopus. Trouble with the Indians brought Governor Peter Stuyvesant up from New Amsterdam in 1658. He directed his troops to build a stockade and ordered the Dutch farmers to move their homes within the protective walls of the settlement, then called Wiltwyck (Wild Woods). Trading continued with the Indians, who were only allowed in the stockade from dawn to dusk, but relations remained uneasy. In 1663, the Indians attacked Wiltwyck, massacring citizens and burning many homes. A year later when the Dutch lost New Netherlands, the town, renamed Kingston, came under English rule.

In the Revolutionary War, Kingston strongly supported the patriot cause. Strategically located on the Hudson River, the town was able to supply the Continental Army with food from its rich farmlands. The newly formed Convention of Representatives of the State of New York, forced to flee upriver from British-occupied New York City, met first in White Plains, then in Fishkill and then in Kingston in 1777. British General John Vaughan, on his way to join forces with General Burgoyne at Saratoga, burned Kingston, destroying over one hundred fifty buildings, including portions of the house where the State Senate had been meeting.

Well into the nineteenth century, Kingston was an important transfer center for raw materials and goods between New York City and the mid-Hudson Valley. Canal boats brought coal from the mines of Pennsylvania along the Delaware and Hudson Canal to steamships and barges waiting at Rondout Landing. Bricks, cement and native bluestone, used to pave the sidewalks of Manhattan and the Bronx, were loaded onto vessels and transported to New York. As roads and highways superceded the water routes, Kingston's economy slowed. Today, its stone houses, its waterfront district and the old stockade area recall its 300-year history.

STOCKADE DISTRICT

Governor Peter Stuyvesant's stockade around the settlement of Kingston was built with tree trunks thirteen feet high and seven inches thick. No traces of this barrier against Indian attack remain today, but archaeologists have uncovered post holes into which the original timbers were sunk. During the Revolutionary War, the major threat to Kingston came not from the Indians but from British troops under General John Vaughan. Kingston was a hotbed of patriot activity, and Vaughan called it "a nursery for almost every villain in the country." As General Dave R. Palmer in his book *The River and the Rock* goes on to say, Vaughan encountered musket fire from Kingston which "induced me to reduce the place to ashes, which I accordingly did, not leaving a house."

Actually, one house, the Van Steenburgh House (97 Wall Street), did survive, probably because of the Tory sympathies of its owner. Many of the others were rebuilt, and these old stone houses can be seen today. There is even an intersection, where Crown Street meets John Street, with an eighteenth-century stone house on each corner—the only such intersection in the country. Interspersed with modern day shops and restaurants are buildings with architectural features of the past. Dutch stepped gables, fluted columns, mansard roofs and elaborate Victorian cornices—all can be found within the old Stockade District. Two buildings in particular recall Kingston's past: the Senate House where New York State's first Senate met and the Old Dutch Church with George Washington's thank-you letter to the congregation for their hospitality.

DIRECTIONS:
From West Point and New York City: New York State Thruway (87) north to Exit 19 Kingston. Take second road off traffic circle (becomes Washington Avenue). Follow signs to Stockade District.

SENATE HOUSE AND MUSEUM

Renting a room in the home of Abraham Van Gaasbeek, the New York State Senate convened for the first time on September 9, 1777. Sitting on boxes and barrels in what had been Van Gaasbeek's store, the seventeen Senators debated procedures for governing the new state. Since April when the constitution was adopted, Kingston had been the capital of New York, and in July, George Clinton was sworn in as the first governor on the steps of the Kingston Courthouse. By the time the Senate met, the British were advancing up the Hudson. Only four weeks into the session, the Senators abandoned Kingston and fled inland to Hurley. They took with them the minutes of their meetings which are now in the Senate House Museum Archives. Van Gaasbeek's house burned along with the rest of Kingston in the British attack on October 16, 1777. It is believed that Abraham Van Gaasbeek rebuilt it sometime before his death, and additions were made in the nineteenth century. In 1887, the State of New York purchased the house and has preserved it as an historic site.

Since details about the original house are sketchy, curators have furnished it to represent a typical house of the period. The room in which the Senate convened is set up as a meeting room. The boxes and barrels are gone, replaced by a gateleg table and Windsor chairs. The kitchen with a beehive oven contains implements used for cooking in the eighteenth century. In the bedroom, which also served as an office, is a letter written in 1772 by Van Gaasbeek to his son Peter. Tiles surrounding the

Meeting place of New York State's first Senate, Kingston.

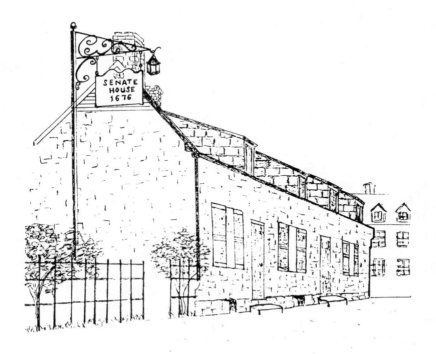

fireplace in the parlor are original to the house, and the complete set of delftware, painted only on one side, was meant for display on the mantel.

The separate museum building has an exhibit of works by John Vanderlyn, a native Kingston artist. A painter in the neoclassic style, he never embraced the trend toward naturalism which culminated in the Hudson River School. Another exhibit, entitled Senate House Recollects, was opened in 1987 on the one hundredth anniversary of the purchase of the Senate House, New York State's second oldest historic site. (The oldest is Washington's Headquarters in Newburgh. See Chapter 5.) An eclectic collection, it includes sketches of the original Senators, local artifacts, candlesticks from the courthouse at Appomattox, hair from the tail of Robert E. Lee's horse, and photographs showing the Senate House through the years. Another gallery recounts the research behind the continuing restoration of the Senate House.

312 Fair Street
(914) 338-2786

OLD DUTCH CHURCH

In November of 1782, George Washington rode up from West Point to Kingston where he was received by the ministers, elders and deacons of the Dutch Reformed Church. They praised him for his wisdom, integrity and fortitude during the War for Independence, and he in turn thanked them for their "concern for my temporal and eternal life." A copy of his words in his own hand hangs in the vestibule of the present church.

The original church was built within the Stockade on land specifically designated by Governor Peter Stuyvesant for a house of worship. Religion was an integral part of the settlers' lives. Yet, unlike other colonists in the New World, they welcomed those whose beliefs differed from their own. The French Huguenots, fleeing persecution in Europe, found refuge among the Dutch. In fact, the Huguenots became so much a part of the community that some feared that their children were becoming too Dutch. A number of families resettled inland in Hurley (see

Old Dutch Church, Kingston.

Chapter 7) and in New Paltz (see Chapter 6) in order to maintain their own identity.

The Dutch Reformed congregation grew over the years, and in 1852 built the present Renaissance Revival church, designed by Minard Lafever. The vaulted ceiling, the elaborately carved galleries and the liberal use of gilding add elegance to the typical Dutch classical style. The Tiffany stained glass window behind the pulpit was added in 1891. In the vestibule items on display chronicle four centuries of the church's history. A tablet commemorates the date 26 December 1660 when Communion was first celebrated by the congregation. George Washington's letter recalls the eighteenth century, and Civil War battle flags, the nineteenth century. A Book of Remembrance signed by Queen Juliana and Princess Beatrix of Holland, who visited the church on the congregation's three hundredth birthday, represents the twentieth century.

The church's exterior is of native bluestone, and its magnificent spire can be seen for miles around. A statue entitled "Patriotism," commissioned by Civil War General George H. Sharpe, is in the churchyard. It is the only known monument erected by a general to honor his troops. George Clinton, first Governor of New York and Vice President under Jefferson and Madison, is buried in the graveyard.

227 Wall Street
(914) 338-6759

RONDOUT LANDING

The waterfront district, Rondout Landing, is being restored in an attempt to recapture its days as a busy port on the Hudson River. As the terminus of the Delaware and Hudson Canal, Rondout Landing attracted shipbuilders, shopkeepers and immigrant workers to service the active maritime industries. Today, it has several restaurants, small shops and the dock from which river boat cruises depart.

DIRECTIONS:
From West Point and New York City: New York State Thruway (87) north to Exit 19 Kingston. Follow Route 587 to Broadway. Turn left (east) and follow Broadway down to the waterfront.

Hudson River Maritime Center

Limited exhibits in this small museum present information on lighthouses, riverboats and the industries which were dependent on the Hudson River. Adjacent to the museum is a boat-building shop where workers can be seen constructing large wooden boats. The Center also maintains the old lighthouse which guides ships in and out of the harbor (914/338-0071).

Rondout Lighthouse

After completion of the Delaware and Hudson Canal in 1828,

the volume of traffic on the Hudson River near Kingston dramatically increased. To ensure safety, a lighthouse was built in 1837 where Rondout Creek meets the river. Made of wood, it was replaced in 1867 with what became known as Rondout Light No. 1. The Murdock family lived in this lighthouse and operated it for almost seventy years.

In 1913, the lighthouse had to be relocated because of changes in the river channels. Rondout Light No. 2, the last lighthouse built on the Hudson, still guides ships today. Its signal is now automated, but the rooms where the lightkeeper once lived are open to the public. The *Rondout Belle* ferries visitors out to tour the lighthouse from May through October (914/338-0071).

Rondout Lighthouse, Kingston.

Boat Trips on the Hudson

Three companies offer boat trips on the Hudson, departing from Rondout Landing. In addition to the lighthouse tour, the *Rondout Belle* has lunch and dinner cruises and can be chartered by private groups (914/338-6280). The *Rip Van Winkle*, a 500-passenger motor vessel, makes three-hour afternoon, dinner or music cruises, passing lighthouses and great estates along the way. Also available on the *Rip Van Winkle* is a full day excursion to West Point (914/255-6515). Myles Gordon's Great Hudson Sailing Center provides sailing instruction, rents sailboats and on weekends offers a sunset cruise on the forty-three foot sailing yacht *Champagne* (914/338-7813).

CHAPTER 9

Hudson

HIGHLIGHTS...

—Olana, Hudson River School artist Frederick Church's Persian style villa overlooking the river

—Fire engines of bygone days in the American Museum of Firefighting

—Antiques and collectibles: Trash to Treasures

If there ever was a town fit to be the home of the American Museum of Firefighting, Hudson is it. Back in 1785 when Hudson became the first city chartered by the new nation, its Proprietors required each family to have a water bucket for every fireplace and chimney in the house. Even today within a seven block area, there are four different firehouses. On Park Place is the J. W. Edmonds Hose Company, the oldest active volunteer fire company in New York State. It was established April 17,

1794. A short distance from the downtown area, the American Museum of Firefighting displays an impressive collection of fire engines—hand pulled, horse drawn and motorized—along with memorabilia from the lives of volunteer firemen.

Hudson was settled by seamen from Nantucket and Rhode Island who, fearing British aggression, loaded their families and even their houses onto ships and sailed to the safer inland harbor at Hudson. Here they reconstructed their houses and resumed their whaling activities. The town prospered and declined along with the demand for whale oil. In later years, the fortunes of Hudson rose and fell with the railroad and light industries. In good times, the city expanded. Many of the existing homes were built during the nineteenth century—over half the buildings in town are on the National Register of Historic Places.

Today Hudson is a city of contrasts. Nicely restored examples of Federal, Greek Revival and Queen Anne houses sit beside shabby, dilapidated buildings in various stages of disrepair. Antique shops abound, but merchandise ranges from elegant, formal English and European pieces to flea market castaways. Old-fashioned corner stores stand amidst pockets of poverty. Nevertheless, in spite of these contrasts or perhaps because of them, Hudson is worth a visit.

ARCHITECTURAL HIGHLIGHTS

A detailed walking tour brochure entitled "Historic Hudson" is available in many town shops or through the Chamber of Commerce (729 Columbia Street, Hudson, NY 12534). This house-by-house survey is difficult to follow and catalogs a great number of buildings, many of which are not superb examples of the architectural styles they represent. Some of the highlights are listed below.

Parade Hill
Overlooking the Hudson River is a park given in perpetuity to the citizens of Hudson by the original Proprietors. Steps from Front Street at the foot of Warren lead to the green, open space

of the Promenade with a view of the river, the Athens Lighthouse and the Catskills beyond. It is easy to imagine hoop-skirted young ladies on the arms of frock-coated gentlemen parading by on a Sunday afternoon. The twelve-foot statue of St. Winifred, given to the city in 1896, is nearby. Today, the well-maintained park is still popular with Hudson's citizens.

Walking Lower Warren Street

The two blocks of Warren below 2nd Street have some of Hudson's finest examples of eighteenth- and early nineteenth-century buildings. Each of these has a plaque documenting its style of architecture and approximate date of construction. Along the north side of Warren, several structures are noteworthy: **Shiloh Baptist Church** (#14) was built in 1909. The Stars of David on the upper facade indicate its original use as a synagogue. **Curtiss House** (#32) was built by a whaler in 1834. This Greek Revival house with Ionic columns has a lovely wrought iron enclosed garden and boasts an octagonal widow's walk. **Bank of Hudson** (#116) an 1809 Adam-style house, encompasses both Federal and Greek Revival architecture. When the bank failed during a depression, its owner converted the building into his private residence. Don't miss the carved faces capping the columns. One of the few cast iron homes ever built in the United States is the **Ezra Waterbury House** (#124). The facade simulates stone and wood so accurately that it is necessary to tap the exterior to verify its cast iron construction.

Across the street, two homes clearly similar in style are the **Robert Jenkins House** (#113) and the **Seth Jenkins House** (#115). The brothers, who were sons of the first mayor, lived next door to each other in these two brick Federal homes. The Daughters of the American Revolution received the Robert Jenkins House from Robert's granddaughter Frances Hartley and maintain it as a geneological library and museum of local artifacts (open only Wednesday and Sunday afternoons during July and August). Unfortunately, the house no longer reflects a true Federal style due to modifications to the interior over the years. However, anyone interested in the Hudson River School of Art will want to visit. The five paintings on view here, while not the finest examples of the School, are works rarely seen by the general public. Henry Ary's "Mount Merino" depicts the view from Hudson looking out over South Bay toward the mountains. Ernest Parton's "Pond at Olana" is also of local interest. Other works include those by Arthur Parton and Bert Phillips. While there, be sure to see the Zouave uniform worn during the Civil War, one of only five complete outfits in the country.

Touring Union and East Allen Streets by Car

On the way to Union Street, a short detour leads to what is probably the oldest house remaining in Hudson. Drive south on Front Street and make a left onto Cross. Around the bend at the end of Tanners Lane is an old gambrel-roofed two story home, a relic from the original Dutch settlers of Hudson. Originally it was a farmhouse on the edge of old South Bay before the harbor was filled in at the coming of the railroad.

Retrace the route to Front Street towards Warren. Make the third right onto Union (a block before Warren). Number 211 on the right is the **General William Jenkins Worth House.** Son of one of the thirty-one original Proprietors, Worth was a hero of the Battle of Chippewa in 1814 and served brilliantly under General Winfield Scott in the war with Mexico. In 1820, he was appointed the fourth Commandant of Cadets at West Point. (Fort Worth, Texas and Lake Worth, Florida, are named for him.) Up the street the tiny house at #343, built in 1828, is the **Friends' Meeting House.** Many of Hudson's early families were Quakers whose plain lifestyle is reflected in the simplicity of this building. On the next block at #445 is a fanciful example of Hudson River Bracketed architecture, a style which employs ornate brackets to support the elaborately carved cornices of Italianate Victorian buildings.

South 5th Street becomes East Allen, a section that was once a showplace of Victorian prosperity. Each large gracious home has a style of its own. Some have been carefully renovated, and there is an obvious neighborhood pride. A stroll along East Allen reveals towers, bay windows, gables, comfortable porches and Gothic details characteristic of the Victorian style.

Antiques and Collectibles

Hudson boasts over fifteen antique shops, most of them clustered on the 500 and 600 blocks of Warren Street. Merchandise ranges from superbly crafted eighteenth-century pieces to tag sale items. All offer copies of "Hudson Shopping Guide for Antiques and Collectibles." Clearly the most spectacular pieces are at the English Antiques Centre at Union and South 4th. Customers are welcomed into the magnificent 1830s Federal style house, built for Judge Gaul, lawyer to the Hudson River School painter Frederick Church. (See the description of Church's home Olana below.) Room after room of exceptional English, French and other Continental furniture is attractively arranged with porcelains, prints, crystal and *objets d'art*. Amid the formality are some Scandanavian painted and French country pieces along with excellent English-made reproductions. Several shops include new merchandise along with the old, and the eclectic collections offer a golden opportunity for browsing. With a bit of luck and an eye for quality, it is possible to stumble upon a real find.

DIRECTIONS:
From West Point and New York City: New York State Thruway (87) north to Exit 21 Catskill. Follow signs to Rip Van Winkle Bridge. Cross bridge and follow Route 9G north to Hudson.

THE AMERICAN MUSEUM OF FIREFIGHTING

Lovingly tended by retired New York State firemen who live in the adjacent home, the American Museum of Firefighting preserves over two hundred fifty years of the history and spirit of volunteer firefighters in America. The carved wooden figure of a volunteer fire chief (circa 1850) points you toward rooms filled with equipment, uniforms, photographs and "firematic ornaments." Engine Hall Number One displays horse-drawn and hand-pulled engines, while Engine Hall Number Two exhibits steam- and motor-powered vehicles. Although in the early days of our country, most firemen were volunteers (there was no paid force in New York City until 1865), firefighting activities played a central role in their lives. Display case upon display case portrays state conventions, hose-pulling contests, family picnics, ladies' auxiliaries and medals for bravery. Uniforms and fire engines made solely for parades reveal the firemen's dedication and the community's pride in their service. Fire, always a threat, was even more of a menace in days before fire hydrants

Wooden statue of volunteer fire chief, American Museum of Firefighting, Hudson.

and mechanized equipment. The games and contests at social gatherings served the practical purpose of developing volunteers' necessary physical strength and teamwork.

Clearly worded texts accompany the various exhibits. An 1883 Parade Carriage from Jamestown, New York, sits regally on six-foot wheels with silver hub bands. The central reel cylinder, decorated with diamond-shaped French plate glass mirrors, is topped by a bronze figure of a nineteenth-century firefighter flanked by winged serpents. On a Brooklyn parade engine are four painted panels depicting the American heroes George Washington, Thomas Jefferson and Henry Clay along with Alfred Carson, Chief Engineer of the New York Volunteer Fire Department. Known for its speed and power, this was one of the most famous engines of its kind. Wagons with sleigh runners and others lined with wooden buckets were used to fight fires in all kinds of weather and brought aid to the outlying districts.

Some of the photographs are fascinating. In a 1910 enlargement, muscular horses pulling steaming engines rush to fight a fire in New Haven, Connecticut. Their breathless race vividly portrays the desperate need for speed and strength to overcome the terror of fire's destruction. Another display shows closets of firemen's gear—coats, hats and boots—some with smoke smudges and grit still clinging. Cast iron toys and miniature engines recall the attraction to firefighting children experience; a display of engines used as late as the 1950s rekindles this fascination.

Harry Howard Avenue
(518) 828-7695

DIRECTIONS:
From West Point and New York City: New York State Thruway (87) north to Exit 21 Catskill. Follow signs to Rip Van Winkle Bridge; cross bridge and take Route 9G north to Hudson. Museum is on Harry Howard Avenue opposite the Middle School.

OLANA

Olana is Frederick Church's masterpiece. His Persian style villa is itself a work of art, and the setting was created as a Hudson River School landscape. Today, the house is filled with Church's paintings and the furnishings he designed himself. Church (1826-1900), a prominent Hudson River School artist, transformed his property high above the river into a living landscape. Working with his architect Calvert Vaux, Church immersed himself in every detail of planning, construction and decoration. He arranged tiles and bricks in mosaic patterns to outline Moorish arches and cover stone walls two-and-one-half feet thick. He personally mixed paint colors for every room and stenciled elaborate gold and silver designs around windows and doorways. With an artist's eye, he carved out miles of carriage roads so that the approach to Olana revealed scene by scene the finished work.

Church would find few changes in his home today. Although some of the colors may have faded, his son Louis and daughter-in-law Sally preserved Church's furnishings and possessions almost exactly as he had placed them. After Sally died in 1964, the house complete with contents was maintained by Olana Preservation until it became a New York State Historic Site in 1966.

Just as Church left it is the Court Hall, reminiscent of the center courtyard of Persian dwellings. It is here that he let his imagination run free. Intricate grillwork, heavy Oriental tapestries, hammered metal trays and water jugs—all transform a Victorian room into a Middle Eastern stage set. Church's children used the landing to entertain family and guests, illuminated by light streaming through the amber-colored glass of the window behind. As in a Hudson River School painting, the eye is drawn to the light above. Windows are designed to frame vistas beyond. In his studio addition, Church aligned a large picture window with the front door. He wanted his visitors' first view to be of the Catskill Mountains, beloved by Hudson River School artists.

Art of this school fills the house. Many of Church's sketches and canvases line the walls. In some rooms it is possible to trace a work's progression from sketch to oil, as in the East Parlor where "After Glow" hangs above the fireplace with a preliminary sketch nearby. The colors of the family Sitting Room were determined by the pink tones in "El Khasned in Petra," a painting of the Hidden City in Jordan visited by Church and his wife on their Middle Eastern tour. Also in the room is Church's "Charter Oak" as well as "Protestant Cemetery in Rome" by Thomas Cole, Church's teacher and the founder of the Hudson River School. A sketch of one of Church's most famous paintings, "Heart of the Andes," is in the Long Hall.

In a completely different style, signed copies of famous seventeenth-century paintings decorate the walls of the dining room, also called the Old Masters Gallery. Created by Church as a period room, the gallery features seventeen-foot ceilings and four windows bringing in northern light. While we might scoff at copies, Church wanted to recall the days when reproducing great works was an honored and skilled profession. Before

**Detail from Olana, Hudson River School artist Frederick Church's
Persian style villa, Hudson.**

photographs and prints, there was no other way to make these
masterpieces available.

The Olana estate is truly a work of art. It took four years to
build and decorate, and for many years thereafter, Church continued his mission to integrate art and nature. The whole con-
cept of a Moorish villa set in a Hudson River landscape seems
incongruous. But Church's creation works (518/828-0135).

DIRECTIONS:
From West Point and New York City: New York State Thruway (87) north to Exit 21 Catskill. Follow signs to Rip Van Winkle Bridge. Cross bridge and take Route 9G south. Entrance is on 9G, one mile south of the bridge.

THOMAS COLE HOUSE

For those who are dedicated students of the Hudson River School of Art, a short side trip to the home of Church's teacher and mentor, Thomas Cole, is worthwhile. Cedar Grove, Cole's home from 1836 until his death in 1848, remained in the family until its purchase by a conservation group in 1979. Even though renovation has been ongoing since the early 1980s, the house is still in a state of major disrepair. Only the first floor is open to the public. The rooms are unfurnished, and there are no original Coles on view. Instead, copies, both prints and oils, of some of his works are on display. In the back room, more than thirty slides and photographs of Cole's major paintings trace his development over twenty-three years. This may be the only place such a "retrospective" exists. The accompanying text details Cole's life and notes the museums and galleries owning these works.

In the East Parlor, a display case contains some of Cole's brushes and paint tubes along with pressed leaves and flowers he brought back from his European tour in 1841. An engraving of one of Frederick Church's most famous paintings, the 1859 "Heart of the Andes," hangs behind the stairway in the front hall. On the bottom border in a faded, flowing hand, the inscription reads: "To Mrs. Thomas Cole, with kind regards of Frederick Church." Flanking the doorway of the East Parlor, two Charles Herbert Moore oils portray Cole's first Catskill studio and Cedar Grove in more prosperous days. After Cole's death, the family fortunes fell, and as years passed even the Hudson River School he founded fell into disfavor. In 1964, when family members were forced to sell his last paintings, a small Cole oil could be purchased for as little as five hundred dollars. More notable works brought only one thousand to three thousand dollars. Now, of course, Hudson River School paintings command enormous prices. Therefore, it is unlikely even when renovations are completed that Cedar Grove will ever own a major collection of Cole's work.

218 Spring Street
Catskill, N.Y.
(518) 943-6533

DIRECTIONS:
From West Point and New York City: New York State Thruway (87) north to Exit 21 Catskill. Take Route 23 east to Route 385. Make a right onto Spring Street. House is almost immediately on left.

BRONCK HOUSE

Further afield and open only in the summer is Bronck House Museum. Begun in 1663 by Pieter Bronck whose family gave its name to the Bronx in New York City, this homestead remained in the family for nine generations. Over the years, the Broncks extended Pieter's 1663 stone house to include a 1685 stone addition and a 1738 brick house attached to the original structures by a hallway. The property also includes a thirteen-sided "freedom" barn, a kitchen dependency and other outbuildings dating from the time when this was a working farm. By 1840, Bronck House was no longer the family's primary residence. Tenant farmers worked the land, and few improvements or changes were made to the buildings so that this compound still appears as it did in the early nineteenth century. All but the caretaker's cottage are listed on the National Register of Historic Places, and today, the three-in-one family house is open to visitors.

In 1663, Pieter Bronck built a stone house in the Dutch style with one large living area and a loft above. As the family grew, his son Jan extended the house to include a dining room, a hallway and extra loft space. By 1738, the Bronck family was prosperous enough to bring builders from Albany to design and construct what was essentially a town house in the country. Built of brick rather than the native rubble stone, this Dutch, Federal style house was elegant and spacious. Today, each room contains family pieces as well as furnishings from Greene County, typical of the period.

One of the outstanding features of the house is its varied collection of paintings. In the bedroom of the 1738 brick house are three works by Thomas Cole, the founder of the Hudson River School of Painting. "The Clove," a mountain landscape, hangs near two small oils; one of a European ruin and the other of a fishing scene. In 1964, Cole's descendants were forced to auction off many of his effects. Bronck House acquired his hatbox, traveling trunk and his sketch box, which are on display in this bedroom along with other of his personal possessions. Also in the bedroom is B.B.G. Stone's "Sunrise in the White Mountains." Stone studied under Cole's pupil, Frederick Church, whose Persian style villa lies across the river just south of Hudson. In the parlor is a portrait of a woman by Ammi Philips as well as two unsigned landscapes, "Shoreline of Lake Champlain" and "Mount Marcy," attributed to John Frederick Kensett. Another unsigned work, "Near West Point on the Hudson," shows a site often painted by Hudson River School artists.

The oldest work in the house is a 1710 painting of Samuel Van Vechten by Nehemiah Partridge, an early limner or portrait painter. It hangs in the 1663 stone house near an oil of Judge Leonard Bronck (1751-1828), who was the first judge of the Court of Common Pleas in Greene County. In the hallway connecting the 1663 stone house with the 1685 addition are portraits of the last three generations of the Bronck family. These portraits were commissioned by Leonard Bronk Lampman, the last of the line, who bequeathed the house to the Greene County Historical Society in 1939. While he approved the paintings of his parents and grandparents, he did not like his own and refused to pay for it. It remained in the artist's studio until 1954 when it came to Bronck House through the artist's estate.

The outbuildings have now been adapted for other uses. One houses the archives of the Greene County Historical Society, including Bronck and Cole family papers. The Dutch barn, dating from the late 1700s, contains carriages and farm-related equipment. The "freedom" barn at the edge of the property is the oldest documented multi-sided barn in New York State, and its thirteen sides most probably represent the original thirteen colonies.

Behind a white wooden fence is the family cemetery. Tombstones identify the graves of Judge Leonard Bronck, his wife and children, while the graves of family slaves lie back in the woods, marked only by stones from the field. A small marker carved with the name Ezra Bronk, a colonel in the Spanish-American War, lies between the two. It is thought that Colonel Bronk was a freed slave who claimed family ties. For over three hundred years, the history of the Bronck family was interwoven with this farm, and today it is preserved by the Greene County Historical Society.

Pieter Bronck Road
Coxsackie, N.Y.
(518) 731-8862

DIRECTIONS:
From West Point and New York City: New York State Thruway (87) north to Exit 21 Catskill. North on 9W; at Red Barn, turn left onto Pieter Bronck Road (opposite New York State Vocational Institution).

CHAPTER 10

Rhinebeck

HIGHLIGHTS...

—Picturesque country village with America's oldest inn

—Clermont, home of the Livingstons, Revolutionary War Patriots

—World War I vintage airplanes in flight

—Five restored gardens of nineteenth-century Montgomery Place

Once a stage coach stop halfway between New York City and Albany, the small town of Rhinebeck played an important role in the country's early history. In 1688, only two years after Hendrick and Jacob Kip purchased 2200 acres from the Indians, Judge Henry Beekman received the land by grant from King James II of England and established the village of Rhinebeck on its present site. During the Revolutionary War, George Washington watched his troops drill on the lawn outside the Bogardus Tavern, now the Beekman Arms. Lafayette, Hamilton, Burr and other notable men of the time stayed in Rhinebeck, and General Richard Montgomery, killed in the Battle of Quebec, was a citizen of the town. Henry Beekman's granddaughter Margaret married Judge Robert Livingston. Their eldest son, Chancellor Robert Livingston, helped draft the Declaration of Independence and later served as Minister to France. The Livingstons, along with other Hudson River families, such as the Delanos, Roosevelts, Astors and Vanderbilts, became the aristocracy of New York society in the nineteenth century.

VILLAGE OF RHINEBECK

Today, Rhinebeck's center is still the intersection of the old Sepasco Trail (Market Street) and the King's Highway (Route 9, Mill Street). The Beekman Arms, built in 1766 and the oldest inn in continuous operation in America, stands on the southwest corner. Just across the road, a smoke shop, a bookstore, a five-and-ten-cent store, and a drugstore-turned-ice-cream-parlor line Market Street. Down Mill Street is the Dutch style, fieldstone post office and the Reformed Dutch Church with its cemetery containing the graves of forty-three veterans of the Revolutionary War. Up and down the side streets, small houses exhibit the brackets, porches, cornices, bay windows and gables typical of nineteenth-century architecture. Since 1979, the village of Rhinebeck has been listed on the National Register of Historic Places.

DIRECTIONS:
From West Point and New York City: New York State Thruway (87) north to Exit 19 Kingston. Route 199 east. Cross Kingston-Rhinecliff Bridge. South on Route 9G to Route 9 south to Village of Rhinebeck.

Beekman Arms

Known as America's oldest inn in continuous operation, the Beekman Arms was built by the Traphagen family in 1766 on the site of their original, two-room stone tavern. With its huge oak beams, wide-plank floors and stone walls two-to-three feet

America's oldest inn, the Beekman Arms, Rhinebeck.

thick, the Inn provided comfortable lodging for travelers on the King's Highway and a refuge for the villagers in case of attack. When the town of Kingston just across the Hudson was burned by the British in 1777, the citizens of Rhinebeck retreated to the Inn and prepared to defend their town. Although several houses along the river were hit by cannon fire, the British never marched inland to attack Rhinebeck.

The Beekman Arms' register records the signatures of famous guests—George Washington, the Marquis de Lafayette, Alexander Hamilton, Aaron Burr, Benedict Arnold, Martin Van Buren and William Jennings Bryan. In more recent times, Franklin Delano Roosevelt, who lived in nearby Hyde Park, delivered his traditional eve of the election address to local residents from the Beekman Arms' porch. With its tap room and restaurant, its public rooms hung with muskets, maps and corn cob pipes and its private meeting rooms, the Beekman Arms remains a gathering place for the families of the Hudson River Valley. Many of the guest rooms are furnished with colonial antiques and reproductions, and those in the Carpenter Gothic Delamater house just a block away are in the Victorian style.

Post Office

Built on land where Continental soldiers once drilled under the watchful eye of their commander, George Washington, the Rhinebeck Post Office stands next to the Beekman Arms on Route 9, the old King's Highway. President Franklin Roosevelt designed the building to replicate as accurately as possible the 1700 home of Hendrik Kip, one of the original settlers of the area. Roosevelt insisted that native materials, including fieldstone salvaged from the ruins of Kip's dwelling, be used in the building's construction. Dedicated on May 1, 1939, this Works Projects Administration (WPA) project reflected F.D.R.'s pride in his own Dutch heritage and that of the Hudson Valley. The cornerstone was laid by His Royal Highness, Crown Prince Frederik of Denmark and Iceland, at a ceremony attended by Roosevelt, Henry Morgenthau and James Farley.

Inside is a mural by local artist Olin Dows, who also painted the mural at the Hyde Park Post Office. In twelve panels, he traces the town's history beginning with Hendrik Hudson's 1609 journey up the river and concluding with the Rhinebeck of his day. On display is the lintel stone from the basement door of the Kip House, carved with its 1700 date of construction and the initials of Hendrik Kip and his wife Annatje. A sash from the house, rescued from fire by John Jacob Astor, is also on view. The Post Office's round window represents the cannonball fired by the British into the Kip home during the Revolutionary War.

With its hardwood floors, brass chandelier and Dutch style architecture, the Rhinebeck Post Office illustrates F.D.R.'s belief that public buildings should reflect the historical background of the communities they serve.

Reformed Dutch Church

The Reformed Dutch Church of Rhinebeck was built in 1808 at the corner of South Street and the Albany Post Road to replace the congregation's smaller 1773 church. Its exterior walls of brick and stone represent a compromise by the congregants, some of whom wanted to use only native fieldstone and others who preferred the more elegant brick. The bells in the four-sided clock tower have called to worship such notable local families as the Beekmans and the Livingstons. Legend has it that Colonel Henry Beekman, founder of Rhinebeck, is buried beneath the pulpit. Typical of Reformed Dutch churches, the walls are painted white and the wooden pews have red velvet cushions. The large clear glass windows on the east and west walls flood the church with light. In keeping with the Church's belief that man cannot improve upon nature, no stained glass is used. Outside is the church cemetery with graves dating back to the eighteenth century, including those of forty-three Revolutionary War veterans. Also in the churchyard is a cannon in memory of General Richard Montgomery who was killed in the Battle of Quebec in 1775. A citizen of Rhinebeck and husband of Janet Livingston, Montgomery was the first general to lose his life in the Revolution. (914/876-3727)

OLD RHINEBECK AERODROME

Just off Route 9 on Stone Church Road is the Old Rhinebeck Aerodrome. In hangars and barns, Cole Palen has assembled a collection of aircraft dating from the earliest days of aviation. Gliders, mono-, bi- and tri-planes, World War I vintage fighters and their engines show the development of the machines which allowed men to fly. Daily from May through October, visitors may examine these planes at close range, and on weekend afternoons in July and August, pilots fly many of the planes in the Old Rhinebeck Aerodrome Show.

Surrounded by aircraft in three large metal hangars, visitors can see how uncomfortable and precarious these early planes were. The Thomas Pusher Model 2 (American, 1912) has a hard wooden chair seat. Open cockpits in many of the planes exposed pilots and passengers to wind and cold. The wings of the famous German Fokker Triplane seem as flimsy as the balsa wood wings of model planes.

Despite the fact that flight was in its infancy, both sides in World War I developed fighter planes. Guns were mounted both forward and rear, but mistimed firings and bullets ricocheting off propellers often proved more dangerous to the gunner than to his enemy. The F. E. 8 (British, 1916), displayed in Hangar II, had not only its gun, but also its propeller, mounted

Old Rhinebeck Aerodrome and Air Show, Rhinebeck.

in the back. Very unstable, all the original F. E. 8s were lost during the war, most to Baron von Richthofen, the "Red Baron." The well-designed Morane-Soulvier "N" (French, 1914) with forward firing machine gun is considered the forerunner of all modern fighter planes.

While it is fascinating to see these planes on the ground, it is truly exciting to see them fly. Seeing planes taking off at the mercy of the wind, floating above, suspended on air currents, and landing on a narrow grassy runway without brakes, visitors understand both the romance and danger pilots encountered in the early days of flight. Aviator goggles were a necessity as were the flowing, white silk scarves, used to wipe away gasoline and oil spatters. The show lasts an hour and a half, but planes are in the air for only about fifteen minutes. Unfortunately, the time between takeoffs is filled with silly skits and commentary. Before and after the show, rides are available to visitors in a 1929 open cockpit biplane. Both these barnstorming rides and the show itself depend upon good weather.

Stone Church Road
(914) 758-8610

DIRECTIONS:
From West Point and New York City: New York State Thruway (87) north to Exit 19 Kingston. Route 199 east; cross Kingston-Rhinecliff Bridge. Take Route 9G south to Route 9 south to Stone Church Road. Watch for Aerodrome signs.

CLERMONT

The country seat of the Livingston family for seven generations, Clermont was rebuilt in the late eighteenth century after the original 1730 brick residence was destroyed by the British in the Revolutionary War. Georgian in style, Clermont stands in a park-like setting overlooking the Hudson River and the Catskill Mountains beyond. Robert of Clermont (1688-1775), who built the first house, bought much of the surrounding countryside, including one-third of the Catskills, in order to preserve his view. Formal gardens, designed between 1909 and 1935 by Alice Livingston, the last of the family to live at Clermont, are being restored, and much of the landscape is being returned to its eighteenth-century appearance.

The Livingstons were a prominent family in colonial times. Robert Livingston (1718-1775) was Judge of the Admiralty Court and of the Supreme Court of New York under British rule, but nonetheless gave his allegiance to the patriot cause. A delegate to the Stamp Act Congress, he reputedly wrote the Congressional Letter of Protest to King George III. His son Robert R. Livingston (1746-1813) was a member of the Continental Congress and served with Thomas Jefferson on the committee to draft the Declaration of Independence. Appointed Chancellor of New York in 1777, he held this position, the state's highest judicial office, for twenty-four years and as Chancellor administered the oath of office to George Washington as the first President of the United States. Later, as Minister to France, he negotiated the Louisiana Purchase.

After the British burned Kingston in 1777 (see Chapter 8), they sailed upriver to set fire to Clermont. Knowing that the enemy might retaliate for the family's political stand, Margaret Beekman Livingston (1724-1800), wife of the Judge and mother of the Chancellor, buried the valuables, loaded wagons with household goods and fled with her servants to Connecticut. Clermont was burned to the ground. Immediately thereafter, Margaret Livingston began to rebuild. Successfully petitioning Governor Clinton to excuse her workmen from military service, she was able to complete construction quickly, and in 1782, George and Martha Washington were among her first guests at the new house. The letter she sent to Governor Clinton is in Clermont's small library.

Many family portraits hang throughout the house. In the main hall is a Gilbert Stuart portrait of the Chancellor along with portraits of his father Judge Robert Livingston, his grandfather Robert of Clermont who built the 1730 house and his great-grandfather first Lord of the Manor, Robert Livingston who emigrated from Scotland in 1674.

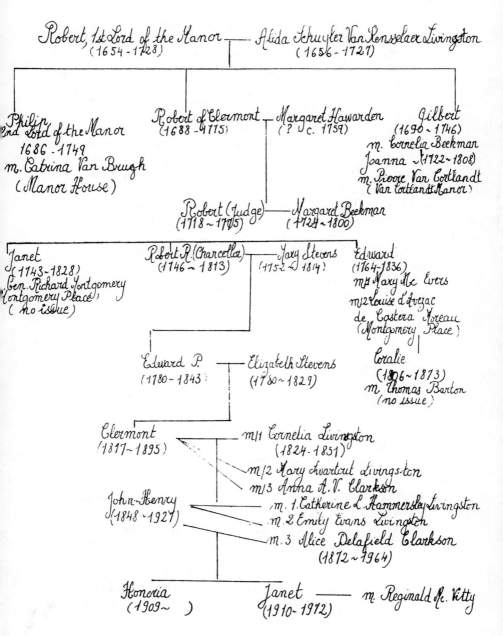

Robert, 1st Lord of the Manor (1654-1728) — Alida Schuyler Van Rensselaer Livingston (1656-1727)

Philip 2nd Lord of the Manor 1686-1749 m. Catrina Van Brugh (Manor House)

Robert of Clermont (1688-1775) — Margaret Hawarden (? c. 1759)

Gilbert (1690-1746) m. Cornelia Beekman Joanna (1722-1808) m. Pierre Van Cortlandt (Van Cortlandt Manor)

Robert (Judge) (1718-1775) — Margaret Beekman (1724-1800)

Janet (1743-1828) Gen. Richard Montgomery (Montgomery Place) (no issue)

Robert R. (Chancellor) (1746-1813) — Mary Stevens (1752-1814)

Edward (1764-1836) m/1 Mary McEvers m/2 Louise d'Avezac de Castera Moreau (Montgomery Place)

Edward P. (1780-1843) — Elizabeth Stevens (1780-1829)

Coralie (1806-1873) m. Thomas Barton (no issue)

Clermont (1817-1895) — m/1 Cornelia Livingston (1824-1851)
m/2 Mary Swartout Livingston
m/3 Anna A. V. Clarkson

John Henry (1848-1927) — m.1 Catherine L. Hammersley Livingston
m.2 Emily Evans Livingston
m.3 Alice Delafield Clarkson (1872-1964)

Honoria (1909-)

Janet (1910-1972) — m. Reginald R. Kitty

In the dining room are pictures of John Henry Livingston and his wife Alice, sixth generation, and their daughters Honoria and Janet. Over the fireplace is the only portrait of a non-family member, Andrew Jackson. Edward, the Chancellor's youngest brother and heir of Montgomery Place (see below), fought with Jackson in the Battle of New Orleans and served as Minister to France in his administration.

Most of the furnishings in the house belonged to the Livingstons. The chandelier and mantel clock in the drawing room were brought back from France by the Chancellor. In the small library is a mirror given by Lafayette. It originally hung in Robert Fulton's steamship *Clermont* and was given to the Livingstons when the ship was decommissioned. Fulton named this first steam-powered vessel after Clermont in recognition of the support and financial aid given to him by the Chancellor. A model of "Fulton's Folly" is displayed in the exhibit room along with other photographs of the Livingston family. Clermont, acquired by New York State in 1962, has been preserved as a tribute to a remarkable family.

Germantown, N.Y.
(518) 537-4240

DIRECTIONS:
From West Point and New York City: New York State Thruway (87) north to Exit 19 Kingston. Take Route 199 east and cross Kingston-Rhinecliff Bridge. North on Route 9G to County Route 6. Follow signs to Clermont.

MONTGOMERY PLACE

Montgomery Place was built in 1804 by Janet Livingston Montgomery, widow of Revolutionary War hero General Richard Montgomery who was killed in 1775 at the Battle of Quebec. Only five miles from her childhood home at Clermont, the Federal style country house was set on four hundred thirty-four acres of land overlooking the Hudson River. Twice remodeled by the well-known nineteenth-century architect Alexander Jackson Davis, the mansion took on a Neoclassical appearance with the addition of the north and south pavilions and the Corinthian-columned portico. For one hundred eighty-two years, Montgomery Place was the summer home and weekend retreat of Livingstons, Bartons, Hunts and Delafields, all tracing their ancestry back to Janet who died childless in 1828.

The family never threw anything away. Over 80,000 papers—letters, invoices, inventories, even birthday cards—were acquired with the house and document the restoration. All the pieces in the house belonged to the Livingstons and their descendants. Furniture, paintings, rugs and table settings reflect the family's tastes and interests over the years. The Empire style dining room chairs were sent from France by Janet's brother Chancellor Robert Livingston. The 1856 chandelier above the table, made of Austrian glass, was purchased by an early Delafield who was in Europe reporting on the Crimean War. In the Montgomery Room where Janet once entertained Lafayette are her husband's Revolutionary War campaign chest and telescope. Photographs signed by four twentieth-century presidents—Calvin Coolidge, Herbert Hoover, Franklin D. Roosevelt and Dwight D. Eisenhower—hang in the game room. Three of the pictures are inscribed with personal notes from the Presidents to John Ross Delafield. The picture of F.D.R., the lone Democrat, bears no message and was tolerated only because Roosevelt was a county resident and neighbor.

A number of the documents acquired with the house relate to the gardens on the estate, and horticulturists are in the process of restoring them to their original beauty. In the formal Rose Garden, flowers are arranged by color, and some of the pink Livingston roses, planted by Janet, still remain. In the 1930s, the Herb Garden, the Ellipse, the Brook Garden and the Rock Garden were all planned by Violetta White Delafield. Mrs. Delafield wanted her gardens to be a series of experiences, each evoking a different emotion, and they were recognized by the Garden Club of America as some of the most beautiful in the country. Today, Montgomery Place offers special tours just of the gardens as well as tours of the house.

When Historic Hudson Valley bought the estate in 1986, the decision was made to present Montgomery Place as it had been used by the family over the years—as a place of recreation, leisure and family entertainments. In addition to touring the house and gardens, visitors are encouraged to explore the trails, to picnic on the grounds and to play croquet, badminton and board games which can be borrowed for the day. In summer, produce from the estate and from farms around the area can be purchased at the roadside market, and in fall, visitors can pick their own apples from Janet Montgomery's orchards.

Annandale-on-Hudson, N.Y.
(914) 758-5461

DIRECTIONS:
From West Point and New York City: New York State Thruway (87) north to Exit 19 Kingston. Route 199 east across the Kingston-Rhinecliff Bridge. Continue two miles to Route 9G. North on Route 9G for two and one-half miles. Left on Barrytown Road (Route 82). One-quarter mile to River Road (Route 103). Right on River Road three-quarters mile to Montgomery Place entrance on left.

EDITH C. BLUM ART INSTITUTE, BARD COLLEGE

A few miles north of Montgomery Place on Route 9G is the Edith C. Blum Art Institute at Bard College. Rotating exhibits, some of which pertain to the Hudson River Valley, are open to the public. Bard College, an unusual school in an unusual setting, was founded as an Episcopal men's school in 1860 by John Bard. Now a coeducational liberal arts college, it emphasizes writing and the creative arts. The elegant Neoclassical manor Blithewood is now the Jerome Levy Economics Institute. Its Victorian hexagonal gatehouse was designed by famed nineteenth-century architect Alexander Jackson Davis. Bard's campus is comprised of several old homes, two of which were once main houses of river estates, in addition to a number of modern buildings. Visitors driving along River Road may wonder when they are actually on college grounds since several of the buildings are far from the small campus center.

Annandale-on-Hudson
(914) 758-6822

DIRECTIONS:
From West Point and New York City: New York State Thruway (87) north to Exit 19 Kingston. Follow 199 east and cross Kingston-Rhinecliff Bridge. North on Route 9G. Bard is five miles on left.

Franklin Delano Roosevelt's lifelong home, Springwood, Hyde Park.

CHAPTER 11

Hyde Park

HIGHLIGHTS...

—F.D.R.'s lifelong home, Springwood

—Eleanor Roosevelt's weekend hideaway, Val-Kill

—Vanderbilt Mansion, opulent symbol of the Gilded Age

—C.I.A., Culinary Institute—America's foremost academy of haute cuisine with four restaurants open to the public

Hyde Park has become synonymous with the Roosevelts. It is the site of Springwood, the Roosevelt family estate and of Val-Kill, Eleanor Roosevelt's private retreat. F.D.R. was born at Springwood, spent his boyhood there and throughout his life he returned to find both refuge and renewal. He inspired the nation in the dark days of the Depression and World War II with his famed fireside chats, many of which were delivered from

Springwood. Despite the burdens of public office, he never lost his love for his native town and his pride in his family's place within it. Even as President, he involved himself in the smallest details of community life. He designed the town's new post office in 1939 and had local resident Olin Dows paint murals of Hyde Park's history on its walls. He brought distinguished visitors to enjoy the town's hospitality and proudly took King George VI of England and his Queen to worship with him at St. James Church.

Hyde Park was home to other influential Hudson Valley families as well. The Vanderbilts, Rodgers, Dinsmores and Millses all built mansions here and entertained the social elite of the day. Pillars of the community, they supported numerous philanthropic causes and offered employment to many village residents. Still, the Roosevelt name remains foremost in people's minds. "Dateline: Hyde Park" conjures up memories of world leaders gathered together to discuss strategy during World War II; of a precedent shattering campaign for a third term in office and of a smiling host driving his guests around the estate. In this town, momentous decisions were made, and today history remains a living presence.

SPRINGWOOD, HOME OF FRANKLIN DELANO ROOSEVELT

His dressing gown lies ready on the daybed. His suit hangs neatly pressed in the closet. His books and magazines are strewn about the room. It is as if F.D.R. will enter at any moment. His boundless enthusiasm for life fills every room, and Springwood is a national memorial to this remarkable man.

Springwood was purchased by F.D.R.'s father James Roosevelt in 1867, and enlarged when James married Sara Delano in 1880. It was in this seventeen-room, clapboard house that F.D.R. was born on January 30, 1882. He almost died at birth. The attending physician administered too much chloroform to his mother, and the baby needed mouth-to-mouth resuscitation to survive. Although James had wanted to name his son Isaac, he was named Franklin Delano after his Uncle Franklin Hughes Delano. It was traditional in the Roosevelt family to name first born sons James in one generation and Isaac in the next, but Sara objected. She wanted the baby to be named for her side of the family, and as usual, Sara's will prevailed.

Both the Delanos and the Roosevelts were prominent Hudson River families. The Roosevelts owned sugar refineries and later the Delaware and Hudson Railroad. The Delanos made their fortune in the China tea trade, and Sara actually lived in China for several years. Throughout the house many items suggest the family's background and interests. The Buddhist temple gong on the front hall landing came from the Orient. It was rung one-half hour and one-quarter hour before each meal to ensure that no one would be late. Also in the entrance hall are model ships which F.D.R. built and sailed with friends. The naval prints that line the walls attest to his love of the sea. Glass cabinets display his boyhood collections of birds and Indian artifacts. James Roosevelt allowed his son to take only one bird of each species and taught him to respect and care for his environment, laying the groundwork for later conservation policies.

Down the hall to the left is the wood paneled living room, part of the extensive renovation work carried out in 1915. With the addition of two new wings, the house grew to thirty-five rooms. Stucco and local fieldstone replaced the clapboard exterior, and Springwood assumed its present day Georgian Revival appearance. Despite its size and elegance it remained a family home. The living room with its two large fireplaces, its books and its comfortable chairs was the gathering place for the family. The five Roosevelt children played here with their dogs while their parents read nearby. The Dresden Room, in contrast, was proper and formal. Its gilt-edged furniture and Dresden chandelier reflect the taste of Sara Delano Roosevelt. This was a room that Sara loved and Eleanor hated.

In fact, Springwood was Sara's home, not Eleanor's. Sara held title to the estate and controlled the family monies until her death in 1941. A strong-willed and determined woman, she easily overshadowed her daughter-in-law and remained mistress of the household. Always retiring in her presence, Eleanor needed a place of her own and had Franklin build her a Dutch style stone cottage a few miles away. It is at Val-Kill (see below) that Eleanor's true personality can be seen. Her bedroom at

Springwood is marked more by her absence than her presence.

F.D.R.'s bedroom was thoroughly his own. His treasured books and photographs, the chair on which his dog Fala slept and the fedora that he wore as he campaigned paint a picture of this vigorous man undaunted in the face of the polio which left him crippled. In his dressing room is his wheelchair, left in place at his request. He preferred this cut-down kitchen chair with wheels to the bulky, unmaneuverable models of his day. At his bedside is a telephone which gave him a direct line to the White House. During World War II, it was secretly coded to protect the President's conversations.

Springwood is very much a house of history. F.D.R.'s ground floor office, his "Summer White House," was the room where he and Winston Churchill signed the agreement to build the first atomic bomb. Winston Churchill was one of many famous visitors to the house. King George VI and his Queen occupied the Pink Room on their state visit just before World War II. Their daughter, Queen Elizabeth II, once stayed in the Chintz Room. It was at Springwood that F.D.R. awaited election results, tallying up the votes with his advisers. On the porch he delivered acceptance speeches and received the congratulations of neighbors and friends.

Several outbuildings are open to the public. In the stables, the name plates of the Roosevelt family horses are still in place above the stalls. Past the icehouse a path leads to the Rose Garden where both Franklin and Eleanor are buried. Springwood truly chronicles F.D.R.'s life, and his energy and magnetism pervade every room.

The Franklin D. Roosevelt Library and Museum

Recognizing that some of the most momentous events in our country's history were occurring during his presidency, F.D.R. as early as 1938 took steps to ensure that his papers would be available to scholars. He wanted to provide historians with immediate access to behind-the-scenes strategies and negotiations and hoped that the records of his administration would give insight to future policy makers. Therefore, F.D.R. set aside sixteen acres of his Hyde Park estate and built the first presidential library. With more than fifteen million pages of manuscripts and documents, photographs and books, the library set a precedent for leaders to come.

Using some of this material, the museum wing of the building chronicles F.D.R.'s life. The first section follows him from his birth in 1882 through his first presidential campaign in 1932. On display are his childhood toys, letters from prep school (even a less than spectacular report card) and news articles about his early political career. Descriptions of F.D.R.'s bout with polio in 1921 culminate in a 1924 photograph showing his triumphant walk to the podium to nominate Al Smith as the Democratic candidate for President. In 1932, he astonished his party by flying to the convention in an airplane and by accepting the nomination in person, two things no other presidential candidate had ever done.

The second section of the library traces F.D.R.'s career from 1933 to his death in 1945 during his fourth term as President. The exhibits cover the two cataclysmic events of the time—the Depression and World War II. Official documents include Roosevelt's message to Congress requesting a declaration of war after the Japanese attack on Pearl Harbor. Downstairs is his 1936 Ford Phaeton specially designed with hand controls. Nearby are ice boats he raced as a young man. A new wing opened in 1972 is devoted to Eleanor Roosevelt. Her childhood portrait shows a shy, quiet young girl who through adversity and determination became the eyes and ears of a President and First Lady of the World.

The museum is filled with Roosevelt family pictures and personal items which give visitors an intimate sense of the Roosevelts' personalities and lives. F.D.R.'s exuberance and indomitable spirit sparkle, and his ability to enjoy life without losing the seriousness of purpose shines through.

(914) 229-9115

DIRECTIONS:
From West Point: Route 9W north to Route 84 east, cross Newburgh-Beacon Bridge; north on Route 9D to Route 9 north to Hyde Park; Springwood is on the left.

From New York City: New York State Thruway (87) north to Exit 17 Newburgh; Route 84 east, cross Newburgh-Beacon Bridge; north on Route 9D to Route 9 north to Hyde Park; Springwood is on the left.

VAL-KILL

Eleanor Roosevelt had no place to call her own. From the moment she married F.D.R. in 1905, her mother-in-law was ever present. Sara Delano Roosevelt dominated the household at Hyde Park, summered with Eleanor and Franklin at Campobello and even built them a townhouse next to hers in New York City. When Franklin offered to build her a cottage of her own on her favorite part of the Hyde Park estate, Eleanor accepted enthusiastically. The Dutch fieldstone house he designed became her sanctuary from the turbulence of both politics and domestic affairs. She named this refuge Val-Kill, which means "valley stream."

"The shack on the crick for the missus and her friends" was completed in 1925. Her friends Marion Dickerman and Nancy Cook moved in, and Eleanor joined them for weekends and summer vacations. In 1926, the three women along with Caroline O'Day started Val-Kill Industries to train local farmers in furniture making. For ten years the industry, housed in another F.D.R.-designed fieldstone building on the premises, helped to supplement the farmers' incomes and to keep them on the land. (The twin beds in the Chintz Room where Queen Elizabeth II stayed at Springwood are products of Val-Kill Industries.) Unfortunately, the business failed in 1936 because of the Depression. Two years later, Eleanor converted the larger factory building into her own residence and called it Val-Kill Cottage. For the next seven years Val-Kill Cottage was her weekend hideaway, and after F.D.R.'s death, it became her permanent home. Her days at Val-Kill afforded her the solitude and time necessary to pursue her many political and humanitarian activities.

Eleanor was a shy, reserved young matron until her husband's bout with polio in 1921 forced her into a public role. Determined to help him resume his career, she became active in the Democratic Party and traveled throughout New York State in F.D.R.'s gubernatorial campaigns in 1928 and 1930. During F.D.R.'s years as President, Eleanor championed the causes of the unemployed, the poor and the young. Journeying to places her husband could not go, she kept him in touch with the American public. During World War II, she was his ambassador to servicemen overseas and met with Allied leaders in his stead. After his death, she served as a delegate to the United Nations General Assembly and helped draft the Universal Declaration of Human Rights. Born to wealth and position, Eleanor Roosevelt chose to devote her life to those in need, and her simple unassuming manner won her friends throughout the world.

It is at Val-Kill Cottage that Eleanor's informal and relaxed style is most apparent. The slipcovered chairs arranged for conversation, the knotty-pine walls and photographs of family and friends suggest a gentle, kind woman concerned with the comfort of others. In her office is the desk where she wrote her daily column "My Day," answered her mail and worked to further the humanitarian causes dear to her. In this unpretentious setting, she entertained dignitaries from around the world. Adlai Stevenson, Nikita Khrushchev, John Kennedy and Winston Churchill were all her guests. Haile Selassie felt so much at home that he kicked off his shoes and watched footage of himself on television. Instead of another formal state meal, the King and Queen of England picnicked happily on hot dogs grilled outdoors on the grounds at Springwood and then sat by the pool at Val-Kill. While she loved being surrounded by family and friends, Eleanor was also happy to be here alone. She relished her privacy and the natural beauty of the spot. It was at Val-Kill that she was truly at home.

DIRECTIONS:
Take shuttle bus from F.D.R. Museum and Library.

VANDERBILT MANSION

Extravagance, opulence and lavishness were hallmarks of America's Gilded Age, and Vanderbilt Mansion manifests them all. Two hundred craftsmen camped in tents on the lawn and worked for more than two years to create a Beaux-Arts mansion for Frederick Vanderbilt and his wife Louise. Its fifty-four rooms contain pieces from the former home of Napoleon near Paris as well as tapestries, statuary and furnishings from other French and Italian villas. It cost over $1.5 million for decoration alone and included custom-made fireplaces, bathroom fixtures and breakfast china that matched the wallpaper in each guest room. Louise Vanderbilt's bedroom has a copy of a bed at Versailles with ornately carved railing and an embroidered silk canopy. The dining room ceiling was brought intact from Italy, and in the main hall a tapestry with the Medici coat of arms hangs above the fireplace. Gold leaf is everywhere—in reception rooms, bedrooms and hallways. Even the Steinway grand piano is decorated with gold. Sixty-five people were needed to run this simple country home, although the family was in residence only in the spring and fall.

Even for 1898 this was life on a grand scale, but the Vanderbilts could afford it. Beginning with a hundred dollars borrowed from his mother when he was only sixteen, Cornelius Vanderbilt started a ferry service between New York City and Staten Island. With his profits he invested in a line of steamships (becoming known as the "Commodore") and went on to own a number of railroads. By the time of his death in 1877, he had amassed a fortune of $1 million. In the days before income and property taxes, before anti-trust and labor laws, a huge family fortune could be made and passed on to succeeding generations without inheritance taxes. The Commodore's son, William Henry, followed in his father's footsteps and parlayed his $85 million legacy into $200 million.

The members of the next generation devoted much of their time to philanthropy and leisure. The Commodore's grandchildren became known as "the Mansion Builders" and constructed homes throughout the Northeast. In the Gilded Age it was considered important to demonstrate the enormity of one's resources through boundless displays of wealth. The Vanderbilts were masters of such display, and Frederick's mansion in Hyde Park is an example of such excess.

An entire underclass of servants was necessary to run these great estates, and within this class a hierarchy developed. The butler and the housekeeper held the highest positions, and all employees, whether footmen, parlor maids, gardeners or ladies' maids, knew their place. There was also a hierarchy among employers. Since the Vanderbilts were considered near royalty, holding high positions in their household conferred special status.

At Vanderbilt Mansion, downstairs servants ate in the kitchen, but those of higher rank had a dining room of their own, set with Villeroy and Boch china. The butler and housekeeper each had a private suite with sitting room, while a lounge was available for the others. Still, the house was not designed with the servants' comfort in mind. The coal chute was in the front of the house, and coal had to be transported to the furnace in back. Ice had to be carried from its delivery point at one end of the house to the ice box at the other. And the bushes and shrubs planted to enhance the beauty of the estate often covered servants' windows.

Vanderbilt Mansion was a home built for show. Its grandeur and impersonality are reminiscent of a Hollywood movie set. More a museum than a family home, its magnificence symbolizes its era.

(914) 229-9115

DIRECTIONS:
From West Point: Route 9W north to Route 84 east; cross Newburgh-Beacon Bridge; north on Route 9D to Route 9 north to Hyde Park; continue on Route 9 through Hyde Park; Vanderbilt Mansion is on the left.

From New York City: New York State Thruway (87) north to Exit 17 Newburgh; Route 84 east; cross Newburgh-Beacon Bridge; north on Route 9D to Route 9 north to Hyde Park; continue on Route 9 through Hyde Park; Vanderbilt Mansion is on the left.

MILLS MANSION

The first view of Mills Mansion is astonishing. The drive winds through rolling parkland, and around a bend, the stately Greek Revival mansion suddenly appears on the hill above. Marble stairs lead through fluted columns to the portico of this majestic home. Originally built by Morgan Lewis, third governor of New York State, the house was extensively enlarged and remodeled in 1895 by his great-granddaughter Ruth Livingston Mills and her husband Ogden. Every possible convenience—central heating, electricity, gas, indoor plumbing—was added for the comfort of the family even though they spent only September through New Year's here. They divided the rest of the year among their residences in New York, Paris, Newport and California.

The enormous oak paneled entrance hall contains Oriental art objects along with portraits of Ruth's Livingston ancestors. The 30 × 50 foot dining room was designed to showcase the seventeenth-century tapestries which hang on the green marble walls. With its eighteen leaves, the black walnut Regency table could seat twenty-four guests in grand style. Windows looked out upon lawns sweeping to the Hudson below, and dinners were timed to catch the sunset. (This is one of the few estates on the east side of the Hudson where the view of the river is not interrupted by train tracks.) The very best furnishings and art were placed in the drawing room. Three Greek vases purchased by Ogden Mills at a 1909 auction date back to 400-500 B.C.

The real life of the family centered in the library. Two thousand books from the 1700s to the 1930s line the shelves. Reading, board games and piano music filled the evenings. An oil painting of Morgan Lewis attributed to John Trumbull hangs above the fireplace, and an untitled work by the Hudson River School artist Albert Bierstadt hangs nearby. Ogden Mills, a gracious host, had seventy different newspapers delivered for his guests on Sunday mornings and urged his visitors to enjoy his thirty-five foot yacht, his nine-hole golf course and the miles of walking and carriage trails.

One of the more interesting rooms in the house is the butler's pantry. The polished wooden counters and paneled walls attest to the butler's high position. Not only did he bear responsibility for the family silver and fine china, but he also enforced the high standards of service and deportment expected of the male servants. (The housekeeper was in charge of the female servants.) Posted on the wall are rules governing behavior which include: "No smoking allowed in pantry until after dinner is served. Refrain from profanity and loud talking." The butler directed staff to the stations where they were needed. His call box was activated by white ivory buzzers in each room. When the buzzer was pushed, a light appeared on the panel identifying the room from which the call was made. Servants were loyal and well cared for. One butler, Mr. Thompson, remained with the family for twenty-five years.

The third floor, not open to the public, contained ten identical bedrooms for the female servants. A reproduction of one of these rooms can be seen on the second floor. All ten rooms shared one bath. In its floor was a trap door leading to hidden stairs for use in case of fire.

With its elegantly proportioned rooms and exquisite interiors, with its sweeping view of the Hudson River, Mills Mansion is a grand and opulent estate. Yet strange as it may seem, this sixty-five room Beaux-Arts mansion has the feel of a home. It is not difficult to imagine yourself as a guest of a warm and welcoming family.

Staatsburg, N.Y.
(914) 889-4100

DIRECTIONS:
From West Point: Route 9W north to Route 84 east; cross Newburgh-Beacon Bridge; north on Route 9D to Route 9 north to Hyde Park; continue on Route 9 through Hyde Park; Mills Mansion is located in the Mills-Norrie State Park just south of Staatsburg.

From New York City: New York State Thruway (87) north to Exit 17 Newburgh; Route 84 east; cross Newburgh-Beacon Bridge; north on Route 9D to Route 9 north to Hyde Park; continue on Route 9 through Hyde Park; Mills Mansion is located in the Mills-Norrie State Park just south of Staatsburg.

CULINARY INSTITUTE OF AMERICA (C.I.A.)

Secrets abound at the Culinary Institute of America (C.I.A.)—culinary secrets. One of America's foremost cooking schools, the C.I.A. trains students in all aspects of food preparation. In the twenty-one month course, apprentices serve as chefs, waiters, captains and maîtres d's, learning the restaurant profession from every angle. Founded in New Haven in 1946, the C.I.A. moved to its present quarters, an old Jesuit seminary, in 1972. Walking through the halls, the visitor sees students in aprons and toques hurrying to classes in pastry making, bread baking or Chinese cooking. Often special exhibits of student creations are on display, but even more impressive are the meals they prepare in the four C.I.A.-sponsored restaurants.

Escoffier Room

French cuisine, both classic and nouvelle, is served in the elegantly appointed Escoffier Room overlooking the Hudson. Seasonal dishes using the freshest of ingredients are prepared by students nearing the completion of their studies at the Institute. The service is attentive and gracious. Silver and crystal glow in the candlelight, and fresh flowers adorn the tables. The extensive and reasonably priced wine list offers selections of French, California and Hudson Valley wines to complement the meals. The Escoffier Room is highly recommended, but reservations are required well in advance. If you only have time to sample one of C.I.A.'s restaurants, this is the one to choose.

American Bounty

Less formal than the Escoffier Room, American Bounty specializes in what the C.I.A. calls regional American cuisine. Although current and up-to-date, it offers a combination of many cuisines rather than the strictly American fare that the name suggests. Near the tables, past a cornucopia overflowing with breads, student chefs can be seen at work in the kitchen. Descriptions of the innovative menu offerings are so tantalizing that they may inspire guests to recreate them in their own kitchens. The hunter green and cream dining room overlooks what was once the courtyard of the old seminary.

Caterina de Medici

Those who enjoy Italian food should try the newest of the C.I.A.'s dining rooms, Caterina de Medici. It specializes in traditional and modern foods from Italy and features Italian wines. Small and intimate, the restaurant seats only forty diners. Caterina de Medici is highly rated by the C.I.A. students themselves. As in the other Institute restaurants, care is evident in both preparation and service.

St. Andrew's Cafe

Emphasizing healthy and low calorie foods, the chefs of St.

Andrew's Cafe concentrate on dishes that provide high nutritional value. Vegetables, fruits, soups and pastas are specialties here along with other foods low in fat, salt and sugar. Housed in what looks like an old diner, St. Andrew's Cafe is surprisingly attractive inside. Linen cloths covering the tables, soft lighting and solicitous service make this a pleasant setting for a three-course meal. After dessert, diners are given a print-out detailing the vitamin, mineral and calorie content of the dishes they consumed.

(914) 471-6608

DIRECTIONS:
From West Point: Route 9W north to Route 84 east; cross Newburgh-Beacon Bridge; north on Route 9D to Route 9 north to Hyde Park; C.I.A. is on the left.

From New York City: New York State Thruway (87) north to Exit 17 Newburgh; Route 84 east; cross Newburgh-Beacon Bridge; north on Route 9D to Route 9 north to Hyde Park; C.I.A. is on the left.

LOCUST GROVE: THE YOUNG-MORSE HOUSE

Just a few miles south of Hyde Park is Locust Grove, the home that Samuel F.B. Morse bought with the royalties from his famous invention, the telegraph. The property had been owned by several prominent Hudson River families—the Schuylers, Livingstons and Montgomerys. When Morse acquired the estate in 1847, he hired the famous architect Alexander Jackson Davis to transform the small Georgian house on the grounds into a Tuscan villa. Morse himself designed the lawns and gardens. Before the telegraph brought him fame and fortune, he was a portrait painter. Trained at Yale and at London's Royal Academy, he used his artistic talent in his landscape design. To preserve the sweeping view of the river from his porch, he topped the trees along the banks of the Hudson. Today, visitors may walk the woodland paths and picnic on the 155 acres of this old estate.

The house itself is more reminiscent of the Youngs, who bought it in 1901, than of the Morse family. All the furnishings belonged to the Youngs. Their collections fill cabinet after cabinet in every room. They owned more than one hundred candlesticks, many sets of china, and dozens of mirrors, hatpins, diaries, rocking chairs—even scissors and twine holders. So extensive were their acquisitions that collections must be rotated since they cannot all be exhibited at one time.

In the basement, a room is set aside to highlight Morse's career. Telegraph equipment, a letter in Morse's own hand and blueprints of his additions to the house are displayed along with a print of his most famous painting, "A Gallery of the Louvre" (1830). There is even an unsigned landscape attributed to him. (Because it was his custom to include a man wearing a red sash in his landscapes, experts believe this painting is an original Morse.)

Poughkeepsie, N.Y.
(914) 454-4500

DIRECTIONS:
From West Point and New York City: New York State Thruway (87) north to Exit 17 Newburgh; cross Newburgh-Beacon Bridge to route 9D north to route 9 north to Locust Grove on left.

CHAPTER 12

Cold Spring

HIGHLIGHTS...

—Boscobel, a gracious Federal mansion overlooking the Hudson River

—A small river town with charming bed-and-breakfast inns

Directly across the river from West Point is the small nineteenth-century town of Cold Spring. Main Street slopes down to the water and loops around the bandstand at the river's edge. (A favorite pastime of residents and visitors is to "Scoop the Loop"—drive or walk down Main Street and circle the bandstand.) Small shops and restaurants line the street, and several bed–and–breakfast inns offer accommodations to overnight visitors. Essentially a weekend town, Cold Spring seems to close up on Mondays and Tuesdays and for the entire month of January. The real draw is nearby Boscobel, a restored Federal mansion located only minutes from Main Street.

BOSCOBEL

Flower-bordered brick paths and formal gardens give way to manicured lawns sweeping to the banks of the Hudson below. Amidst this tranquil beauty stands Boscobel, one of the loveliest homes ever built in America. The classical symmetry and stately proportions of the facade and rooms furnished with early nineteenth-century pieces make this Adam style mansion a perfect showcase of the decorative arts of the Federal period.

Boscobel ("beautiful woods" in Italian) was named for the forest in England which sheltered King Charles II as he fled the armies of Oliver Cromwell in 1651. States Morris Dyckman who built Boscobel was a Loyalist and during the Revolutionary War was employed by Sir William Erskine, the Quartermaster General of the English Army. When Erskine left British-held New York City in 1779, Dyckman accompanied him and remained in England for ten years. In this period, he developed a fondness

Boscobel, a museum of decorative arts of the Federal period, Garrison.

for all things British and for the life of a country gentleman. His service was rewarded with an annuity from Erskine, enabling Dyckman to make extensive investments in the London stock market. By 1789, animosity against the Loyalists had waned, and Dyckman returned to America a wealthy man. He settled on the 1000 acres he had instructed his brother to purchase for him near the Hudson River.

In 1794, at the age of thirty-nine, Dyckman married eighteen-year-old Elizabeth Corne who came from a neighboring Loyalist family. Soon after the marriage, his annuity was stopped, and he was forced to sell his London stocks to cover his debts. He sailed to England and spent almost four years in the successful attempt to have his stipend reinstated. While in London, Dyckman made extensive purchases, sending home china, prints, crystal and candelabra for the mansion he planned to build.

On his return, he immediately began construction on his property overlooking the Hudson in Montrose, New York. He never saw his home finished. He died in 1806, and his wife Elizabeth carried on with the project. Two years later she moved in with the couple's only son Peter and spent the last fifteen years of her life completing the mansion according to her husband's designs.

Years later as family fortunes fell, Boscobel passed into the hands of creditors and was finally sold for demolition in 1955 for only $35. Saved at the last moment by Lila Acheson Wallace, co-founder of the *Readers Digest*, Boscobel was dismantled, and pieces were stored in houses and barns all over Cold Spring and Garrison. The house was reconstructed on its present site and today is a museum dedicated to the decorative arts of the Federal period.

Neoclassical details found throughout Boscobel are characteristic of the Federal period's renewed interest in ancient Rome, brought about by the discovery of Pompeii in 1763. In the entrance hall, layers of oil paint brushed with turkey quills simulate a marble floor. Triple arches frame the wide, graceful staircase, and walls papered in a cut stone pattern are reminiscent of the friezes of antiquity. Emphasizing the importance of light, the house abounds with windows, looking glasses and gold detailing. Eagles with torches and swag designs carry out the Federal motif. Dark mahogany tables and sofas attributed to New York cabinetmaker Duncan Phyfe feature reeding, brass ornaments and low relief carving. While the furnishings are authentic to the period, few are original to the Dyckman family. However, the museum room features the Dyckman's mono-grammed flatware, Coalport porcelain and a specially commis-sioned snuffbox decorated with a likeness of King Charles II.

In addition to the formal areas, rooms used by servants such as a maid's bedroom and the butler's pantry suggest what life was like below stairs. Tours at Boscobel end in the recreated kitchen of the period. On cold, winter days, hot cider and cookies are offered in front of a blazing fire. Each season has its own delights. The tulips in spring, the rose garden in June and the magnificent fall foliage showcase this architectural gem of the Hudson Highlands.

Garrison, N.Y.
(914) 265-3638

DIRECTIONS:
From West Point: Route 9W south to Bear Mountain Bridge; cross bridge and take Route 9 north; eight miles to Boscobel, on the left.

From New York City: Palisades Parkway north to Bear Mountain Bridge; cross bridge and take Route 9 north; eight miles to Boscobel, on the left.

VILLAGE OF COLD SPRING

A stroll up and down Cold Spring's Main Street is a pleasant way to spend a couple of hours. Boutiques, craft shops and restaurants are interspersed with private residences. At last count, there were twenty stores calling themselves antique shops. Some have quality pieces while others merely offer scores of items for the weekend bargain hunter. On the second floor of Mycroft Holmes Antiques, 144 Main, Burt Murphy has recreated Sherlock Holmes' study at 221B Baker Street complete with wainscoting, heavy Victorian wallpaper and wine-colored drapes. (The upstairs room is not always open.) Just down the block, Salmagundi Bookshop, 66 Main, is an especially good bookshop with a surprisingly extensive collection of regional materials.

At the foot of Main Street, in the old train station, is The Depot, a great spot for burgers, snacks and old-fashioned soda fountain treats. Near the outside dining area, a marker identifies the spring from which George Washington drank when he visited his troops encamped nearby. A delightful but questionable story claims that he was so refreshed by his drink that he named the town Cold Spring. The Old Foundry Gun Shop, 92 Main, recalls the time when Cold Spring's West Point Foundry manufactured much of the nation's weaponry. The Foundry, established by Gouverneur Kemble, forged the famous Parrott gun of Civil War times. So vital were these guns to the North that cadets from West Point were dispatched to guard the Foundry in the summer of 1863 when threats were made against it by Southern sympathizers.

It was to serve the Catholic workers of the Foundry that Gouverneur Kemble had the Chapel of Our Lady built on Market Street in 1834. One of Cold Spring's most celebrated buildings, this simple Greek Revival chapel, perched on a bluff high above the river, was a popular subject of many Hudson River School painters. It is now used only for weddings and special services. Two other spots recalling Cold Spring's earlier days are the Julia L. Butterfield Memorial Library and the Foundry School Musuem.

DIRECTIONS:

From West Point: Route 9W south to Bear Mountain Bridge; cross bridge and take Route 9 north; at intersection with Main Street (Route 301), Cold Spring, make a left.

From New York City: Palisades Parkway north to Bear Mountain Bridge; cross bridge and take Route 9 north; at intersection with Main Street (Route 301), Cold Spring, make a left.

Julia L. Butterfield Memorial Library

The endearing, small-town Julia L. Butterfield Memorial Library is notable for its two Hudson River School paintings, both by Thomas Pritchard Rossiter. Rossiter, who lived in Cold Spring for the last eleven years of his life (1860-1871), delighted in the views of the Hudson Highlands, inspiration for many of his works. "The Hudson from His House at Cold Spring" hangs in the back reading room. His famous "Pic-Nic on the Hudson" portrays several important Cold Spring residents and includes Rossiter himself on the far left. Seated on the far right is Gouverneur Kemble, Director of the West Point Foundry; standing behind him is Robert Parrott, inventor of the Parrott gun, and his wife. The legendary West Point drawing master Robert Weir is seated on a mossy stone in front of his two daughters, Louisa and Cora. Julia L. Butterfield in a flowing dress with violet sash holds a fan in her right hand. A patron of the arts, Mrs. Butterfield left much of her considerable fortune to fund the town's library, hospital and school. In her ninety years, she traveled extensively and entertained such notables as the Empress of Russia. The portrait of the Tsarina in the library was a thank-you gift to her Cold Spring hostess. General Daniel Butterfield, one of Julia's three husbands, is credited with commissioning taps and is buried in West Point's cemetery.

Morris Avenue (Route 9-D, near the corner of Main St.)
Cold Spring, N.Y.
(914) 265-3040

Foundry School Museum

Built in 1830 as a school for foundry workers' children, the small Foundry School Museum features a nineteenth-century classroom setting with benches, slates, old books and even a dunce cap on a stool in a corner. One room is devoted to the history of the Foundry and the items forged there. A model of the famous Civil War Parrott gun designed by West Point graduate Robert Parrott (Class of 1824) is on view along with a fragment of an actual gun barrel. Prints and paintings of the Hudson River Valley include "The Gun Foundry" by John Ferguson Weir, son of West Point's famous drawing master, Robert Weir. Some exhibits change periodically. In the collection is the Butterfields' Russian boat sleigh, purportedly presented to them as a hostess gift by the Tsarina of Russia. The museum's hours are limited.

63 Chestnut Street
Cold Spring, N.Y.
(914) 265-4010

CHAPTER 13

Tarrytown

HIGHLIGHTS...

—Van Cortlandt Manor, 1750 stone manor house of Revolutionary War Patriots

—Philipsburg Manor, working gristmill and farm owned by the Loyalist Philipse family

—Storybook Cottage of Washington Irving, author of *Rip Van Winkle* and the *Legend of Sleepy Hollow*

—Lyndhurst, Railroad Tycoon Jay Gould's Gothic Revival mansion on the Hudson

The lands that make up modern day Tarrytown were settled by the Dutch in the 1600s. It was the wheat crop grown by the early farmers that gave the town its name. "Tarwe" is the Dutch word for wheat; thus, Tarrytown. The famous writer Washington Irving, a nineteenth-century resident, had a somewhat more intriguing explanation. He attributed the name to the custom of local residents who tended to "tarry" too long in the town's taverns.

All the land was at one time part of the 52,000-acre Manor of Philipsburg, granted by royal patent to Frederick Philipse I in 1693. During the Revolutionary War, the population was divided, with almost one-third of Westchester County remaining loyal to the King. The area was the borderland between British-controlled New York City and the American fortifications at West Point. Territory changed hands often, and there was a constant threat from raiding parties of both sides. Houses were burned, and others were commandeered as operational headquarters. The staunchly patriotic Van Cortlandts of Van Cortlandt Manor abandoned their house in 1776 and spent the rest of the war further north. Frederick Philipse III, who owned the mill at Philipsburg as well as a manor house in Yonkers, was imprisoned for his Tory politics and eventually fled with his family to the British stronghold of New York City.

By 1800, the large land holdings along the Hudson River were no more. Many had been divided among family members, while others were sold to satisfy war debts. The Manor of Philipsburg was seized by the government and sold at auction. Present-day Tarrytown is part of the 750-acre parcel purchased by Gerard and Cornelia Beekman at this sale. The Beekmans administered their lands and mills along the Pocantico River for thirty years. When Gerard died in 1822, the Widow Beekman and her sons divided their property into residential lots and laid out a plan for Tarrytown, then called Beekmantown.

In 1835, celebrated author and diplomat Washington Irving purchased a tenant farmhouse on the old Philipsburg Manor and transformed it into his whimsical cottage Sunnyside. His good friend, General William Paulding, built The Knoll, a home for his retirement, half a mile north of Sunnyside. With the coming of the railroad in 1851, Tarrytown became easily accessible from New York City, and prosperous industrialists fixed upon the Hudson Valley as a site for weekend and country homes. Wealthy merchant George Merritt bought The Knoll and renamed it Lyndhurst. He commissioned famous architect Alexander Jackson Davis to double it in size, and when railroad tycoon Jay Gould purchased it in 1880, Lyndhurst became a symbol of wealth and opulence. The Rockefellers, too, found the area attractive and acquired land in nearby Pocantico Hills for a family compound. In the 1930s, lawyer and investment banker Walter Rosen built Caramoor, a Mediterranean style villa in Katonah, New York, to house his extensive collection of Chinese and European art. As rail service improved, Tarrytown also became home to businessmen who commuted daily to their jobs in New York City. Today, it is a thriving town along the Hudson River, and its citizens, while retaining their strong ties to New York City, have a deep sense of their community's past.

VAN CORTLANDT MANOR

Baron, Ranger, Sheriff and Lord of the Manor by Royal Patent of King William III of England, Stephanus Van Cortlandt held title to 86,000 acres in the Province of New York. His land stretched from the Kitchewanc Creek (Croton River) to the red cedar tree on Anthony's Nose (near Bear Mountain Bridge) and from the Hudson River to the Connecticut border. The original charter, which now hangs in the main hall of the manor house, has the King's picture on the front and his seal and signature on the back.

Sometime between 1697 and 1700, Stephanus built the fortress-like lower level of Van Cortlandt Manor. Two rooms with stone walls two feet thick provided shelter when Stephanus came north from his home in New York City to hunt and to trade with the Kitchewanc Indians. At his death, Stephanus's oldest surviving son Philip received the rustic lodge and surrounding land. In 1750, Philip's son Pierre added the more formal second story, and the Manor became his family's permanent residence.

The Van Cortlandts were prominent in colonial times and played an important role in the establishment of the new nation. In 1774, Royal Governor William Tryon visited the Manor in an attempt to persuade Pierre to remain loyal to the Crown and offered him elevation to the nobility and a commission in the British Army. Pierre refused and risked all for the patriot cause. With the approach of the enemy in 1776, the Van Cortlandts abandoned their house for the duration of the war.

Pierre became a member of New York's Provincial Congress and voted to ratify the Declaration of Independence. He presided over the convention which drafted New York State's first constitution and was elected the State's first Lieutenant Governor in 1777. He served in that capacity until 1795, essentially running the government for the seven years that Governor George Clinton spent on the battlefield.

Philip Van Cortlandt, Pierre's oldest son, became a Brigadier General in the Continental Army. A close friend of Lafayette, he was present at Valley Forge, at Burgoyne's surrender at Saratoga and led a charge in the final battle at Yorktown. When funds ran low, he paid his men out of his own pocket. After the war, he served in the House of Representatives for fifteen years during the Washington, Adams and Jefferson administrations.

Van Cortlandt Manor was badly damaged during the Revolution, and Philip made extensive repairs when he returned from the war. Today, visitors enter through the massive Dutch door that he restored. All the hardware is original, including the brass dolphin doorknocker. The two glass ovals in the upper portion of the door are characteristic of the period. Most of the pieces in the house once belonged to the family. Some are part of the twenty to thirty cartloads Pierre took with him when he evacuated the house during the Revolutionary War, and others belonged to later family members. In the parlor is Philip's secretary, and the Queen Anne game table and the Chinese porcelain are Van Cortlandt pieces as well. Benjamin Franklin slept in this room on May 25, 1776, when he visited Pierre; other famous men who visited the house during this period include Lafayette, Rochambeau, John Jay and George Clinton.

In the main hall is a portrait of Abraham Van Cortlandt, brother of Pierre. The draperies in the picture were reproduced by curators, using bolts of eighteenth-century silk. These draperies hang on the windows in the parlor. The magnificent mahogany sideboard in the dining room was brought back to the Manor by John D. Rockefeller, Jr. who traced its whereabouts through an auction house. In fact, it was Rockefeller who bought most of the Van Cortlandt furnishings in 1941, when the house was sold by the family. In 1953, he acquired the Manor and began major restoration work. Today, it is owned by Historic Hudson Valley, which maintains the Manor, gardens and Ferry House down by the river.

Ferry House

At the end of the Long Walk is the brick and clapboard Ferry House by the banks of the Croton. From around 1788-1819, ferry service was provided from this point, and the house offered food and lodging for farmers and cattle drovers waiting to cross the river. Today, the Ferry House is set up as an inn of the period with a common room, a barroom and several bedchambers. It is furnished with old country pieces including a rare, 300–year–old Hudson Valley painted kas and several hutch tables. In the barroom, there are five different kinds of Windsor chairs and a smoker's companion, a device which held clay pipes and the candles used to light them. Innkeepers often rented pipes by the evening and always kept a supply of them on hand. In the back bedroom is an acutal British war map detailing the position of troops under General Sir William Howe against those of George Washington in October and November of 1776. Just outside is the 1799 bell which stood on the opposite bank and was rung to summon the ferry master.

Croton-on-Hudson, N.Y.
(914) 631-8200

DIRECTIONS:
From West Point: Route 9W south to Tappan Zee Bridge. Cross bridge and take Exit 9 for Tarrytown. Go north on Route 9 nine miles to signs for Van Cortlandt Manor.

From New York City: New York State Thruway (87) north to Exit 9 for Tarrytown. Go north on Route 9 nine miles to signs for Van Cortlandt Manor.

PHILIPSBURG MANOR

Philipsburg Manor recreates the 1720-1750 period when the property was the site of a thriving gristmill and working farm. Today, costumed guides in the reconstructed mill demonstrate

Upper Mills, Philipsburg Manor, Tarrytown.

how wheat and corn were ground into flour and explain the workings of the waterwheel and grindstones. There are sheep, cows, chickens and other animals on the property as well as kitchen gardens, orchards and a New World Dutch barn.

This holding, known as the Upper Mills, was in the northern portion of the Manor of Philipsburg, the 52,000-acre estate granted to Frederick Philipse I in 1693. Never a permanent family residence, the Upper Mills was administered from Frederick's homes in New York City and the Lower Mills in Yonkers (see below). Frederick built a small stone structure which served as an office for the Upper Mills and as a place for him to stay when he came north to supervise its operations. When he died, his son Adolph inherited the Upper Mills, and sometime between 1720 and 1730, Adolph doubled the size of the house. Still simple and austere, this manor house remained a place of business rather than a comfortable home.

Adolph's office on the first floor allowed him to oversee the activity at the mill and to keep track of river traffic. On the wall is a 1746 French map which locates the Upper Mills, indicating the importance of the site to New World commerce. While furnishings in the manor house are not family pieces, an extensive inventory taken at Adolph's death in 1750 has allowed curators to replicate rooms of the period. In the parlor is a Dutch country cupboard painted with the Biblical scene of Tobias and the Angel. The chest in the reception room dates back to the time of William and Mary. Upstairs, one bedchamber is set up as a room in a tenant farmer's house. Another chamber shows how rooms were used for storage and warehouse space.

Philipsburg Manor reached the height of its prosperity under Adolph's management. At his death, the Upper Mills passed first to his nephew Frederick II, and a year later to Frederick's son, Frederick III. Frederick III preferred the life of a country gentleman to that of a merchant and lived in luxury at his home in Yonkers. During the Revolutionary War, he was a Loyalist and as a result, his entire estate was confiscated after America won her independence. General Philip Van Cortlandt from neighboring Van Cortlandt Manor, the Commissioner of Forfeiture for the Southern District of New York, presided over the dissolution and sale of the Philipse property. (As a commissioner, Van Cortlandt received a commission, a percentage of the revenues from the sale.) The land was divided into parcels and auctioned off to 287 different families. Gerard and Cornelia Beekman became the owners of the Upper Mills along with 750 acres of surrounding farm land.

In subsequent years, the property passed through many hands until 1940 when the Tarrytown Historical Society acquired the house and grounds with funds from John D. Rockefeller, Jr. They built a nineteenth-century mill modeled after one in a Currier & Ives lithograph and removed some of the manor house's later additions. In 1951, Sleepy Hollow Restorations took over from the Historical Society and began a long process of research and reconstruction. Deciding to return the site to the period when it was most prosperous, Sleepy Hollow replaced the mill and dam with eighteenth-centruy reproductions built on the foundations of the original structures. Using as models such extant Dutch stone houses as the Bevier-Elting and Jean Hasbrouck homes in New Paltz (see Chapter 6) and studying seventeenth-century paintings of Dutch interiors, they recreated the manor house as it would have appeared in Adolph's time. The restoration is documented in the Reception Center where Historic Hudson Valley, which now administers the site, has prepared a ten-minute film as an introduction to the tour.

(914) 631-8200

DIRECTIONS:
From West Point: Route 9W south to the Tappan Zee Bridge. Cross bridge and take Exit 9 for Tarrytown. Take Route 9 north two miles to Philipsburg Manor.

From New York City: New York State Thruway (87) north to Exit 9 for Tarrytown. Take Route 9 north two miles to Philipsburg Manor.

PHILIPSE MANOR HALL IN YONKERS

The years and changing neighborhoods have taken their toll on what was once a lovely Georgian country home. Quite rundown and unfurnished, Philipse Manor Hall retains few traces of its past elegance. Its park-like setting and formal gardens are gone, replaced by dilapidated commercial buildings and parking lots. Yet, Philipse Manor Hall was once the country seat of one of the wealthiest and most prominent citizens of colonial New York.

Frederick Philipse I (1617-1702), a carpenter employed by Peter Stuyvesant, came to the New World in the 1650s. He became a successful merchant and landowner and acquired vast holdings which, in 1693, were consolidated by Royal Patent into the 52,000-acre Manor of Philipsburg. Administering his property from his New York City home, he built small residences at both his Upper Mills property on the Pocantico River (see above) and at his Lower Mills site in what is now Yonkers. At his death, the Lower Mills passed to his grandson, Frederick Philipse II, who became second Lord of the Manor when he attained his majority in 1717. Educated in England, Frederick II served in New York's Provincial Assembly and encouraged his son Frederick III to value all things English.

It was Frederick III who, with his immense fortune, was able to live the life of a country gentleman. He transformed the house in Yonkers into a Georgian manor hall and lived there year round. Unsympathetic to the patriot cause, he remained staunchly loyal to King George III. He headed a convention at White Plains which, on November 26, 1776, issued a Declaration of Dependence upon England. At one point, he was arrested and imprisoned in Connecticut by the Continental forces. Released after six months, he fled with his family behind British lines to New York City. When the peace treaty recognizing America's independence was signed in 1783, Frederick Philipse sailed to England. His vast holdings were forfeited and sold at public auction. He died three years later, a poor and broken man. He was buried in Chester, England, where a plaque at the cathedral honors his loyalty to king and country.

Philipse Manor Hall is a site more important as the home of a Loyalist family than for what can be seen there today. After its years as a boarding house and as Yonkers City Hall, all that remains is the shell of Frederick III's once grand manor. The wide plank floors with wooden dowels, the hand-turned spindles of the main staircase and the intricately carved woodwork suggest the attention to detail of Frederick III's Georgian addition. Fireplace frontispieces bear Tudor roses, Prince of Wales plumes and other symbols of English royalty. The Rococo ceiling in the East Parlor is the house's most outstanding architectural feature. Its complex design includes eight figures at the corners pointing to a central arabesque, all sculpted from papier-maché in 1756.

Pictures of men of the Revolution (Jefferson, Lafayette, Knox) and of our early presidents (Madison, Monroe, Lincoln) hang in several rooms of the house. There are a number of pictures of George Washington, a one-time suitor of Frederick III's daughter Mary who grew up in this house. A display relating the history of Yonkers explains the derivation of the town's name. It came from Adriaen van der Donck "the Youncker" (the Young Gentleman) who first owned this property in the seventeenth century.

Warburton Avenue and Dock Street
Yonkers, N.Y.
(914) 965-4027

DIRECTIONS:
From West Point: Route 9W south to Tappan Zee Bridge. Cross bridge and take New York State Thruway (87) south to junction with Saw Mill Parkway. Take Saw Mill Parkway south to Yonkers Ave. Go west one and one-quarter miles. Right onto Riverdale Avenue which becomes Warburton. Take the left immediately past third traffic light into driveway of Philipse Manor Hall.

From New York City: Saw Mill Parkway north to Yonkers Ave. Go west one and one-quarter miles. Right onto Riverdale Avenue which becomes Warburton. Take the left immediately past third traffic light into driveway of Philipse Manor Hall.

MONUMENT TO THE CAPTORS OF MAJOR JOHN ANDRÉ

On September 23, 1780, an event took place in Tarrytown that most likely prevented the British from winning the Revolutionary War. Major John André, a British spy, was captured with the plans of West Point's fortifications hidden in his boot. West Point, under the command of Benedict Arnold, was the most important bulwark of the Continental Army in the north. Had it fallen, the British would have seized control of the Hudson River and divided the colonies. Arnold had sought this command with the specific intent to betray the post to the British. Although a hero at Quebec and Saratoga, he was passed over by Congress for promotion, and while stationed in Philadelphia, felt himself unjustly accused of misconduct. Through his wife's Loyalist family, he made contact with British General Sir Henry Clinton and formulated plans for his treason.

In August 1780, Arnold took control of West Point, and on the night of September 21, he met with Clinton's adjutant-general, Major John André, near Stony Point. He handed André detailed information which would enable the British to take the fort. Arnold returned to his headquarters while André, dressed as a civilian, began the dangerous journey back to British lines. On the morning of September 23, he was captured by three Tarrytown militiamen—John Paulding, Isaac Van Wart and David Williams. Although offered bribes to set him free, the young men turned him over to the authorities. Benedict Arnold received word of André's capture while breakfasting with General Washington's aides. Realizing that André carried incriminating evidence written in his own hand, Arnold fled immediately. He was taken aboard the British warship *Vulture* and eventually made his way to England.

André was tried and convicted as a spy and executed on October 2 in Tappan (see below). In 1853, the citizens of Tarrytown erected a monument on the actual spot where André was captured in honor of the three militiamen who saved West Point and their country.

North Broadway (Albany Post Road)
near the North Tarrytown line

TAPPAN

Site of the imprisonment, trial and execution of British spy Major John André, Tappan was George Washington's Headquarters at three different times during the Revolutionary War. From September 28 to October 7, 1780, Washington resided in the DeWint House to oversee André's trial. André had been captured on September 23 in Tarrytown (see above). His trial was held on September 29 in the Tappan Reformed Church across from the Village Green. André was brought to Tappan the day before from West Point, where he had been held for two nights. He was taken to the Mabie Tavern on Main Street (now the Old '76 House restaurant) and confined under heavy guard. Washington stipulated that while André was to be closely watched, his quarters were to be pleasant and comfortable. Fourteen generals, including the Marquis de Lafayette, Baron von Steuben, Henry Knox and Arthur St. Clair, heard evidence at a court-martial presided over by Major General Nathanael Greene.

André was found guilty and sentenced to be hanged as a spy. Washington, who was not present at the trial, signed the death warrant at the DeWint House and scheduled the execution for October 1. When the possibility of exchanging André for Benedict Arnold arose, the execution was delayed. Nothing came of the exchange, and the date was reset for October 2. Large crowds followed André, guarded by three hundred soldiers, as he was taken from the Mabie Tavern up the hill to the gallows. Many onlookers felt great sympathy for this brave young man who met his death with courage. He was buried at the site, but in 1821, his remains were transferred to Westminster Abbey. On the centennial of his death, a monument to André was erected on the site.

DIRECTIONS:
From West Point: Route 9W south through Stony Point; Route 202 west to Palisades Interstate Parkway south to Exit 5, Route 303 to Tappan. Right onto Kings Highway into center of village.

From New York City: Palisades Interstate Parkway north to Exit 5, Route 303 to Tappan. Right onto Kings Highway into center of village.

DeWint House

To commemorate the bicentennial of George Washington's birth, the DeWint House was purchased in 1932 by the Grand Lodge of Free and Accepted Masons of New York. Four times between 1780 and 1783, Washington took up residence in this house while Commander-in-Chief of the Continental Army. In August 1780, he stopped here on his way to a meeting with General Rochambeau in Hartford. The next month he made the DeWint House his headquarters while supervising the trial of Major John André. In May of 1783, he entertained British General Sir Guy Carleton at the house while they negotiated the evacuation of the English from New York City. Washington's last visit was unplanned. On his way to West Point in November 1783, he took shelter with the DeWints when he was caught in a snowstorm.

The DeWint House, the oldest building in Tappan, was built in 1700 of local sandstone and bricks from Holland. Visitors take a self-guided tour through its four rooms, each of which is protected by plexiglass walls. In the brick-floored kitchen is a mahogany Chippendale dropleaf table, reputed to be the table on which George Washington signed André's death warrant. In the other first floor room, original purple Dutch Delft tiles surround the fireplace.

The carriage house contains displays devoted to George Washington. Over forty-six likenesses of Washington appear in paintings, prints, busts and ceramic plates. There is also a model of the H.M.S. *Perseverance*, the ship which carried Sir Guy Carleton to his meeting with General Washington. When Washington boarded the ship, the Royal Navy fired a salute—the first formal recognition of the independent American nation. In 1966, the DeWint House was designated a National Historic Landmark.

Livingston Avenue and Oak Tree Road
Tappan, N.Y.
(914) 359-1359

JOHN JAY HOMESTEAD

Winding country roads past miles of stone walls and white picket fences lead to the John Jay Homestead in Katonah, New York. It was to this farmhouse that John Jay retired in 1801 after years in his country's service. Here for the last twenty-eight years of his life, Jay devoted himself to his farm, his family and his church.

Beginning with his election to the first Continental Congress in 1774, Jay held more public offices than any other man of the period. As a member of New York's Provincial Congress, he drafted the resolution endorsing the Declaration of Independence. During the war, he was Minister to Spain and, in an effort to secure a loan for his fledgling government, offered his own funds as surety. At the request of Benjamin Franklin, Jay went to Paris and participated in the peace negotiations with

Britain. In 1785, he became Secretary of Foreign Affairs. Holding this office under the Articles of Confederation, he came to realize that a stronger national government was a necessity. Along with Alexander Hamilton and James Madison, he wrote the *Federalist Papers* urging ratification of the Constitution. When George Washington was elected President, he appointed Jay the first Chief Justice of the United States Supreme Court.

The greatest controversy of Jay's public career came in 1794 when he traveled to Great Britain in an attempt to settle the differences that remained between the two nations after the war. The Jay Treaty won several concessions from the English government but failed to satisfy the anti-Federalists. The resulting storm of protest destroyed any chance he may have had to become president. His last public office was that of Governor of New York, a position he held until his retirement in 1801.

Much of the John Jay Homestead remains as it was when Jay lived there. In the parlor, the floors and woodwork are original, and the wallpaper is a carefully documented reproduction of the pattern he originally chose. Over the piano is a portrait of John Jay in his academic robes, a copy of the Gilbert Stuart painting in the National Gallery in Washington. An oil of his beloved wife, Sarah Livingston Jay, hangs above the fireplace. She was a member of the distinguished Livingston family, and her father William Livingston was the first Governor of New Jersey. The tapestries covering the settee and two chairs were presented by Lafayette to John Jay when he was in France negotiating the Peace of Paris.

The table in the dining room was made for Jay and used in the Governor's Mansion in Albany. The portrait in the alcove over the sideboard is of Jay's grandfather Auguster. A Huguenot from La Rochelle, France, Auguster fled to the New World at the age of twenty and later married a relative of Peter Stuyvesant. Their son Peter (John Jay's father), whose picture hangs over the fireplace, also aligned himself with a prominent New York family, the Van Cortlandts.

The family library served as John Jay's office during his lifetime. All pieces in the room, with the exception of the wing chair, belonged to Jay. Three of the chairs are from the first United States Senate which met in New York City. They were sent to Jay's Albany office by mistake, and although he offered to send them down to Washington, he was told not to incur the expense.

Jay's years here were happy ones. Despite the loss of his wife soon after he moved in, he was surrounded by family and free to pursue his interests in farming. He owned over 900 acres, and from his porch he could see the Hudson River and the mountains beyond. Today, the homestead still has sweeping lawns and the feel of the country although only sixty acres of the property remain. For one hundred and fifty-two years, it was home to the descendants of John Jay, a man who played a pivotal role in the establishment of our nation.

Katonah, N.Y.
(914) 232-5651

DIRECTIONS:
From West Point: Route 9W south to Bear Mountain Bridge. Cross bridge and take Route 9 south to Peekskill. Take Route 35/202 east past Route 684 to Route 22. Go south on Route 22 (Jay Street) to John Jay Homestead.

From New York City: Route 684-Saw Mill Parkway north to Exit 6 Katonah-Cross River. Go east on Route 35 to stoplight. South on Route 22 (Jay Street) to John Jay Homestead.

SUNNYSIDE

The storybook cottage of Washington Irving, America's first great storyteller, Sunnyside combines Dutch stepped gables, a Spanish tower and ivy-covered walls to create the cozy home Irving called his "snuggery." Top-hatted, frock-coated guides lead visitors through rooms "as full of angles and corners as an old cocked hat." From 1835 when he bought the house until his appointment as Minister to Spain in 1842, Irving worked and slept in his study while extensive renovations were made to the rest of the house. Everything in the study belonged to Irving, including the leather manuscript chair and the thousand-volume library. At the desk, presented to Irving by his publisher

Sunnyside, Washington Irving's storybook cottage, Tarrytown.

G. P. Putnam's Sons, he wrote his detailed *Life of George Washington*, a standard work for many years. Irving was the first American to earn his living as a writer, and he was well known both in this country and in Europe for his satires, essays, folktales and historical novels.

The dining room looks out over the Hudson River. Irving loved the view from Sunnyside, and though he traveled and lived in Europe for over twenty years, he never found another view to equal it. He was known as a gracious host. John Jacob Astor, Oliver Wendell Holmes, Martin Van Buren and William Cullen Bryant were among his dinner guests. Although conversation was lively, religion, politics and money were forbidden topics at his table. Guests and family often gathered in the back parlor for musical evenings. In summer, the outside doors were flung open, and there was dancing on the porch.

When renovations were completed, Washington Irving moved from the study into a bedchamber upstairs. Near his bed is a picture of Matilda Hoffman, his fiancée who died in 1809. Grief-stricken by her death, he never married and kept a lock of her hair with his prayerbook. A picture entitled "The Chieftain and the Child" is also in the bedroom. The scene recalls the time when the six-year-old Washington Irving was introduced to George Washington by his nurse. Another bedroom belonged to his brother Ebenezer, who moved to Sunnyside with his five daughters at the time of his wife's death in 1838. The spartan, unheated room reflected Ebenezer's taste and the frugality of both Irvings. The brothers combined the two households so that they need only maintain one home and one set of servants. The guest bedroom, Irving's favorite room, reminded him of an apartment in Paris. In this light, airy room overlooking the river, he kept his French, Spanish and Italian books.

Irving built the Spanish Tower to house his servants. In the kitchen below, he installed a copper water-heating system, patterned after one he had seen in Spain when he was writing *The Alhambra*. The water came from the pond outside that he called his "little Mediterranean." Irving designed his grounds as carefully as he did his cottage. Winding paths led him down to the Hudson River, and he felt intimately connected with the early inhabitants of the Hudson Valley, both real and imaginary. Of all his works, Irving is best remembered for his tales of Ichabod Crane and Rip Van Winkle, stories set in the surrounding hills and hamlets. His fanciful imagination and romantic spirit are captured in his enchanting home, Sunnyside.

(914) 631-8200

DIRECTIONS:
From West Point: Route 9W south to Tappan Zee Bridge; cross bridge and take Exit 9 for Tarrytown. Go south on Route 9 one mile to Sunnyside.

From New York City: New York State Thruway (87) north to Exit 9 for Tarrytown. Go south on Route 9 one mile to Sunnyside.

OLD DUTCH CHURCH OF SLEEPY HOLLOW

The only remaining example of seventeenth-century Dutch religious architecture in the United States, the Old Dutch Church was built by Frederick Philipse, first Lord of the Manor of Philipsburg. Erected in 1697 to serve the tenants who farmed his land and ran his mills, the Church was attended by Frederick Philipse and his wife Catherine when they were in residence at the Upper Mills. The Church still owns the Philipses' silver baptismal bowl and beakers as well as the bell, cast in the Netherlands in 1685 and purchased for the bell tower by Frederick Philipse. Both Frederick and his wife are buried in the Church.

The Old Dutch Church was immortalized by Washington Irving in the "Legend of Sleepy Hollow." It was from its churchyard that the headless horseman began his nightly ride and where he flung his pumpkin head at Schoolmaster Ichabod Crane. Gravestones date back to the 1730s, and several record the names of soldiers who fought in the Revolutionary War. Washington Irving's grave lies in the Sleepy Hollow Cemetery directly to the north of this Old Dutch Burying Ground.

Route 9 near Philipsburg Manor
(914) 631-1123

DIRECTIONS:
From West Point: Route 9W south to the Tappan Zee Bridge. Cross bridge and take Exit 9 for Tarrytown. Take Route 9 north two miles. Church is just past the Manor, on the right.

From New York City: New York State Thruway (87) north to Exit 9 for Tarrytown. Take Route 9 north two miles. Church is just past the Manor, on the right.

LYNDHURST

Not only does the Gothic Revival mansion Lyndhurst symbolize the Romantic movement that swept America in the nineteenth century, but the grounds themselves reflect the Victorian vision of nature as art. Built in 1838 for General William Paulding, twice Mayor of New York City, Lyndhurst sits high atop a hill overlooking the Hudson River. The winding drive teases visitors with glimpses of the villa and draws the eye to its marble turrets and Gothic battlements. Paulding commissioned renowned architect Alexander Jackson Davis to build him a home near his good friend Washington Irving at Sunnyside. By mid-century, wealthy industrialists discovered the Hudson Valley and began an era of mansion building. In 1864, George Merritt, a prosperous New York merchant who had purchased Lyndhurst a few years before, engaged Davis to double its size. Railroad magnate Jay Gould moved in in 1880, and his descendants owned Lyndhurst until 1961.

No expense was spared in decorating the house. The massive statue of Cupid in the drawing room was put on rollers so that it could be turned to face outside for parties on the lawn. The popular faux finishes were used lavishly throughout. In the entrance hall, wooden door frames were made to look like stone, and the walls were painstakingly painted with turkey feathers to simulate the veined appearance of marble. The hollow pine beams on the ceiling in the dining room were made to look like heavy oak, and the walls appear to be stamped leather. It is interesting to note that in some cases, it was more costly to simulate a finish than to use the authentic material. Tiffany windows abound—in the drawing room, the smoking room, the library, the master bedroom. In the room the Merritts used as an art gallery and billiard room, a twenty-four foot Tiffany window looks out over the Hudson River. Because they owned so many paintings, the Merritts chose to cover this magnificent window and view in order to display their art.

In spite of its formal elegance, Lyndhurst was a home for children as well. The Goulds' four sons and two daughters often watched from the gallery for their father's yacht to return from New York City. Three panes of magnified glass had been specially inserted in the Tiffany window so they could better see his approach. Gould frequently conducted business meetings in the Cabinet Room within earshot of his children in the library. He wanted them to be prepared for the time when they would take over his empire.

Furnishings in the house belonged to the Pauldings, Merritts and Goulds. When architect Alexander Jackson Davis planned the house, he designed specific pieces of furniture for its interior as well. In the entrance hall is a wheel-back chair pictured in Davis' well-known book on architecture. The table he designed for the dining room could seat up to twenty-two people, and his benches in the outer entry bear a serpentine motif, suggesting the winding Hudson River below.

Specimen trees, flowering shrubs and 127 varieties of roses embellish the sixty-seven acre estate. The Rose Cottage was a children's playhouse, and at one time, a stable complex held horses for the family's use. Today, summer concerts are held on the lawn, and tours are conducted by the National Trust for Historic Preservation.

635 South Broadway
(914) 631-0046

DIRECTIONS:
From West Point: Route 9W south to Tappan Zee Bridge; cross bridge and take Exit 9 for Tarrytown. South on Route 9 one-half mile to Lyndhurst.

From New York City: New York State Thruway (87) north to Exit 9 for Tarrytown. South on Route 9 one-half mile to Lyndhurst.

CARAMOOR

A Mediterranean style villa set in one hundred acres of park-like grounds and woodland gardens, Caramoor was the summer home that Walter Tower Rosen built for his wife Lucie in Katonah, New York. It took a decade (1929-1939) to complete this showcase for the Rosens' vast collection of European and Chinese art. Paintings, tapestries, statuary, furniture and porcelain spanning 2000 years of art and history fill the house. Entire rooms from French chateaux, English country estates and Italian palazzos were transported from Europe and reassembled at Caramoor for the Rosens.

The famous Monkey Bedroom came from a chateau in Artois. It was named for the monkeys hand-painted on its Chinese silk wallcovering. The 1678 library is also from a French chateau. Its vivid blue vaulted ceiling features murals of Biblical scenes, and the wooden fold-up chair bears the insignia of King Ferdinand and Queen Isabella of Spain. The dining room is from an eighteenth-century palazzo in Northern Italy. Around the table are many Grendey chairs, made by English cabinetmaker Giles Grendey for a Spanish palace in 1740. Other pieces of this set, which once numbered seventy-two, are in the Victoria and Albert and the Metropolitan Museums.

In the hall outside the dining room is the most famous piece in the house, a forty-paneled Chinese spinach jade screen. Crafted for the Emperor, it was one of three made during the Ch'ien Lung period (1736-1795). The only one remaining intact, the screen is carved on one side with images from nature. The other side depicts the Taoist view of man's journey through life and his encounters with gods, sages, immortals and mythical beasts.

The music room, the last to be completed, epitomizes the family's eclectic tastes and interests. With its Flemish tapestries, Louis XV lamps, Renaissance paintings, Venetian draperies and Russian ikons, it represents the breadth and depth of their collections. The family's real passion was music, and this eighty-foot-long, forty-foot-wide and thirty-foot-high room was designed for their musical evenings. Walter Rosen and his daughter Anne played the piano, and many felt that either could have become a concert pianist. Lucie Rosen was an accomplished violinist, and the family loved to share their musical interests with friends. Guests were invited to hear performances by great artists of the time, and in 1946 the Rosens held three concerts, the beginning of the Caramoor Music Festival.

After Walter's death in 1951, Lucie continued the couple's commitment to establish Caramoor as "a center for music and the arts." Concerts were offered in the villa's open Spanish Courtyard, and in 1957 construction began on the 1600-seat Venetian Theater on the grounds. At the Theater's opening performance the next summer, Marian Anderson sang the title role in "Orpheo ed Euridice." Over the years, the Music Festival has grown, and it has become a treasured part of New York's summer music schedule. Chamber music, opera and solo performances fill the evenings, and concertgoers enjoy the serenity of the Rosens' beautiful estate.

Girdle Ridge Road
Katonah, N.Y.
(914) 232-5035

DIRECTIONS:
From West Point: Route 9W south to Bear Mountain Bridge. Cross bridge and take Route 9 south to Peekskill. Take Route 35/202 east past Route 684 to Route 22. Make right turn onto Route 22 (Jay Street). Continue to the junction of Girdle Ridge Road (3 miles). Follow signs to Caramoor.

From New York City: Route 684-Saw Mill Parkway north to Exit 6 Katonah-Cross River. Go east on Route 35 to stoplight. Turn right onto Route 22 (Jay Street). Continue to the junction of Girdle Ridge Road (3 miles). Follow signs to Caramoor.

UNION CHURCH OF POCANTICO HILLS

The small stone Union Church on a country road in North Tarrytown is famous for its stained glass windows commissioned by the Rockefeller family. Eight windows by Marc Chagall comprise his only cycle of church windows in this country. Painting directly on the glass, Chagall was able to create vivid tones of blue, green, yellow and red. Combining time-honored artistry with modern techniques, he presents his contemporary interpretation of Old Testament prophets and a dramatic rendering of the Crucifixion ("Seek and Ye Shall Find," *Matthew* 7:7). The more traditional Rose Window above the altar was the last work Henri Matisse completed before his death in 1954. It was dedicated on Mother's Day 1956 to the memory of Abby Aldrich Rockefeller who had been a prominent member of the Union Church. Tours of the sanctuary highlighting its windows are conducted by Historic Hudson Valley.

North Tarrytown, N.Y.
(914) 631-8200

DIRECTIONS:
From West Point: Route 9W south to Tappan Zee Bridge; cross bridge and take Exit 9 for Tarrytown. Route 9 north to Route 448 to Church on right.

From New York City: New York State Thruway (87) north to Exit 9 for Tarrytown. Route 9 north to Route 448 to Church on right.

CHAPTER 14

Hudson Valley Wineries

HIGHLIGHTS...

—See old oak casks in underground cellars

—Learn the age-old art of winemaking

—Picnic in vineyards overlooking the Hudson River

—Taste Chardonnays, Seyval Blancs and Estate Reds in America's oldest grape growing region

Ever since the French Huguenot settlers planted their vineyards in the seventeenth century, grape growing and winemaking have played an important role in the Hudson Valley. The town seal of Marlboro, incorporated in 1788, bears a cluster of grapes acknowledging the significance of the crop to the region. In fact,

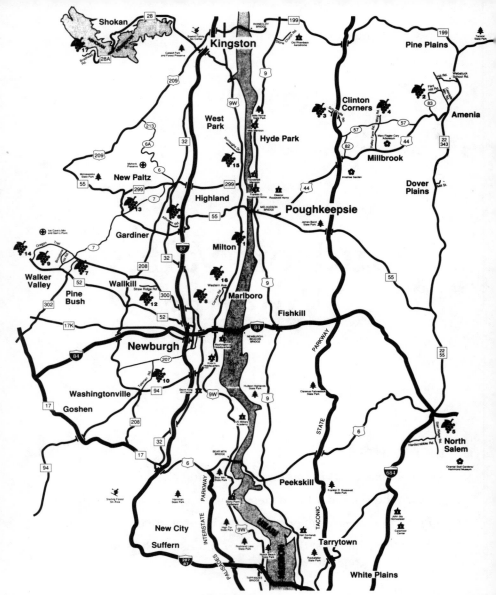

Hudson Valley Winery Directory

East Side of the Hudson River

2. Cascade Mountain Vineyards, Flint Hill Rd., Amenia, NY 12501, (914)373-9021. Open daily 10-6, year 'round. Follow signs 3 miles north on Amenia on Rt. 22. Winery is 4 miles from Rt. 22.

3. Clinton Vineyards, Schultzville Rd., Clinton Corners, NY 12514 (914)266-5372. Open Saturdays, Sundays, Holidays by appointment only. Take Taconic Parkway north to Salt Point Turnpike exit, proceed north through Clinton Corners to Schultzville Rd. Winery 1/4 mile.

4. Millbrook Vineyards, Wing and Shunpike Roads, RR 1, Box 167D, Millbrook, NY 12545, (914)677-8383. Open daily, 11-5. Take Taconic Parkway to Route 44 exit, proceed west on Rt.44, take Rt. 82 north to Shunpike Rd. Go 3 miles to Wing Rd. Winery entrance ahead on right.

5. North Salem Vineyard, Hardscrabble Rd., North Salem, NY 10560 (914)669-5518. Open daily Jun.-Oct. from 1-5. Nov.-May open Sat. and Sun., 1-5. Take Route 684 north to Exit 8. Hardscrabble Road. Proceed east on Hardscrabble 2 1/4 miles to North Salem Vineyard.

West Side of Hudson River

6. Adair Vineyards, 75 Allhusen Road, New Paltz, NY 12561, (914)255-1377. Open daily Apr. - Nov. 12-6. Proceed south on Route 32 from New Paltz for about 6 miles to Allhusen Road. Make left, winery is less than 1/2 mile from intersection on right.

7. Baldwin Vineyards, Hardenburgh Rd., Pine Bush, NY 12566,(914)744-2226. Open weekends 11-5 May, Nov. and Dec., 11-5, Thurs. through Mon., 11-5, June - Oct. Take Rt. 302 North from Rt.17 or Rt.17K. Proceed to Pine Bush and Route 52. Follow signs for one mile to the 1786 Hardenburgh Estate and Baldwin Vineyards.

8. Benmarl Vineyards, Highland Avenue, Marlboro, NY. 12542, (914)236-4265. Open year 'round Mon. - Sun., 11-4. On Route 9W 2 miles south of Marlboro, turn west on Conway Rd. 1 mile to stone gate posts on right.

9. Brimstone Hill Vineyard, Brimstone Hill Road. R.D.2. Pine Bush, NY 12566. (914)744-2231. Open June. July. Aug., Thurs. - Mon., 12-6. Sept. thru May, open weekends. Take Rt. 302 North to Pine Bush and Route 52. Make left on Rt. 52 to New Prospect Road. Make right and follow signs to winery.

10. Brotherhood, America's Oldest Winery. Ltd., 35 North Street, Washingtonville. NY 10992, (914)496-9101. Winery outlet open year 'round except Christmas and New Year's: Tours: Daily May - Oct., 11-6. Weekends only, Jan.-Apr. Nov., Dec., 12-5. Take NY Thruway North to Exit 16 (Harriman) onto Route 17 West. Take Exit 130 onto Route 208 North to Washingtonville. Follow signs to winery.

11. Kedem Royal Winery, Route 9W and Dock Rd. Milton. NY 12547 (914)795-2240. Open May 1 - December 31. Sunday-Friday. 10-4. Open Sundays. year 'round. Closed Saturdays. Take 9W to Milton. Follow signs to Kedem Winery.

12. Magnanini Farm Winery, 501 Straw Ridge Rd., Wallkill, NY (914)8[...] Open Apr. 1 - Dec. 31. Tues.-Sun., 10-6. Closed Jan. - Mar. From Rt. 84[...] 10S, take Rt. 32 north to Rt. 300, go 5 miles and make left on Plains Rd[...] mile and make right on Straw Ridge Rd. Winery 1/2 mile ahead on left.

13. Rivendell Winery, 714 Albany Post Rd., New Paltz, NY 12561, (914[...] 0892. Open all day, every day, year 'round. Closed major holidays. Follo[...] 299 West from New Paltz to Route 7 South (Albany Post Road). Follow [...] miles, winery is on right.

14. Walker Valley Vineyards, Rt. 52. Walker Valley, NY 12588 (914)74[...] Open weekends year round 10-5; open every day June 20-Oct. 20, 10-5[...] Rt. 17 or Rt. 17K proceed on Route 302 North to Pine Bush and Route 5[...] Make left on Rte. 52 and follow to Oregon Trail Rd. Make right and follo[...] yds. to winery.

15. West Park Wine Cellars, Route 9W and Burroughs Drive, West Par[...] 12493, (914)384-6709. Open May - Jan., Fri., Sat. and Sun., 11-6. Loca[...] the corner of 9W and Burroughs Dr. 5 miles north of the Mid-Hudson B[...]

16. Windsor Vineyards, 104 Western Avenue, Marlboro, NY 12542 (91[...] 4233. Open daily 10-5 except Christmas, Thanksgiving and Easter. Take[...] Marlboro. Proceed east on Western Ave. 1/10 mile. Winery is on right.

17. Woodstock Winery, 628 Brodhead Rd., West Shokan. NY 12494 (914) 657-2018 Open Fri.-Mon. for tours, tasting and retail sales by app[...] Take Exit 19 on NY Thruway. Take Route 28 for 12 miles to Shokan. Ma[...] Reservoir Rd. and make next two rights. Make left on Brodhead Road. [...] mile ahead on right.

Marlboro is home to Benmarl, the oldest continuously operated vineyard in the United States. It is the Hudson Valley's intense summer heat and the high shale content of its soil that provide an environment favorable to viticulture. However, the vines native to North America produce grapes more suitable to jam and jelly making than to top quality wines. The *vinifera* varieties from which the fabled European wines are made seemed unable to withstand the harsh New York State winters or the various insects and fungi to which the native vines were immune. For years the Hudson Valley's potential as a winemaking region remained unrealized. It was not until extensive experimentation yielded hybrid vines, combining the characteristics of European grapes with the resiliency of indigenous stock, that wine of good quality could be produced.

Still America was not a wine drinking nation, and wine production along the Hudson was limited. With the culinary revolution of the early 1970s, Americans changed their attitude toward food and drink and began to appreciate fine wine. Winemaking itself has always exerted a fascination upon its enthusiasts. We were told time and time again how what had begun as a hobby had become all-consuming. The passage of the New York State Farm Winery Act in 1977 enabled many backyard vintners to open wineries. Today there are more than thirty along the banks of the Hudson, each one unique. Some produce a single wine while others offer a wide range of whites and reds. The microclimate of each winery dictates to a certain degree the types of grapes that can be grown. Most vineyards are on the west side of the Hudson where it can be ten degrees warmer than across the river to the east. Many vintners believe the future of the Valley lies only in white wines. Lou Fiore of West Park produces only chardonnay, and Ben Feder of Clinton Vineyards has only seyval blanc. However, John Dyson at Millbrook sees great potential in red wines as well. He now sells seven different reds along with his whites and is experimenting with dozens of European rootstocks to produce more reds.

No matter what grapes they grow, most vintners share a belief that the Hudson Valley can produce great wines. Mark Miller of Benmarl, who spent years learning about wines in Burgundy, believes that in the near future demand for the region's wine will far exceed its supply. The Valley now stands where California did in the late 1960s, and people are just beginning to realize its potential. Already good wines are available. Many have been compared to the *vins de pays*, the wines of the European countryside, and like these wines, are at their best when drunk young and served with local fare. As you tour the Valley and taste the wines, the excitement and commitment of these vintners become apparent, and you too may find yourself toasting Hudson Valley wine.

We have highlighted some Hudson Valley wineries that we feel are of special interest because of their quality, their location or their winemaking process. If you've never toured a winery before, you may want to start with Brotherhood Winery where guides take you step by step from grape to bottle and explain the history of the craft. If you're well acquainted with the process, a self-guided tour such as West Park's may be more appropriate for you. The interest in Hudson Valley wines continues to grow, and you may discover wineries newly opened to the public. In addition to the wineries we've described, you may want to try some of the others listed at the end of the chapter.

ADAIR VINEYARDS

Jim Adair makes wine, and Adair Vineyards is as close to a one-man operation as you will find. From the harvesting of the grapes to the monitoring of fermentation to the final bottling, Jim is there. He has equipped his two-hundred-year-old Dutch barn with custom built stainless steel tanks and Italian-made, hand-operated machinery. His label is a story in itself. Even before he purchased the site, Jim had chosen Asher Durand's Hudson River School landscape "Solitary Oak" as his trademark.

Perhaps it was Fate. Not only does an old oak tree stand near a brook in his vineyard, but he later learned that Adair means "ford by the oak" in Gaelic.

Like the operation itself, the tour is truly personal. Jim Adair is expert at explaining his winemaking process. He demonstrates how he presses the grapes, how fermentation takes place and then how he fills his bottles, corks them and glues on labels. Jim says that the hardest part of his business is the cleaning up. "All you're doing is doing dishes." He may hate the cleaning, but he does a great job. The winery is immaculate.

75 Allhusen Road
New Paltz, N.Y.
(914) 255-1377

DIRECTIONS:
From West Point: Route 9W north to Route 84 west; take Route 32 north past Route 55 and make a right onto Allhusen Road. Winery is one-half mile on right.

From New York City: New York State Thruway (87) north to Exit 18 New Paltz. West onto Route 299 to Route 32 south. Go six miles on Route 32 south to Allhusen Road. Make left. Winery is one-half mile on right.

BENMARL WINERY

In 1971, when Benmarl Winery's proprietor Mark Miller went into Manhattan to market his wines, he found only six wine shops in the whole city, none of which was interested in selling Hudson Valley wines. Not even California wines were acceptable to the few people who drank wine at the time, since European wines were considered the only wines worth drinking. But Mark Miller had a mission. He believed in the potential of the Hudson Valley as a wine producing region, and he had over thirty years worth of knowledge and experience behind him.

While living in Burgundy and pursuing a career as an illustrator, Miller was befriended by many *vignerons* and *négociants.* They took him through their vineyards, into their cellars and shared with him their skills and traditions. Miller was even given the rare honor of membership in *La Confrérie des Chevaliers*

du Tâstevin. He returned to the United States with renewed
enthusiasm, and what had begun as a backyard hobby became
his profession. Planting his upper vineyard with one hundred
different vines, he began his search for the varieties that would
thrive and produce wines equal to those he had known in

Burgundy. He was determined to make wine an integral part of American culture, just as important as it has always been in France. He firmly believed that each course of a meal should be complemented with an appropriate wine. His years of experimentation have paid off. From his light seyval blancs to his Nevers oak-aged reds, Mark Miller's wines are a testimony to his belief that future demand for Hudson River wines will far exceed the supply.

Benmarl's acres of vines sloping down toward the Hudson and the view of the Berkshires beyond make it easy to understand why this artist-turned-winemaker says he bought the property for the landscape alone. When visiting the winery, allow time for a picnic lunch and for a tour of the galley displaying Mark Miller's art and illustrations. If this winery captures your imagination, you can join its *Société des Vignerons*. Members sponsor plots or "vinerights," and for their patronage they receive a case of personally labeled wine every vintage year. *Société* members are also feted at special winery events throughout the year. Mark Miller's dedication to excellent wines is helping to win recognition for the Hudson Valley as a fine wine producing region.

Highland Avenue
Marlboro, N.Y.
(914) 236-4265

DIRECTIONS:
From West Point: Route 9W north past town of Middlehope. Left onto Conway Road. Right onto Highland Avenue. Look for signs to Benmarl Winery on the right.

From New York City: New York State Thruway (87) north to Exit 17 Newburgh. Route 84 east to Route 9W north past town of Middlehope. Left onto Conway Road. Right onto Highland Avenue. Look for signs to Benmarl Winery on the right.

BROTHERHOOD WINERY

Twenty-eight feet underground, surrounded by old oak casks and the yeasty smell of fermentation, visitors to Brotherhood

Winery realize they are in the cellars of America's oldest winery. In continuous operation since 1839, Brotherhood weathered the years of Prohibition by producing its sacramental wine Rosario. In fact, it is said that during those years the nearby town of Washingtonville boasted the highest number of priests per capita in the nation, each household listing at least one. Today under Winemaster Cesar Baeza, Brotherhood is focusing its production on premium varietal wines. To achieve this goal, they are buying European style *vinifera* grapes grown in the Finger Lakes and Long Island regions of New York State. (Brotherhood no longer owns its own vineyards.)

Brotherhood's tour begins in a vaulted wine storage room with a slide presentation on the history of winemaking and of the winery. Leading the way through cool cellars, guides point

out barrels of wine in various stages of development and champagne in riddling racks, while describing how the one-hundred-year-old oak casks flavor the wine within. In addition, guides provide practical information on the care of wine, explaining that the cellars, registering fifty-five degrees, are the perfect climate for wine storage. Room temperature for wines actually means fifty-five degrees, and chilling a wine means serving it only ten degrees cooler. At the end of the tour, visitors have an opportunity to sample the final product and compare a number of Brotherhood's traditional wines, albeit in plastic cups. For an extra fee (reimbursable with a purchase), the premium varietals may also be tasted.

35 North Street
Washingtonville, N.Y.
(914) 496-9101

DIRECTIONS:
From West Point: Route 293 south to Route 6 west to Route 17 west. Take Exit 130 onto Route 208 north to Washingtonville. In town, make left at Gulf Station onto North Street. Winery is a short distance on right.

From New York City: New York State Thruway (87) north to Exit 16 Harriman. Route 17 west to Exit 130. Route 208 north to Washingtonville. In town, make left at Gulf Station onto North Street. Winery is a short distance on right.

CASCADE MOUNTAIN VINEYARDS

Chef Melissa Bernard believes that local foods and local wines go together. At Cascade Mountain's restaurant, her menus feature creative regional dishes designed with the vineyard's wines in mind. She uses goats' milk cheese from nearby farms, fruits from neighboring orchards and garden vegetables—whatever is fresh and in season. The dining room is simple and bright. Whitewashed walls, wooden beams and dried flowers surround tables covered in country French chintz. In warm weather, guests may eat outside on the deck.

Laminated on the back of the restaurant's menu are directions for a quick walk-through of the winemaking operation downstairs. Tastings are offered, and some of the products used by

Chef Bernard can be purchased along with the wine.

Flint Hill Road
Amenia, N.Y.
(914) 373-9021

DIRECTIONS:
From West Point: Route 9W north to Route 84 east. Cross Newburgh-Beacon Bridge and continue on Route 84 east to Taconic Parkway north. Take Millbrook exit, Route 44 east through Millbrook to Amenia. Left onto Route 22 north for 3 miles to sign on left for winery.

From New York City: Taconic Parkway north to Millbrook exit. Route 44 east through Millbrook to Amenia. Left onto Route 22 north for 3 miles to sign on left for winery.

CLINTON VINEYARDS

Against the advice of the experts at Cornell University, Ben Feder decided to plant only one variety of grape at Clinton Vineyards. Encouraged by fourth generation winemaker Herman Wiemer, he determined that seyval blanc was the grape most suitable for producing excellent wine in the Hudson Valley. In fact, Mr. Feder believes that this region's future success in winemaking lies in the white wines for which its climate is most appropriate. Good red wines require a longer growing season in which grapes can continue to mature well into the fall months. In the Hudson Valley, the ripening process can sometimes stop as early as Labor Day.

His fourteen acres of seyval blanc grapes are terraced in rows just above the old barn where the wine is made. Visitors can walk among the vines and see the clusters of grapes ripening throughout the summer months. Clinton Vineyards turns a small amount of its seyval blanc into sparkling wine using the French *méthode champenoise.* Both the wine and the champagne have been very well received. (Twenty cases of champagne were once sent to New York City to serve President Bush at a gala dinner.) Mr. Feder has modeled Clinton Vineyards after the small wine estates of Europe, and he does not foresee expansion. Thus, the demand for these wines may continue to exceed the supply.

Schultzville Road
Clinton Corners, N.Y.
(914) 266-5372

DIRECTIONS:
From West Point: Route 9W north to Route 55 east. Cross Mid-Hudson Bridge to Route 44 east to Taconic Parkway. Go north on Taconic Parkway to Salt Point Turnpike exit. Follow signs north through Clinton Corners. Make left onto Schultzville Road. Winery is on left.

From New York City: Taconic Parkway north to Salt Point Turnpike exit. Follow signs north through Clinton Corners. Make left onto Schultzville Road. Winery is on left.

MILLBROOK VINEYARDS

A gravel road winds its way to Millbrook Vineyards through rows and rows of vines with lush, leafy canopies and cluster upon cluster of grapes. Here in the heart of Dutchess County, John Dyson, the former New York State Commissioner of Argriculture and Commerce, has set out to prove that the noble *vinifera* grapes of Europe can thrive in the Hudson Valley. He has planted over thirty varieties of these vines including chardonnay, pinot noir, merlot, cabernet sauvignon and riesling. In a controlled, scientific manner, he has developed innovative viticultural techniques which have shown that these grapes can be successfully grown in the Hudson Valley despite the harsh winters. The red *vinifera* varieties must have an abundance of sunlight and sufficient time on the vine to develop their full potential. With the shade-producing traditional trellis system and the early frosts in New York State, this was frequently impossible. To overcome these obstacles, John Dyson developed the goblet trellis which allows greater penetration of sunlight and better air circulation around the vines. Growing the pinot noir grape on both types of trellises, he has demonstrated that the grapes from the goblet trellis are more plentiful and make better wine.

On his one hundred thirty acres of rolling farmland, Mr. Dyson has planted forty-five acres of vines and is continually committing more acreage to established and experimental varieties. The old Dutch hip-roofed dairy barn is now a state-of-the-art winery complete with a modern laboratory, Tuscan-arched barrel aging room, and automated bottling facility. Upstairs the old hay loft is a tasting room where Millbrook's varietals and Hunt Country table wines can be sampled. Looking out over the vineyards, visitors may see tractors terracing the hillside, workers pruning the vines or grapes being harvested, testimony to Dyson's belief in the Hudson Valley as a premium wine producing area and his commitment to its future.

Wing and Shunpike Roads
Millbrook, N.Y.
(914) 677-8383

DIRECTIONS:
From West Point: Route 9W north to Route 84 east. Cross Newburgh-Beacon Bridge. Remain on 84 east to Taconic Parkway north. Exit Route 44 east to Millbrook. Take Route 82 north three and one-half miles to Shunpike Road (Route 57). Right onto Shunpike Road three miles to Wing Road. Left onto Wing Road to winery.

From New York City: Taconic Parkway north to Route 44 east to Millbrook. Take Route 82 north three and one-half miles to Shunpike Road (Route 57). Right onto Shunpike Road three miles to Wing Road. Left onto Wing Road to winery.

WEST PARK WINE CELLARS

West Park produces only one wine—a chardonnay. Despite the belief that the chardonnay grape could not flourish in the Hudson Valley, Lou Fiore was determined to produce a wine as fine as those he had tasted in France. There the chardonnay grape produces chablis, Montrachet and Merseault among others, and it was wines of such quality to which he aspired. So far the experiment has met with success. Even with his "silent partners"—one year the birds and deer ate twenty percent of his crop; another year the rain took its toll—Lou Fiore has been able to produce a consistently good wine. His first vintage, released in 1984, received good reviews, and all vintages since have sold out. West Park's chardonnay appears on the wine lists of some of the finest restaurants of New York City and the Hudson Valley.

On his 800 acres of land, Lou Fiore has built his winery and cafe. In the old dairy barn wooden panels explain the history of winemaking and describe the special care taken at West Park to ensure that the highest standards are maintained in every step of the winemaking process. Visitors are invited to taste the wine as they watch a ten-minute video about West Park's operations. Picnic lunches are available. You can eat in the cafe near the sixty-gallon Limousin oak aging barrels or lunch outdoors. Just outside is a vine-covered arbor, and tables are scattered along the vineyard. A steep path leads to a picnic area on a ridge high above the Hudson River. Lou Fiore's wine should convince others that the chardonnay grape has an important future in the Hudson Valley.

Route 9W and Burroughs Drive
West Park, N.Y.
(914) 384-6709

DIRECTIONS:
From West Point: Route 9W north to Burroughs Drive (five miles north of Mid-Hudson Bridge). Left onto Burroughs Drive and follow signs to winery.

From New York City: New York State Thruway (87) north to Exit 17 Newburgh. Route 84 east to Route 9W north. Left onto Burroughs Drive and follow signs to winery.

OTHER HUDSON VALLEY WINERIES

Baldwin Vineyards
Hardenburgh Road
Pine Bush, NY 12566
(914) 744-2226

Brimstone Hill Vineyard
Brimstone Hill Road
R.D. 2
Pine Bush, NY 12566
(914) 744-2231

North Salem Vineyard
Hardscrabble Road
North Salem, NY 10560
(914) 669-5518

Rivendell Winery
714 Albany Post Road
New Paltz, NY 12561
(914) 255-0892

Kedem Royal Winery
Route 9W and Dock Road
Milton, NY 12547
(914) 795-2240

Magnanini Farm Winery
501 Straw Ridge Road
Wallkill, NY 12589
(914) 895-2767

Walker Valley Vineyards
Route 52
Walker Valley, NY 12588
(914) 744-3449

Windsor Vineyards
104 Western Avenue
Marlboro, NY 12542
(914) 236-4233

Woodstock Winery
62B Brodhead Road
West Shokan, NY 12494
(914) 657-2018

APPENDIX I

Restaurants and Lodging

Restaurant listings precede lodging information. All information was accurate at the time of publication. However, readers should be aware that changes often occur in chefs, management, ownership and hours of operation. (A) following a restaurant or lodging description indicates that the authors have personally visited the establishment.

AMENIA

Cascade Mountain Winery
Flint Hill Road
(914) 373-9021

Lunch—May-December, daily
   12:00 P.M.-3:00 P.M.
Dinner—Saturday only
   7:00 P.M. seating, reservations
   needed.

C.I.A. graduate chef Melissa Bernard prepares creative dishes featuring local foods with Cascade Mountain wines. Whitewashed walls, wooden beams, country French chintz. (A)

CATSKILL

Mike's
7 Main Street
(518) 943-5352

Kitchen opens at 4:00 P.M.
Closed Mondays.
 Charbroiled steak and chops
and pizza. Highbacked wooden
booths, dark wood paneling,
white tablecloths. Located near
the water in a marine-industrial
area.

Pegasus
Route 9W, five miles north of
Catskill
(518) 731-9200

Lunch and dinner daily
 11:30 A.M.-9:30 P.M.
 Saturdays open until 10:00 P.M.
 Seafood, sandwiches and omelettes served in large diner-like
setting. (A)

COLD SPRING

Cold Spring Depot
Foot of Main Street
(914) 265-2305

Lunch, dinner and snacks daily
 12:00 P.M.-11:00 P.M.
 Burgers, snacks and old-fashioned soda fountain treats served
in old train station. Clam bar and
outside tables with view of river.
(A)

Dockside Harbor
1 North Street
(914) 265-3503

Lunch—Tuesday-Sunday
 12:00 P.M.-3:30 P.M.
Dinner—Tuesday-Thursday
 5:00 P.M.-9:30 P.M.
Dinner—Friday and Saturday
 5:00 P.M.-11:00 P.M.
Dinner—Sunday
 5:00 P.M.-9:00 P.M.
Closed Mondays.
 Seafood items a specialty. Outside tables with view of river.

Hudson House
2 Main Street
(914) 265-9355

Lunch—Monday-Saturday
 11:30 A.M.-3:00 P.M.
Lunch—Sunday
 12:00 P.M.-3:00 P.M.
Dinner—Tuesday-Thursday
 5:30 P.M.-9:00 P.M.
Dinner—Friday and Saturday
 5:30 P.M.-10:00 P.M.
Dinner—Sunday
 5:30 P.M.-8:30 P.M.
Closed Mondays out of season.
 Yankee fare served in early
nineteenth-century inn with
views of Hudson River. Half
Moon Bar and Lounge, fires blazing in the winter. (A)

Plumbush
Route 9D
(914) 265-3904, -9764

Lunch—Monday-Saturday
  12:00 P.M.-2:30 P.M.
Dinner—Monday-Saturday
  5:30 P.M.-9:30 P.M.
Sunday—brunch
  12:00 P.M.-2:30 P.M.
Sunday—dinner
  2:30 P.M.-8:00 P.M.
Closed Tuesdays.

Nineteenth-century home, former country residence of Marchesa Rizzo dei Ritii (née Agnes Shewan). Heavy Swiss and Continental fare; some lighter meals at lunch. We preferred the smaller, intimate rooms to the larger dark paneled or wallpapered dining rooms. (A)

The River House
45 Fair Street
(914) 265-3166

Lunch—Tuesday-Friday
  11:00 A.M.-3:00 P.M.
Dinner—Tuesday-Sunday
  5:00 P.M.-10:00 P.M.
Brunch—Saturday
  11:00 A.M.-3:00 P.M.
Brunch—Sunday
  12:00 P.M.-4:00 P.M.

Soups, salads, pastas and omelettes served in bright, contemporary dining room. River view with intervening parking lot. Ample portions. Creative preparation. (A)

Vintage Cafe
Main Street (in the courtyard)
(914) 265-4726

Lunch—Monday-Saturday
  11:30 A.M.-2:30 P.M.
Lunch—Sunday
  12:00 P.M.-3:00 P.M.
Dinner daily
  6:00 P.M.-9:30 P.M.

Small cafe with authentic country feel. Creatively prepared dishes with fresh, local ingredients. Exceptional pastas and salads. Homemade desserts. (A)

☆   ☆   ☆

Hudson House
2 Main Street
(914) 265-9355
15 rooms, 2 suites: all have private baths

Second oldest continually operating inn in New York State, pleasant public rooms. Bar and restaurant. Some rooms have lovely river views. The restaurant, lounge area and third floor bedrooms are air conditioned. Second floor bedrooms have ceiling fans. (A)

The Olde Post Inn
43 Main Street
(914) 265-2510
6 air conditioned rooms, furnished with antiques, shared baths

Easy walk from the train station to this 1820 inn listed on the National Register of Historic Homes. Patio and garden. Relaxed atmosphere. Continental breakfast. Jazz in the Tavern (the inn's stone and brick cellar) Friday and Saturday nights. (A)

Pig Hill Bed and Breakfast
73 Main Street
(914) 265-9247
8 rooms, some with fireplaces and private baths

Antique-filled rooms, tastefully decorated (furnishings available for purchase). Breakfast served in room or downstairs in the terraced garden or in the dining room. The innkeeper's careful touch is evident everywhere. With advance notice kitchen will prepare picnic lunches and dinners. (A)

Plumbush
Roue 9D
(914) 265-3904
3 rooms, all with private baths

Rooms nicely appointed. Shared sitting room which can be combined with one or two bedrooms to make a suite. Above restaurant in Victorian country house. (See write-up above.) (A)

CORNWALL-ON-HUDSON

Painter's Tavern
8 Idlewild Ave.
(914) 534-2109

Daily
    11:30 A.M.-10:00 P.M.
Sunday—Brunch
    12:00 P.M.-3:00 P.M.
Friday and Saturday closes at 10:30 P.M.
    Small and informal—just a scenic drive away from West Point in the midst of the Hudson Highlands. Owned by two artists, the restaurant is decorated with contemporary art, much of which is for sale. Light creative meals featuring focaccia, innovative salads, hamburgers, vegetarian specialties and over 50 types of imported beer.

GARRISON

Bird and Bottle
Old Albany Post Road (Route 9)
(914) 424-3000

Lunch—Monday-Saturday
12:00 P.M.-2:30 P.M.
Dinner—Monday-Friday
6:30 P.M.-9:30 P.M.
Dinner—Saturday seatings
6:00 P.M. and 9:00 P.M.
Dinner—Sunday
3:00 P.M.-7:00 P.M.
Pub lunch, Sunday brunch, full course Continental dinner served in country inn established in 1761. Wood burning fireplaces, beamed ceilings and wide plank floors. Could use some work; dining room was damp, cold and dark when we visited. (A)

Xaviar's
Route 9D (on the grounds of Highland Country Club)
(914) 424-4228

Dinner—weekdays
6:00 P.M.-9:00 P.M.
Saturday seatings
6:00 P.M. and 9:00 P.M.
Sunday brunch
Closed month of January.
Fresh, innovative French/American cuisine served in huge, rather bare room softened by flowers and candlelight. Lovely terrace overlooking golf course. Quality service. Harpist and violinist Fridays and Saturdays. (A)

HIGH FALLS

DePuy Canal House
Route 213
(914) 687-7700

Dinner—Thursday-Saturday
5:30 P.M.-9:00 P.M.
Dinner—Sunday
4:00 P.M.-8:30 P.M.
Sunday brunch
11:30 A.M.-2:00 P.M.
Extraordinary dining in 1797 old stone tavern. Astonishingly creative offerings such as cepes sautéd in olive oil and capers served with morel nicoise paté; pheasant breast, calves liverwurst and smoked pork loin on tarragon umebushi sauce; catfish Cajun style with mesquite grilled baby eggplant. Imaginative creations prepared by chef/owner John Novi. Candlelight, fresh flowers, four fireplaces. Comfortable elegance. Menus change weekly. Exceptional restaurant. Call for reservations. (See Chapter 7.) (A)

The Egg's Nest Saloon
Route 213
(914) 687-7255

Daily from 11:30 A.M.-11:00 P.M.
Dinner
6:00 P.M.-11:00 P.M.
Fridays and Saturdays open until
1:00 A.M.
Hot and cold sandwiches, prae-seaux (a crispy pizza). Dinner specialties. Casual atmosphere. (A)

Captain Schoonmaker's Bed and Breakfast
Route 213
(914) 687-7946
9 bedrooms, shared baths

Built in 1760 by Captain Frederick Schoonmaker, a prosperous Ulster County landowner. The Captain spent his entire personal fortune (between $50,000-$60,000 in property and money) in support of the patriot cause in the Revolutionary War. He died penniless. The main house has five bedrooms with shared bath. The carriage house offers four rooms, two baths and overlooks a woodland stream. (One room has a fireplace.) Wine and cheese served on patio in summer and in the library in winter. Closed two weeks in April. (A)

Lock Tender's Cottage
Roue 213
(914) 687-7700
2 bedrooms, 1 suite, all have private baths

A delightful 1853 cottage with two rooms on the first floor, each with private bath and one with fireplace. A suite on the second floor has a small kitchen, dining area and bath with jacuzzi. All rooms are furnished with antiques. Innkeeper John Novi also runs the extraordinary DePuy Canal House restaurant just across the street. (See Chapter 7 and above.) (A)

Tow Path House
Route 213
(914) 687-7946
4 rooms, shared baths

Run by the owners of Captain Schoonmaker's. Four rooms, two baths. Eccentric floor plan (to reach other rooms, guests must walk through first floor bedroom). Wrought iron gate. Townhouse feel. Antique shop across the street. Convenient to DePuy Canal House restaurant. (A)

HIGHLAND FALLS

Park Restaurant
64 Main Street
(914) 446-8709

Wednesday-Friday
11:00 A.M.-11:30 P.M.
Breakfast—Friday, Saturday and
Sunday
8:00 A.M. to 11:00 A.M.
Lunch & Dinner
Friday and Saturday until 12
midnight
Sunday until 11:00 P.M.
Lighter fare after 9:00 P.M.
Soups, sandwiches and cold
platters. Full course meals available until 9:00 P.M. (A)

Schade's
54 Main Street (Directly across
from the United States Military
Academy Visitors' Information
Center)
(914) 446-2626

Lunch served daily in the dining
room
11:00 A.M.-4:00 P.M.
Deli open at 6:00 A.M. for take-out
breakfasts
Homemade soups and sandwiches as well as full dinners;
Mexican specialties and pizzas.
Large selections of beer and
liqueur-flavored coffees. Seating
in comfortable booths. (A)

HOPEWELL JUNCTION

Le Chambord Restaurant and Inn
2075 Route 52
(914) 221-1941

Lunch—Monday-Friday
11:30 A.M.-2:30 P.M.
Dinner—Monday-Saturday
6:00 P.M.-10:00 P.M.
Dinner—Sunday
3:00 P.M.-9:00 P.M.
Elegant French dining in 1863
Georgian colonial. Candlelight,
fireplaces, crystal chandeliers and
oil paintings on the walls. Patio
dining in summer. Gracious service and award-winning food. (A)

Le Chambord Restaurant and Inn
2075 Route 52
(914) 221-1941
24 rooms, private baths

Eight rooms in 1863 Georgian
colonial with sixteen rooms in adjoining Tara Hall. Furnished with
antiques and country pieces. All
rooms have private baths. Lovely
country setting. Four-star French
cuisine served in elegant formal
dining rooms. (See above.)

HUDSON

Brandow's
344 Warren Street (next to Hose Company #2)
(518) 828-2388

Lunch—Tuesday-Saturday
11:00 A.M.-2:30 P.M.
Dinner—Friday and Saturday
5:30 P.M.-10:00 P.M.
Closed Sundays and Mondays.
Fresh, creative meals. Fish, chicken and pasta dishes. Soups and salads for lunch. Homemade pastries. Dinner menu changes weekly. (A)

Charleston
517 Warren Street
(518) 828-4990

Lunch from 11:30 A.M.
Dinner from 5:30 P.M.
Sunday—1:00 P.M.-8:00 P.M.
Closed Wednesdays.
Lunch and dinner served; linen tablecloths, creative American cooking; children's portions available.

The Columbia Diner
717 Warren Street
(518) 828-9083

Open daily for breakfast, lunch and dinner.
Monday-Saturday
6:00 A.M.-9:00 P.M.
Sunday
7:00 A.M.-3:00 P.M.
Typical aluminum-sided diner, surprisingly large inside, neon decor. (A)

The Mouse House
701 Warren Street
(518) 828-4840

Monday-Saturday
9:00 A.M.-4:00 P.M.
Lunch served
11:30 A.M.-2:30 P.M.
Closed Sundays.
Eight tables. Soup and sandwiches, quiches and chili. Baked stuffed potatoes a specialty. Homemade desserts. Daily specials on blackboard. (A)

Sweet Time
12 Park Place
(518) 828-6388

Breakfast and lunch and take-out menu.
Monday-Saturday
7:00 A.M.-3:00 P.M.
Sunday
7:00 A.M.-12:00 P.M.
Counter and six tables; homemade soups, salads and ice cream as well as special ice cream cakes. Fresh deli sandwiches, hamburgers, omelettes. Spanish specials on Thursdays. (A)

HYDE PARK

**Culinary Institute of
America (C.I.A.)**
Route 9
(914) 471-6608
(See Chaper 11)

American Bounty
Lunch—Tuesday-Saturday
11:30 A.M.-1:00 P.M.
Dinner—Tuesday-Saturday
6:30 P.M.-8:30 P.M.
Closed Sundays and Mondays.
American regional cuisine in lovely room overlooking court-yard of old Jesuit seminary. (A)

Caterina de Medici
Lunch—Monday-Friday
12:00 P.M. (one seating)
Dinner—Monday-Friday
6:00 P.M. (one seating)
Closed weekends.
Traditional and regional dishes of Italy. Good selection of Italian wines.

Escoffier Room
Lunch—Tuesday-Saturday
12:00 P.M.-1:00 P.M.
Dinner—Tuesday-Saturday
6:30 P.M.-8:30 P.M.
Closed Sundays and Mondays.
Classic and nouvelle French cuisine served in elegantly ap-pointed dining room, overlooking the Hudson River. (A)

St. Andrew's Cafe
Lunch—Monday-Friday
11:30 A.M.-1:00 P.M.
Dinner—Monday-Friday
6:00 P.M.
Closed weekends.
Healthy and low calorie foods with an emphasis on combining nutrition and good taste. (A)

Easy Street Cafe
Route 9 (south of F.D.R. Home)
(914) 229-7969

Monday-Saturday
11:30 A.M.-10:00 P.M.
Dinner—4:30 P.M.-10:00 P.M.
Sunday lunch and dinner
12:00 P.M.-9:00 P.M.
Spacious family restaurant dubbed cafe/saloon by owners. Soups, salads, sandwich platters, daily pasta and quiche specials. (A)

Springwood Inn
Route 9
(914) 229-2681

Lunch daily—11:30 A.M.-4:00 P.M.
Dinner daily—4:00 P.M.-9:00 P.M.
Soups, sandwiches and salads as well as complete meals. Bright greenhouse room serves as one of the dining areas. Directly across from F.D.R. Home and Library. (A)

KINGSTON

Rondout Landing

Armadillo Bar and Grill
97 Abeel Street
(914) 339-1550

Lunch—Tuesday-Friday
    11:30 A.M.-3:00 P.M.
Lunch—Saturday-Sunday
    12:00 P.M.-3:00 P.M.
Dinner—Tuesday-Friday
    4:30 P.M.-10:30 P.M.
Dinner—Saturday
    5:00 P.M.-11:30 P.M.
Dinner—Sunday
    4:00 P.M.-10:00 P.M.
Closed Mondays.
    Southwestern cuisine. Tex-Mex specialties. Fresh grilled seafood prepared on open grill in kitchen. Outdoor dining in summer.

Mary P's
1 Broadway on the Rondout
(914) 338-0116

Lunch daily—11:30 A.M.-3:00 P.M.
Dinner daily—4:30 P.M.-9:00 P.M.
    Northern Italian specialties, spacious dining room and bar area, lively atmosphere. On the waterfront.

Rosita's
3-5 West Strand
(914) 339-5372

Lunch—Tuesday-Friday
    11:30 A.M.-3:00 P.M.
Dinner—Tuesday-Sunday
    3:00 P.M.-9:30 P.M.
Closed Mondays.
    Mexican cuisine. Family owned.

**Rondout Ice Cream &
Cookie Company**
19 West Strand
(914) 338-0744

Lunch and snacks daily
    Soups, salads, ice cream and sweets, specialty coffees. Gift items.

Stockade District

City Fare
50 John Street
(914) 331-1559

10:00 A.M.-5:30 P.M.
Closed Sundays and Mondays.

Homemade pastries, gourmet salads and sandwiches, breads and main courses to take out. Excellent cappuccino. (A)

Hoffman House
94 N. Front Street
(914) 338-2626

Lunch and dinner daily.
Monday-Saturday
11:30 A.M.-10:30 P.M.
Sunday
1:00 P.M.-10:30 P.M.
Continental cuisine served in historic old stone house. Sandwiches available at lunch. Patio dining in warm weather. (A)

Jane's Homemade Ice Cream
305 Wall Street
(914) 338-8315

Monday-Saturday
9:00 A.M.-9:00 P.M.
Closed Sundays.
Ice cream, cookies and other desserts.

Schneller's Restaurant and Market
61 John Street
(914) 331-9800

Restaurant
Lunch—Monday, Wednesday-Saturday
11:30 A.M.-4:00 P.M.
Dinner—Monday, Wednesday, Thursday, Sunday
5:00 P.M.-9:00 P.M.
Friday and Saturday
5:00 P.M.-10:00 P.M.
Closed Tuesdays.
German cuisine. Meat and fish specialties. Homemade desserts, exceptional strudel. Outdoor beer garden.

Market
Open Monday-Saturday
7:30 A.M.-5:30 P.M.
Friday until 7:00 P.M.
Closed Sundays.
Superb homemade wursts of all types, meats and fowl, cold cuts, cheeses and salads. Large selection of beer. Candy counter. Gourmet items. Toys. A real find. (A)

Elsewhere in Kingston

La Parmigiana
604 Ulster Ave.
(914) 338-1026

Lunch—Tuesday-Friday
11:00 A.M.-2:00 P.M.
Dinner—Tuesday-Friday
4:00 P.M.-10:00 P.M.

Dinner—Saturday
1:00 P.M.-10:00 P.M.
Dinner—Sunday
1:00 P.M.-9:00 P.M.
Closed Mondays.
Wood-fired, brick oven pizza. Fresh pasta. Take out available.

Montauk House
395 Albany Avenue
(914) 331-3474

Dinner only.
Tuesday-Saturday
 4:00 P.M.-10:00 P.M.
Sunday
 1:00 P.M.-9:00 P.M.
Closed Mondays.
 Fresh seafood; steaks and chops. Gourmet shop in front, restaurant in back.

Reginato Ristorante
Leggs Mill Road
Lake Katrine
(914) 336-6968

Lunch—Monday, Wednesday-Friday
 11:30 A.M.-2:30 P.M.
Dinner—Monday, Wednesday-Saturday
 5:00 P.M.-10:00 P.M.
Dinner—Sunday
 1:00 P.M.-10:00 P.M.
Closed Tuesdays.
 Traditional Italian cuisine, prepared with care; each order individually cooked. Accommodating service. (A)

MARLBORO

Benmarl Bistro
Highland Avenue
(914) 236-4265

Lunch on weekends during the season.
 Light French bistro fare. Paté, breads, cheeses, grilled specialties. Pasta salads and sandwiches served in informal country room at Benmarl Winery. Lunches can be taken to picnic tables outside with beautiful view of the vineyards and the Berkshires. (A)

Racoon Saloon
Route 9W, Main Street
(914) 236-7872

Lunch
 11:30 A.M.-3:00 P.M.
Dinner—Tuesday-Thursday
 5:00 P.M.-9:00 P.M.
Dinner—Friday and Saturday
 5:00 P.M.-10:00 P.M.
Dinner—Sunday
 12:00 P.M.-9:00 P.M.
 Tavern setting; homemade soups, sandwiches, fried fish and chips. Full meals at dinner. (A)

NEW PALTZ

DuBois Fort
81 Huguenot Street
(914) 255-1771

Lunch—12:00 P.M.-2:00 P.M.
Dinner—5:30 P.M.-7:30 P.M.
Sundays—12:00 P.M.-4:00 P.M.
Closed Mondays and winter months.

Interior and food do not live up to the promise of the historic stone house and surroundings of Huguenot Street. Full lunches and dinners, heavy and rather unimaginative. (A)

The Locust Tree Inn Restaurant
215 Huguenot Street
(914) 255-7888

Lunch—Tuesday-Friday
11:30 A.M.-2:30 P.M.
Dinner—Tuesday-Saturday
5:30 P.M.-10:00 P.M.
Sunday brunch
11:00 A.M.-2:00 P.M.
Sunday dinner
3:00 P.M.-8:00 P.M.
Closed Mondays.

Three dining rooms each with a fireplace in stone and wood farm house dating back to 1759. Nine-hole golf course, open to the public, was once farmland owned by the Huguenot Elting family. Comfortable country setting. Continental menu, fresh ingredients, lighter lunches available as well as full course meals at lunch and dinner. Patio for outside dining overlooks the golf course. (A)

Mohonk Mountain House
Lake Mohonk
(914) 255-1000
300 rooms

Three hundred room, Victorian resort on glacial lake in Shawangunk Mountains. Family activities; cross country skiing and ice skating in winter; swimming, canoeing, horseback riding in summer; hiking on miles of carriage trails year round. Full American plan. Facilities gracious but beginning to show their age. (A)

NEW YORK CITY

Hudson River Club
250 Vesey Street
(in the World Financial Center)
(212) 786-1500

Lunch—Monday-Friday
12:00 P.M.-2:30 P.M.
Dinner—Monday-Saturday
5:30 P.M.-10:00 P.M.

A taste of the Hudson Valley in New York City. Three-tier dining room overlooking New York Harbor with Hudson River School landscapes hanging on light oak paneled walls. Features foods and wines from the Hudson Valley.

RED HOOK

Green and Bressler's
29 West Market Street
(914) 758-5992

Lunch—Tuesday-Saturday
11:00 A.M.-3:30 P.M.
Dinner—Thursday-Saturday
5:30 P.M.-9:30 P.M.
Sunday brunch
11:00 A.M.-3:00 P.M.
Closed Wednesdays.

Soups, fresh salads made with local produce and open-faced sandwiches on grilled French bread for lunch. Pasta salads, marinated vegetables and cheeses to take out. Great picnic fare. More substantial offerings for dinner. Wonderful desserts. Cafe atmosphere.

Taste Buds
139 South Broadway
(914) 876-1606

Lunch—Wednesday-Sunday
11:00 A.M.-3:00 P.M.
Dinner—Wednesday-Sunday
6:00 P.M.-10:00 P.M.
Sunday brunch
10:00 A.M.-3:00 P.M.
Closed Mondays and Tuesdays.

Gourmet take-out and restaurant. Specializes in pasta, soups and salads. C.I.A.-trained chef.

RHINEBECK

Beekman Arms
Junction of Route 9 and Route 308
(914) 876-7077

Lunch—Monday-Saturday
11:30 A.M.-3:00 P.M.
Dinner—Monday-Saturday
5:00 P.M.-9:30 P.M.
Sunday brunch
10:00 A.M.-2:00 P.M.
Sunday dinner
3:30 P.M.-8:30 P.M.
Colonial dark wood paneled Tap Room and Greenhouse Restaurant. Fresh fish, meat and produce, local whenever possible, prepared with a creative flair. Not the heavy, traditional pub food. Helpful, friendly and leisurely service in a 1766 historic inn. (A)

Le Petit Bistro
8 East Market Street
(914) 876-7400

Dinner—5:00 P.M.-10:00 P.M.
Sunday—4:00 P.M.-9:00 P.M.
Closed Tuesdays and Wednesdays.

Light country French cooking served to perfection by chef/owners Jean-Paul and Yvonne Croizer. Pine paneling, soft lighting, small intimate dining room with attractive bar area. Daily specials. Reservations sometimes necessary. (A)

Schemmy's Ice Cream Parlor
19 East Market Street
(914) 876-6215

Breakfast, lunch and afternoon snacks
Daily 8:00 A.M.-5:00 P.M.
Soups, sandwiches and ice cream treats served in converted circa 1858 drug store. Black and white tile floor, wooden booths, small round tables and counter with stools. Penny scale gives weight and fortunes. (A)

☆　　☆　　☆

Beekman Arms and Delamater House
Route 9 in the center of Rhinebeck
(914) 876-7077
48 rooms, private baths

Forty-eight rooms, all with private baths, located in 1766 historic inn, 1844 Carpenter Gothic Delamater House and their outbuildings. Rooms furnished in colonial, Victorian or more modern styles. Comfortable sitting rooms, fireplaces and Tap Room in main inn building. (A)

STONE RIDGE

1820 House
Route 209
(914) 687-4267

Dinner—Thursday-Monday
5:00 P.M.-10:00 P.M.
Sunday brunch
11:00 A.M.-3:00 P.M.
American regional cuisine in a country colonial atmosphere. Dancing and live music Friday and Saturday 10:00 P.M.-1:00 A.M.

The Globe Cafe
Route 209
(914) 687-7400

Lunch—Wednesday-Saturday
11:00 A.M.-3:00 P.M.
Dinner—Sunday-Tuesday
5:00 P.M.-10:00 P.M.
Dinner—Wednesday-Thursday
6:00 P.M.-10:00 P.M.
Dinner—Friday-Saturday
6:00 P.M.-11:00 P.M.
Sunday brunch
11:00 A.M.-3:00 P.M.
Soups, salads, sandwiches, hot plates. Dinner specialties. Roadside cafe. (A)

Hasbrouck House
Route 209
(914) 687-0055

Dinner daily—6:00 P.M.-10:00 P.M.
Bar opens at 4:00 P.M.
Sunday brunch—12:00-3:00 P.M.
Creative dishes such as Vietnamese fritters, mussels in saffron cream, veal in tarragon mustard, and vegetarian specialties. Menu changes regularly. Served in eighteenth-century stone house listed in the Historical Register. Patio dining in season.

Student Prince Restaurant
Route 213
(914) 687-9911

Lunch—11:30 A.M.-2:30 P.M.
Dinner—5:00 P.M.-9:00 P.M.
Closed Sundays.
German specialties featuring schnitzel and sauerbraten. Casual dining.

☆　　　☆　　　☆

Baker's B & B
R.D. Box 80
(914) 687-9795

A 1780s stone farmhouse lovingly restored. Sits on sixteen acres overlooking horse farm, mountains and pond. Boxed beams, uneven floor boards, narrow stairs. Rooms with full bath, half-bath or shared bath. Third floor suite. Antique furnishings. Home-smoked trout often available for breakfast. (A)

Hasbrouck House Inn Bed and Breakfast
Route 209
(914) 687-0055
8 guest rooms, shared baths

Eighteenth-century stone house listed in the Historical Register. Eight guest rooms, three in sepa-rate cottage. Antiques and country style furnishings. Shared baths. Forty acres. Olympic-size swimming pool. Dinners served in colonial inn dining room. Creative menus. (See above.) Breakfast for guests only. (A)

STORMVILLE

Harralds
Route 52
(914) 878-6595

Dinner—Wednesday-Friday
6:00 P.M.-9:00 P.M.
Dinner—Saturday, two seatings
6:15 P.M. and 9:30 P.M.

Call for reservations.
Continental cuisine served in old Tudor country home. Award-winning restaurant. (A)

SUGAR LOAF

The Barnsider Tavern
King's Highway
(914) 469-9810

Daily from 11:30 A.M.
Sandwiches, soups and salads. Hamburgers a speciality. Casual.

Sugar Loaf Inn
King's Highway
(914) 469-2552

Lunch daily
11:30 A.M.-3:00 P.M.
Snacks daily
3:00 P.M.-5:00 P.M.
Dinner daily
5:00 P.M.-9:00 P.M.
Friday and Saturday open until 10:00 P.M.
Country dining in a circa 1854 Grange Hall and country store. Antique tables and fresh flowers. Entrées range from simple cheese and paté in a basket to seafood, chicken and steaks lightly prepared with creative ingredients. (See Chapter 5.) (A)

TAPPAN

The Old '76 House
Main Street
(914) 359-5476

Lunch—Tuesday-Friday
11:30 A.M.-3:00 P.M.
Dinner—Tuesday-Thursday
5:00 P.M.-9:30 P.M.
Dinner—Friday and Saturday
5:00 P.M.-10:30 P.M.
Dinner—Sunday
4:00 P.M.-8:00 P.M.
Sunday brunch
12:00 P.M.-3:00 P.M.

Built in 1753, this old tavern held British spy Major John André during his trial in 1780. Dark wood, cozy atmosphere, fireplaces with original delft tile. Steak, chops, fish and salads. Homemade popovers. Sandwiches at lunch. Stay with pub fare. (A)

TARRYTOWN

Horsefeathers
94 N. Broadway
(914) 631-6606

Monday-Thursday
11:30 A.M.-11:00 P.M.
Friday-Saturday
11:30 A.M.-midnight
Cozy dining room with dark wood walls. Sandwiches, steaks and chops.

Port of Call
Located in Tarrytown Boat Club (across from Tarrytown train station, on eastbound side of tracks)
(914) 631-2888

Lunch daily
11:00 A.M.-4:00 P.M.
Dinner weekdays
4:00 P.M.-9:00 P.M.
Dinner weekends
4:00 P.M.-10:00 P.M.
Bright, casual restaurant with twenty tables on lower level. On waterfront near boat slips of Tarrytown Boat Club. Italian specialties and broiled seafood. Homemade soups, a variety of salads. Sandwiches available at lunch. Lovely water view. (A)

WEST PARK

West Park Wine Cellars
Route 9W and Burroughs Drive
(914) 384-6709

Lunch, Saturdays and Sundays in season.

Lunch served in old barn cafe next to the wine aging room with sixty-gallon Limousin oak barrels.

Also available is a gourmet picnic for two including fruits, cheeses, breads, salads and wine packed in a wicker basket. Picnic area in arbor among the grapevines or up a steep hill overlooking the Hudson. (See Chapter 14.) (A)

WEST POINT

Hotel Thayer
United States Military Academy at West Point
(914) 446-4731

Daily breakfast, lunch and dinner.
Soups and sandwiches to full course meals in lovely dining room overlooking the Hudson River. Courteous and pleasant staff. (A)

☆   ☆   ☆

Hotel Thayer
United States Military Academy at West Point
(914) 446-4731

Located near Thayer Gate on the post. Doubles, singles, some suites. Major changes in progress. Breakfast, lunch and dinner in dining room overlooking the Hudson River. Comfortable lobby, bar and conference facilities. Gift shop run by Daughters of the U.S. Army.

Museums and Historic Sites: Hours of Operation

All information is accurate at the time of publication. Calling ahead is always advisable since sites are sometimes reserved for school groups and special tours. Days and times of operation may vary with the season.

American Museum of Firefighting
Harry Howard Avenue
Hudson, NY 12534
(518) 828-7695

April 1-October 31, Tuesday-Sunday. Closed Mondays. 9:00 A.M.-4:30 P.M. *Donation suggested.*

Edith C. Blum Art Institute
Bard College
Annandale-on-Hudson,
NY 12504
(914) 758-6822

Wednesday-Monday, 12:00 P.M.-5:00 P.M. Closed Tuesdays. *No Admission fee.*

Boscobel
Route 9D
Garrison, NY 10524
(914) 265-3638

Open daily except Tuesdays. Closed Thanksgiving, Christmas and months of January and February. From April-October, 9:30 A.M.- 5:00 P.M. (last tour at 4:30 P.M.). In November, December and March, 9:30 A.M.-4:00 P.M. (last tour at 3:30 P.M.). *Admission fee.*

Brick House
Route 17K
Montgomery, NY 12549
(914) 457-5951

Mid-April—Mid-October, Saturday and Sunday, 10:00 A.M.-4:30 P.M. Also open Memorial Day and July 4. *Admission fee.*

Bronck House
Pieter Bronck Road (off Route 9W)
Coxsackie, NY 12051
(518) 731-8862

Last Sunday in June—Sunday before Labor Day, Tuesday-Saturday 10:00 A.M.-5:00 P.M. (closed 12:00 P.M.-1:00 P.M. for lunch). Sundays 2:00 P.M.-6:00 P.M. *Admission fee.*

Julia L. Butterfield Memorial Library
Morris Avenue
Cold Spring, NY 10516
(914) 265-3040

Days and hours vary; call ahead. *No Admission fee.*

Caramoor
Girdle Ridge Road
Katonah, NY 10536
(914) 232-5035

June—September, Thursday-Saturday, 11:00 A.M.-4:00 P.M. Concert schedule by request. *Admission fee.*

Clermont
Route 6
Germantown, NY 12516
(518) 537-4240

Memorial Day—last Sunday in October, Wednesday-Saturday, 10:00 A.M.-5:00 P.M. Sunday, 1:00 P.M.-5:00 P.M. *No admission fee.*

Thomas Cole House
218 Spring Street
Catskill, NY 12414
(518) 943-6533

Call for days and hours. *No admission fee.*

Delaware & Hudson Canal Museum
Mohonk Road
High Falls, NY 12440
(914) 687-9311

May 30—Labor Day, Thursday-Monday, 11:00 A.M.-5:00 P.M. Sunday, 1:00 P.M.-5:00 P.M. May, September and October, weekends only, Saturday, 11:00 A.M.-5:00 P.M. Sunday, 1:00 P.M.-5:00 P.M. *Admission fee.*

DeWint House
Livingston Avenue and
Oak Tree Road
Tappan, NY 10983
(914) 359-1359

Year round, daily 10:00 A.M.-4:00
P.M. (Call to verify in winter) *Admission fee.*

Foundry School Museum
63 Chestnut Street
Cold Spring, NY 10516
(914) 265-4010

Wednesday and Sunday afternoons. Call for hours. *Donation suggested.*

Hill-Hold Farm
Route 416
Campbell Hall, NY 10916
(914) 294-7661

Mid-April—Mid-October,
Wednesday-Sunday, 10:00 A.M.-
4:30 P.M. Also open Memorial Day
and July 4. *Admission fee.*

Hudson River Maritime Center
Rondout Landing
Kingston, NY 12401
(914) 338-0071

May—October, Wednesday-Sunday, 12:00 P.M.-5:00 P.M. *Admission fee.*

Huguenot Street
(Old Dutch Stone Houses)
New Paltz, NY 12561
(914) 255-1889

Late May—September, Wednesday-Sunday, 10:00 A.M.-4:00 P.M.
Admission fee.

John Jay Homestead
Route 22 (Jay Street)
Katonah, NY 10536
(914) 232-5651

Memorial Day—Labor Day,
Wednesday-Saturday, 10:00 A.M.-
5:00 P.M.; Sunday, 1:00 P.M.-5:00
P.M. (last tour at 4:00 P.M.). *No admission fee.*

Robert Jenkins House
113 Warren Street
Hudson, NY 12534
(518) 828-5240

July and August, Wednesday,
1:00 P.M.-4:00 P.M. Sunday, 1:00
P.M.-3:00 P.M. *Admission fee.*

Knox's Headquarters
Forge Hill Road
Vails Gate, NY 12584
(914) 561-5498

April—December, Wednesday-
Saturday, 10:00 A.M.-5:00 P.M.
Sunday, 1:00 P.M.-5:00 P.M. Also
open Memorial Day, July 4, and
Labor Day. *No admission fee.*

Locust Grove
(See Young-Morse Historic Site)

Lyndhurst
635 South Broadway (Route 9)
Tarrytown, NY 10591
(914) 631-0046

April 1—October 31, Tuesday-
Sunday, 10:00 A.M.-4:15 P.M. November, December and March,
Saturday and Sunday, 10:00 A.M.-
3:30 P.M. Closed Thanksgiving,
Christmas and the months of January and February. *Admission fee.*

Mills Mansion
Old Post Road
Staatsburg, NY 12580
(914) 889-4100

Memorial Day—Labor Day, Wednesday-Saturday, 10:00 A.M.-5:00 P.M. Sunday, 1:00 P.M.-5:00 P.M. Labor Day—Last Sunday in October, Wednesday-Saturday, 12:00 P.M.-5:00 P.M. Sunday, 1:00 P.M.-5:00 P.M. *No admission fee.*

Mohonk Mountain House
Lake Mohonk
New Paltz, NY 12561
(914) 255-1000

Montgomery Place
River Road
Annandale-on-Hudson, NY 12504
(914) 758-5461

April-October, Wednesday-Monday; 10:00 A.M.-5:00 P.M. closed Tuesday. November, December and March, weekends only, 10:00 A.M.-4:00 P.M. Closed January and February. *Admission fee.*

Museum Village
Museum Village Road
Monroe, NY 10950
(914) 782-8247

May, June and September—December, Wednesday-Friday, 10:00 A.M.-2:00 P.M. Saturday and Sunday, 12:00 P.M.-5:00 P.M. July and August, Wednesday-Friday, 10:00 A.M.-5:00 P.M. Saturday and Sunday, 12:00 P.M.-5:00 P.M. Open Memorial Day, July 4 and Labor Day. *Admission fee.*

New Windsor Cantonment
Temple Hill Road
Vails Gate, NY 12584
(914) 561-1765

Mid-April–October 31, Wednesday-Saturday, 10:00 A.M.-5:00 P.M. Sunday, 1:00 P.M.-5:00 P.M. Also open Memorial Day, July 4, and Labor Day. *No admission fee.*

Olana
Route 9G
Hudson, NY 12534
(518) 828-0135

Late May—Labor Day, Wednesday-Saturday, 10:00 A.M.-5:00 P.M. Sunday, 1:00 P.M.-5:00 P.M. Labor Day—late October, Wednesday-Saturday, 12:00 P.M.-4:00 P.M. Sunday, 1:00 P.M.-4:00 P.M. (Summer weekend tours may sell out early.) *Admission fee.*

Old Dutch Church of Kingston
272 Wall Street
Kingston, NY 12401
(914) 338-6759

Old Dutch Church of Sleepy Hollow
Route 9
Tarrytown, NY 10591
(914) 631-1123

Old Rhinebeck Aerodrome
Stone Church Road
Rhinebeck, NY 12572
(914) 758-8610

May 15—October 31, daily, 10:00 A.M.-5:00 P.M. Air shows: July and August, Saturday and Sunday, 2:30 P.M. and 4:00 P.M. *Admission fee.*

Philipsburg Manor
Route 9
Tarrytown, NY 10591
(914) 631-8200

April—October, Wednesday-Monday, 10:00 A.M.-5:00 P.M. November, December and March, Wednesday-Monday, 10:00 A.M.-4:00 P.M. January and February, weekends, 10:00 A.M.-4:00 P.M. Closed Tuesdays year round. *Admission fee.*

Philipse Manor Hall
Warburton Avenue at Dock Street
Yonkers, NY 10702
(914) 965-4027

Late May—late October, Wednesday-Saturday, 12:00 P.M.-5:00 P.M. Sunday, 1:00 P.M.-5:00 P.M. (Last tour at 4:30 P.M.) Open Memorial Day, July 4, and Labor Day. *Admission fee.*

Reformed Dutch Church of Rhinebeck
1 South Street
Rhinebeck, NY 12572
(914) 876-3727

Rondout Lighthouse
c/o Hudson River Maritime Center
Rondout Landing
Kingston, NY 12401
(914) 338-0071

Eleanor Roosevelt Home
(See Val-Kill)

Franklin Delano Roosevelt Home and Museum, Springwood
Route 9
Hyde Park, NY 12538
(914) 229-8114

March—October, daily, 9:00 A.M.-5:00 P.M. November—February, Thursday-Monday, 9:00 A.M.-5:00 P.M. (Closed Tuesdays and Wednesdays.) Closed Thanksgiving, Christmas and New Year's Day. *Admission fee.*

Senate House and Museum
312 Fair Street
Kingston, NY 12401
(914) 338-2786

April-December, Wednesday-Saturday, 10:00 A.M.-5:00 P.M. Sunday, 1:00 P.M.-5:00 P.M. Closed Thanksgiving, Christmas. *No admission fee.*

Springwood
(See Frankin Delano Roosevelt Home and Museum)

Stony Point Battlefield
Stony Point, NY 10980
(914) 786-2521

Mid-April—October 31, Wednesday-Sunday, 8:30 A.M.-5:00 P.M. *No admission fee.*

Storm King Art Center
Old Pleasant Hill Road
Mountainville, NY 10953
(914) 534-3115

Mid-May–October 31, daily 12:00 P.M.-5:30 P.M. *Donation suggested.*

Sugar Loaf Crafts Village
Sugar Loaf, NY 10981

Most stores open on weekends; some mid-week as well.

Sunnyside
Route 9
Tarrytown, NY 10591
(914) 631-8200

April—October, Wednesday-Monday, 10:00 A.M.-5:00 P.M. November, December and March, Wednesday-Monday, 10:00 A.M.-4:00 P.M. January and February, weekends only, 10:00 A.M.-4:00 P.M. Closed Tuesdays year round. *Admission fee.*

Trotting Horse Museum and Historic Track
240 Main Street
Goshen, NY 10924
(914) 294-6330

Monday-Saturday, 10:00 A.M.-5:00 P.M. Sunday and holidays, 1:30 P.M.-5:00 P.M. *Admission fee.*

Union Church of Pocantico Hills
Route 448
North Tarrytown, NY 10591
(914) 631-8200

Tours given April—December, Wednesday-Friday, 1:00 P.M.-4:00 P.M. Sunday, 2:00 P.M.-5:00 P.M. *No admission fee.*

Val-Kill
Route 9G
Hyde Park, NY 12538
(914) 229-9115

April—October, daily, 9:30 A.M.-5:00 P.M. March and November, closed Tuesday and Wednesday. *Admission fee.*

Van Cortlandt Manor
Off Route 9
Croton-on-Hudson, NY 10520
(914) 631-8200

April—October, Wednesday-Monday, 10:00 A.M.-5:00 P.M. November, December and March, Wednesday-Monday, 10:00 A.M.-4:00 P.M. January and February, weekends only, 10:00 A.M.-4:00 P.M. Closed Tuesdays year round. *Admission fee.*

Vanderbilt Mansion
Route 9
Hyde Park, NY 12538
(914) 229-9115

April—October, 10:00 A.M.-6:00 P.M. March and November, closed Tuesdays and Wednesdays. *Admission fee.*

Washington's Headquarters
84 Liberty Street
Newburgh, NY 12550
(914) 562-1195

April—December, Wednesday-Saturday, 10:00 A.M.-5:00 P.M. Sunday, 1:00 P.M.-5:00 P.M. Also open Memorial Day, July 4, Labor Day and Washington's Birthday weekend. *No admission fee.*

Young-Morse Historic Site
Route 9
Poughkeepsie, NY 12601
(914) 454-4500

Memorial Day—September, Wednesday-Sunday, 10:00 A.M.-4:00 P.M. (Last tour at 3:00 P.M.) *Admission fee.*

Seasonal Events

All information below is accurate at time of publication. Although these events are usually held annually, dates vary from year to year. Call ahead to verify days and time.

FALL

Fall is spectacular in the Hudson Valley. Drives along any country road reveal the brilliant orange, gold and scarlet colors that have inspired artists for centuries. It is a season of harvest festivals and West Point football. . .a time for apple picking and tailgate picnics.

Antique Show and Sale   September
Brick House
Montgomery, N.Y.
(914) 457-3000

Apple Festival   October
Knox's Headquarters
Vails Gate, N.Y.
(914) 561-5498

Apple Harvest Festival and Pick-Your-Own Apples   Early September
Montgomery Place Orchards
Annandale-on-Hudson, N.Y.
(914) 758-6338

Clearwater Pumpkin Sale/Sail   October
Hudson River Sloop *Clearwater*
(914) 454-7673 for locations

Colonial Day   September
DeWint House
Tappan, N.Y.
(914) 359-1184

Country Seats Tour   September
c/o Montgomery Place
Annandale-on-Hudson, N.Y.
(914) 758-5461

Culinary Institute Outdoor Food Fair   September
C.I.A.—Culinary Institute of America
Hyde Park, N.Y.
(914) 471-6608

Encampment of the Brigade of the American Revolution   October
New Windsor Cantonment
Vails Gate, N.Y.
(914) 561-1765

Fall Concerts in Color   October
Union Church of Pocantico Hills
North Tarrytown, N.Y.
(914) 631-8200

Legend of Sleepy Hollow Weekend   October
Sunnyside
Tarrytown, N.Y.
(914) 631-8200

Marketplace at Van Cortlandt Manor   October
Van Cortlandt Manor
Croton-on-Hudson, N.Y.
(914) 631-8200

Museum Village Fall Festival   October
Museum Village
Monroe, N.Y.
(914) 782-8247

Produce—Pick-Your-Own   September-November
New York State Department of
    Agriculture and Markets
Albany, N.Y.
(518) 474-2121
(call for up-to-date locations and information)

Pumpkin Painting Festival   October
Clermont
Germantown, N.Y.
(518) 537-4240

Rhinebeck Antiques Fair   October
Dutchess County Fairgrounds
Rhinebeck, N.Y.
(914) 876-4001

Royal Birthday Celebration of King George II   November
Philipsburg Manor
Tarrytown, N.Y.
(914) 631-8200

Sugar Loaf Art Show   September
Sugar Loaf Crafts Village
Sugar Loaf, N.Y.
(914) 469-4963

Sugar Loaf Fall Festival   Columbus Day Weekend
Sugar Loaf Crafts Village
Sugar Loaf, N.Y.
(914) 469-4963

Thanksgiving at Sunnyside   November
Sunnyside
Tarrytown, N.Y.
(914) 631-8200

West Point Cadet Parades   September-November
United States Military Academy
West Point, N.Y.
(914) 938-2638 (for schedules)

West Point Football Games   September-November
Army Athletic Ticket Office
United States Military Academy
West Point, N.Y.
(914) 446-4996 (for schedules and tickets)

Wineries—Special Fall Harvest Festivals   September-November
See Chapter 14 for addresses and
   telephone numbers

Wreathlaying Ceremony   October 11
Eleanor Roosevelt's Birthday
Rose Garden, Springwood
Hyde Park, N.Y.
(914) 229-9115

WINTER

There are many Christmas Tours in the Hudson Valley:

Candlelight Tours at Boscobel   December
Boscobel
Garrison, N.Y.
(914) 265-3638

Candlelight Tours at Knox's Headquarters   December
Vails Gate, N.Y.
(914) 561-5498

Candlelight Tours at Philipsburg Manor   December
Philipsburg Manor
Tarrytown, N.Y.
(914) 631-8200

Candlelight Tours at Sunnyside   December
Sunnyside
Tarrytown, N.Y.
(914) 631-8200

Candlelight Tours at Van Cortlandt Manor   December
Van Cortlandt Manor
Croton-on-Hudson, N.Y.
(914) 631-8200

Candlelight Tours of Washington's Headquarters   December
Washington's Headquarters
Newburgh, N.Y.
(914) 562-1195

Christmas Open House at Olana   December
Olana
Hudson, N.Y.
(518) 828-0135

Christmas with the Roosevelts   December
Springwood, Home of Franklin D. Roosevelt,
    and Val-Kill, Eleanor Roosevelt's Retreat
Hyde Park, N.Y.
(914) 229-9115

A Gilded Christmas   December
Mills Mansion
Staatsburg, N.Y.
(914) 889-4100

A Gilded Christmas   December
Vanderbilt Mansion
Hyde Park, N.Y.
(914) 229-9115

Holiday Celebration at Montgomery Place   December
Montgomery Place
Annandale-on-Hudson, N.Y.
(914) 631-8200

Washington's Birthday Celebration   February
Washington's Headquarters   (Washington's Birthday Weekend)
Newburgh, N.Y.
(914) 562-1195

Wreathlaying Ceremony   January 30
Franklin Delano Roosevelt's Birthday
Rose Garden, Springwood
Hyde Park, N.Y.
(914) 229-9115

SPRING

Antique Auto Show   May
Dutchess County Fairgrounds
Rhinebeck, N.Y.
(914) 876-4001

Chancellor Livingston's Sheep-Shearing Festival May
Clermont
Germantown, N.Y.
(518) 537-4240

Easter Celebration at Montgomery Place   Spring
Montgomery Place
Annandale-on-Hudson, N.Y.
(914) 631-8200

Hambletonian's Birthday Celebration   May or June
Trotting Horse Museum
Goshen, N.Y.
(914) 294-6330

Harness Racing   Mid-May to Early June
Goshen Historic Track
Goshen, N.Y.
(914) 294-6330

Heritage Day   May
Kingston, N.Y.
(914) 331-0800

May Day Celebration   May
Hill Hold Farm
Campbell Hall, N.Y.
(914) 294-7661

Memorial Day Wreathlaying Ceremony   Memorial Day Weekend
Rose Garden, Springwood
Franklin Delano Roosevelt Home
Hyde Park, N.Y.
(914) 229-9115

Rhinebeck Antiques Show   Memorial Day Weekend
Dutchess County Fairgrounds
Rhinebeck, N.Y.
(914) 876-4001

School of the Soldier Revolutionary War Camp Activities   May
New Windsor Cantonment
Vails Gate, N.Y.
(914) 561-1765

Spring Candelight Tour   May
Boscobel
Garrison, N.Y.
(914) 265-3638

Spring Concerts in Color   Spring
Union Church of Pocantico Hills
North Tarrytown, N.Y.
(914) 631-8200

Sugar Loaf Crafts Fair   May
Sugar Loaf Crafts Village
Sugar Loaf, N.Y.
(914) 469-4963

Washington Irving's Birthday   April
Sunnyside
Tarrytown, N.Y.
(914) 631-8200

West Point Cadet Parades   April and May
United States Military Academy
West Point, N.Y.
(914) 938-2638 (for schedules)

SUMMER

Antique Airplane Shows   July and August Weekends
Old Rhinebeck Aerodrome
Rhinebeck, N.Y.
(914) 758-8610

Boat Cruises from Rondout Landing   Summer
  Hudson River Cruises
  (914) 255-6515

  Hudson Rondout Cruises
  (914) 338-6280

  Myles Gordon's Great Sailing Center
  (914) 338-7313

Celebration of Roses   June
Boscobel
Garrison, N.Y.
(914) 265-3638

Chess Tournament   Labor Day
John Jay Homestead
Katonah, N.Y.
(914) 232-5651

Civil War Weekend   Late August/Early September
Museum Village
Monroe, N.Y.
(914) 782-8247

Clermont 1776 Celebration   July 4
Clermont
Germantown, N.Y.
(518) 537-4240

Concerts on the Lawn   Summer
  Bard College
  Annandale-on-Hudson, N.Y.
  (914) 758-6822

  Benmarl Winery
  Marlboro, N.Y.
  (914) 236-4265

  Boscobel
  Garrison, N.Y.
  (914) 265-3638

  Caramoor Music Festival
  Katonah, N.Y.
  (914) 232-5035

  Cascade Mountain Winery
  Amenia, N.Y.
  (914) 373-9021

  Clermont
  Germantown, N.Y.
  (518) 537-4240

  Knox's Headquarters
  Vails Gate, N.Y.
  (914) 561-5498

  Lyndhurst
  Tarrytown, N.Y.
  (914) 631-0046

Mills Mansion
Staatsburg, N.Y.
(914) 889-4100

Vanderbilt Mansion
Hyde Park, N.Y.
(914) 229-8086

United States Military Academy Band
West Point Amphitheatre
West Point, N.Y.
(914) 938-2638

Corn and Craft Festival   Mid-August
Hurley, N.Y.
(914) 331-7374

County Fairs
   Columbia County   Labor Day Weekend
   Chatham, N.Y.
   (518) 392-4121

   Dutchess County   August
   Rhinebeck, N.Y.
   (914) 876-4001

   Orange County   July
   Middletown, N.Y.
   (914) 343-4826

   Ulster County   August
   New Paltz, N.Y.
   (914) 331-9300

Croquet Tournament   June
Clermont
Germantown, N.Y.
(518) 537-4240

General Knox's Birthday Celebration   July
Knox's Headquarters
Vails Gate, N.Y.
(914) 561-5498

Grain Harvest   July
Philipsburg Manor
Tarrytown, N.Y.
(914) 631-8200

Great American Weekend   Early July
Harness Racing and Country Fair
Village of Goshen, N.Y.
(914) 294-7741

Harness Racing   Early June, Some Weekends
Goshen Historic Track
Goshen, N.Y.
(914) 294-6330

Hudson Fulton Celebration and Boat Trips   August
Clermont
Germantown, N.Y.
(518) 537-4240

Independence Day Celebrations at Sunnyside   July 4
Sunnyside
Tarrytown, N.Y.
(914) 631-8200

Last Encampment of the Continental Army   Summer
New Windsor Cantonment
Vails Gate, N.Y.
(914) 561-1765

Martha Washington's Birthday Celebration   June
Washington's Headquarters
Newburgh, N.Y.
(914) 562-1195

Militia Muster and Market Day   June
New Windsor Cantonment
Vails Gate, N.Y.
(914) 561-1765

Produce—Pick-Your-Own   Summer
New York State Department of
  Agriculture and Markets
Albany, N.Y.
(518) 474-2121
  (call for up-to-date locations
  and information)

Rose Day at Lyndhurst   June
Lyndhurst
Tarrytown, N.Y.
(914) 631-0046

Stone House Day   Second Saturday in July
Hurley, N.Y.
(914) 331-7374

Stony Point Battle Reenactment   Mid-July
Stony Point Battlefield
Stony Point, N.Y.
(914) 786-2521

Victorian Picnic   August
Olana
Hudson, N.Y.
(518) 828-0135

Volunteer Fireman's Field Day Firematics Competition   July
American Museum of Firefighting
Hudson, N.Y.
(518) 828-7695

BIBLIOGRAPHY

Agnew, James B., *Eggnog Riot: The Christmas Mutiny at West Point*. San Rafael, CA, 1979.

Aimone, Alan Conrad and Langowski, John F., *River Guide to the Hudson Highlands*. West Point, NY, 1986.

Ambrose, Stephen E., *Duty, Honor, Country: A History of West Point*. Baltimore, 1966.

American Paradise: The World of the Hudson River School. Metropolitan Museum of Art, New York, 1987.

Atkinson, Rick, *The Long Gray Line*. Boston, 1989.

Baritz, Loren, *Backfire*. New York, 1985.

"Benny Havens," *The Pointer*, March 14, 1925.

Blumenson, Martin, *Patton: The Man Behind the Legend*. New York, 1985.

Bugle Notes. United States Military Academy, West Point, NY, 1989.

Butler, Joseph T., *Van Cortlandt Manor*. Tarrytown, NY, 1978.

Castor, Henry, *America's First World War: General Pershing and the Yanks*. New York, 1957.

Catton, Bruce, *U.S. Grant and the American Military Tradition*. Boston, 1954.

Clifton, Chester V., "A Tribute to ABE," *Assembly Magazine*, December, 1974.

Commager, Henry Steele, *America's Robert E. Lee*. Boston, 1951.

Coolidge, Louis A., *Ulysses S. Grant*. New York, 1983.

Diamont, Lincoln, *Chaining the Hudson*. Secaucus, NJ, 1989.

Ellis, Joseph and Moore, Robert, *School For Soldiers*. New York, 1974.

Faber, Harold, "Foliage Tours on the Farm-Stand Route," *The New York Times*, October 13, 1989.

———, "From Caesar to MacArthur, On the Hudson," *The New York Times*, September 10, 1989.

———, "A Guide to Viewing the Foliage Spectacle by Bus and Train," *The New York Times*, October 9, 1987.

———, "Roosevelt Home Marks Royal Hot-Dog History," *The New York Times*, June 12, 1989.

Feron, James, "Reviewing West Point's Honor Code," *The New York Times*, January 8, 1989.

————, "Revised West Point Honor Code Urged," *The New York Times*, June 14, 1989.

Fleming, Thomas, *Band of Brothers: West Point in the Civil War*. New York, 1988.

————, *West Point: The Men and Times of the United States Military Academy*. New York, 1969.

Foderaro, Lisa W., "Since 1805, a Family Saved It All," *The New York Times*, July 7, 1988.

————, "West Point Picks Woman to Lead Cadet Corps," *The New York Times*, August 9, 1989.

Forman, Sidney, *West Point: A History of the United States Military Academy*. New York, 1950.

Fourth Class System, The. United States Military Academy, West Point, NY, 1989.

Frontero, Vincent, "Leaves Aflame," *New York Magazine*, October 10, 1988.

Galloway, K. Bruce, and Johnson, Robert Bowie, Jr., *West Point: America's Power Fraternity*. New York, 1973.

"Ghostly Cavalry Man Reports for Duty at West Point, A," *The New York Times*, November 21, 1972.

Halberstam, David, *The Best and the Brightest*. New York, 1972.

"Hotel of Many Memories, A," *DAR Magazine*, June, 1927.

Honor Code and Honor System, The. United States Military Academy, West Point, NY, 1989.

Howat, John K., *The Hudson River and Its Painters*. New York, 1983.

Hufeland, Otto, *The Capture of Major André*. Tarrytown, NY, 1960.

Inventories of Structures at West Point. 4 vols. United States Military Academy, West Point, NY, 1984.

"Inside West Point," *48 Hours*, New York, December 7, 1989.

Jacobs, William Jay, *Edgar Allan Poe: Genius in Torment*. New York, 1975.

Kinstlinger-Bruhn, Charlotte, "Leading Lady at the Point," *Hudson Valley Magazine*, February, 1990.

Klaw, Spencer, "West Point: 1978," *American Heritage*, June/July, 1978.

Lee, Susan Dye, *Jefferson Davis*. Chicago, 1978.

Lewis, Lloyd, *Captain Sam Grant*. Boston, 1950.

Livesey, Herbert, "History with a View: Tracing the Hudson's Legendary Past," *Travel-Holiday*, December, 1989.

Lovelace, Delos W., *"Ike" Eisenhower: Statesman and Soldier of Peace*. New York, 1969.

Lueck, Thomas T., "West Point Honor Code Faces Study After Expulsion Furor," *The New York Times*, June 19, 1988.

Manchester, William, *American Caesar: Douglas MacArthur 1880-1964*. New York, 1978.

Martin, Ralph G., *A Hero for our Time: An Intimate Story of the Kennedy Years*. New York, 1983.

Meyer, Howard N., *Let Us Have Peace: The Life of Ulysses S. Grant*. New York, 1966.

Michaels, Joanne and Barile, Mary, *The Hudson Valley and Catskill Mountains*. New York, 1988.

Miller, Mark, *Wine—A Gentleman's Game*. New York, 1984.

Morison, Samuel Eliot, *The Oxford History of the American People*. New York, 1965.

————, and Commager, Henry Steele, *The Growth of the American Republic*. Vol. I, New York, 1962.

Mulligan, Tim, *The Hudson River Valley*. New York, 1985.

"No Slack: A Woman's Touch at West Point," *Newsweek*, August 21, 1989.

O'Donnell, Kenneth P., and Powers, David F., with Joe McCarthy, *"Johnny, We Hardly knew Ye:" Memories of John Fitzgerald Kennedy*. Boston, 1972.

O'Neill, Timothy, *Shades of Gray*. New York, 1987.

Parmet, Herbert S., *JFK: The Presidency of John F. Kennedy*. New York, 1983.

Palmer, Dave Richard, *The River and the Rock: The History of Fortress West Point, 1775-1783*. New York, 1969.

Patterson, Gerard A., *Rebels from West Point*. New York, 1987.

"Phantom of the Point," *Time*, December 4, 1972.

Phillips, Sandra S. and Weintraub, Linda, eds., *Charmed Places: Hudson River Artists and Their Houses, Studios and Vistas*. New York, 1988.

Rapp, Kenneth W., *West Point*. Croton-on-Hudson, NY, 1978.

Reeder, Colonel Red, *The West Point Story*. New York, 1956.

Register of Graduates and Former Cadets, 1802-1980, United States Military Academy, Cullum Memorial Edition. West Point, NY, 1980.

Roper, James H., "Summer Slice of City Life Up the Hudson," *The New York Times*, July 20, 1989.

Sergent, Mary Elizabeth, "Classmates Divided," *American Heritage*, February, 1958.

Simon, John Y., ed., *The Personal Memoirs of Julia Dent Grant.* New York, 1975.

Simpson, Jeffrey, *Officers and Gentlemen: Historic West Point in Photographs.* Tarrytown, 1982.

Smith, Dale O., *Cradle of Valor: The Intimate Letters of a Plebe at West Point Between the Two World Wars.* Chapel Hill, NC, 1988.

Symonds, Craig L., *A Battlefield Atlas of the American Revolution.* 1986.

Tripp, William Henry, *Guide to West Point and the United States Military Academy 1900-.* West Point, NY, 1900.

Thorn, John, and Lockyer, Roger, and Smith, David, *A History of England.* New York, 1961.

Visiting Our Past: America's Historylands. National Geographic Society, Washington, D.C., 1986.

Wallace, William, "Earl (Red) Blaik, 92, Army's Top Football Coach," *The New York Times*, May 7, 1989.

Webster, Nancy and Woodworth, Richard, *Getaways for Gourmets in the Northeast.* West Hartford, CT, 1988.

"West Point: Ghost Story," *Newsweek*, December 4, 1972.

West Point Guide Book, The. Daughters of the U. S. Army, West Point Chapter, West Point, NY, 1989.

West Point: United States Military Academy Catalog. West Point, NY, 1988-1989.

Wood, Oliver E., *The West Point Scrap Book.* New York, 1871.

Wood, Robert T., "Benny Havens," *The Pointer*, May 25, 1945.

Young, Bob and Jan, *Reluctant Warrior.* New York, 1971.

Zukowsky, John and Stimson, Robbe Pierce, *Hudson River Villas.* New York, 1985.

Index

311